To Jack, with love and
thanks for helping to make
this happen.

Guy x

THE
GREAT WIZARDS

OF ANTIQUITY

THE DAWN OF WESTERN
MAGIC AND ALCHEMY

About the Author

Guy Ogilvy studied languages at university and spent a lot of time behind the Berlin Wall in the late 70s/early 80s. Subsequent travels brought him into contact with ancient medicine and religious traditions in South America, the Himalayas, and Ethiopia. He abandoned a promising career in publishing to pursue a personal quest that culminated in an eighteen-month stint as a cave-dwelling hermit in the mountains of Central North Mexico. He returned to England to study alchemy under the guidance of the Philosophers of Nature and Manfred Junius. He began writing on esoteric subjects to support his family and has written several of the books published under the name Francis Melville. His books have been translated into more than twenty languages and sold over 750,000 copies. He has appeared on several television networks in Britain, Japan, and the USA to share his expertise on esotericism and alchemy. He lives near Glastonbury in Somerset, England, with his wife, daughters, and whippets. His favourite activities include foraging, laboratory alchemy, and singing with country band The Johnsons.

THE
GREAT WIZARDS

OF ANTIQUITY

THE DAWN OF WESTERN
MAGIC AND ALCHEMY

GUY OGILVY

Llewellyn Publications
Woodbury, Minnesota

FIRST EDITION
First Printing, 2019

Book design by Ted Riley
Cover art by Eric Hotz
Cover design by Kevin R. Brown
Editing by Annie Burdick
Interior illustrations by Eric Hotz
Map in Preface by the Llewellyn Art Department

Llewellyn Publications is a registered trademark of Llewellyn Worldwide Ltd.

Library of Congress Cataloging-in-Publication Data (Pending)
ISBN: 978-0-7387-4412-4

Llewellyn Worldwide Ltd. does not participate in, endorse, or have any authority or responsibility concerning private business transactions between our authors and the public.

All mail addressed to the author is forwarded but the publisher cannot, unless specifically instructed by the author, give out an address or phone number.

Any internet references contained in this work are current at publication time, but the publisher cannot guarantee that a specific location will continue to be maintained. Please refer to the publisher's website for links to authors' websites and other sources.

Llewellyn Publications
A Division of Llewellyn Worldwide Ltd.
2143 Wooddale Drive
Woodbury, MN 55125-2989
www.llewellyn.com

Printed in the United States of America

Other books by Guy Ogilvy

The Alchemist's Kitchen

Future titles in the Great Wizards of History series by Guy Ogilvy

Great Wizards of the Renaissance

Great Wizards of Secret Societies

Acknowledgment

I would like to thank the following for their part in bringing this book into being:

My family and friends, in particular my mother and Sabrina Rowan Hamilton for insisting and assisting; Jack Price for advising me to attend the London Book Fair; Bill Krause of Llewellyn, who I met there, and the whole team at Llewellyn, particularly Elysia Gallo, for her faith and patience; finally, my wife Victoria and my old mucker Frank Mollett for their unflagging support.

Dedication

For Martha, Joe, Millie, Ivo, and Jack.

CONTENTS

Preface   XI

Introduction   I

SECTION 1: Prehistoric and Mythic Magic   II
Chapter 1: The Return of the Lion Man   13
Chapter 2: Orpheus and the Magic of Music   39

**SECTION 2: The Pre-Socratic Sorcerers
   of Ancient Greece**   73
Chapter 3: Prophets, Caves, and Sages   75
Chapter 4: Plague-Busters, Skywalkers, and Time-Travellers   99
Chapter 5: The Man with the Golden Thigh   133
Chapter 6: Sorcerers in Philosophers' Clothing   149

SECTION 3: The Western Alchemical Tradition   197
Chapter 7: Graeco-Egyptian and Islamic Alchemy   199
Chapter 8: Chrysopoeia in Christendom   213
Chapter 9: The Stranger of One Night's Acquaintance   233

Epilogue: Alchemy Today   253

Appendices   259

Bibliography   285

Index   293

PREFACE

This book is what the great Charles Forte would have described as a "Book of the Damned"; its pages are filled with characters, tales, and notions that the sensible, rationalistic modern world has long since damned as being bogus, beyond the pale, deluded, or just plain preposterous. This is not a book about stage magic, trickery, and sleight-of-hand, although some of the great wizards whose stories I shall be telling certainly resorted to trickery on occasion. Unlike the real wizards of this book, all the most skillful illusionists I know are card-carrying atheists who scoff at the notion of higher powers or inherent meaning at play in the universe. If, gentle reader, you are also of such a mind, fear not; your time may not be entirely wasted. There are plenty of splendid tales to amuse you here, which you may find fascinating even if you believe them to be founded on nonsense. You may even be intrigued to discover that most of the characters I will be parading here played, albeit often unwittingly, an important role in opening the Pandora's box that created the scientistic world of to-day, where orthodox reality is defined by weights and measures and reduced to its constituent material parts. There is, to be sure, great wonder and amazement to be experienced even in such a pragmatically constrained worldview, but the great wizards who form the subject of this book were inspired by the knowledge that there are more things in heaven and earth than are dreamt of in such a philosophy. Their inspiration led them to explore the nature of being, with results that ultimately shed light upon material reality in the same way that a four-dimensional object might cast a three-dimensional shadow. In this respect, an adept might consider scientific realism to be a semantic shadow-play quite incapable of illuminating the true nature of being; a sort of *reductio ad absurdum*. Ha ha! Small wonder that magicians have tended to make rationalists so cross over the centuries.

Traditional magic is as old as human history and has been practiced by all peoples in all times throughout the world. It is, perhaps, hard for many living in the "real world" of today to imagine that magic could ever have been a reality, that it ever could have "worked." There is a well-developed tendency these days to believe that such childish notions were the product of ignorance, superstition, and fear; the hag-ridden, benighted fancies of our repressed forebears, subjugated as they were by domineering theocracies in league with brutal monarchies determined to control them and keep them in the dark. The reality, however, is much more complex and infinitely more interesting.

There was a time, even in historical Western Europe, the cradle of secular materialism, when reality was more fluid, when the world was steeped in magic and mystery. Indeed, if truth be told, the fairy tales, myths, and legends of high medieval gothic Europe remain a nagging part of who we are, still haunting our dreams as vivid and compelling reference points in our cultural imagination, as do the great dramas of Greek and Norse mythology, the magic and romance of the Arabian Nights, and the mystique of ancient Egypt. It is from the latter realm that the magical traditions of Europe are principally drawn, and it is on these traditions and their most inspired and daring practitioners that this book will largely focus.

Over recent decades, a host of brilliant scholars have begun to reveal just how pervasive and significant a role the Western esoteric tradition has played, not just in the history of ideas, but in the unfolding of history itself. I am not one of those brilliant scholars, whose shoulders I am now struggling to clamber upon, but rather an enthusiastic student who has spent many thousands of hours exploring this long-neglected but inexhaustible subject that is now a rapidly developing area of research in the humanities. It is usually referred to as "Western esotericism."

My aim here is not to further scholarship in this subject, but to provide an engaging overview. My imaginary readership includes most of my godchildren, who are now in their late teens and have been avid Harry Potter fans. I am mindful that at Hogwarts School of Witchcraft and Wizardry, History of Magic is considered the most boring subject in the curriculum, so I have chosen not to risk boring my readers with tedious amounts of detail, obscure words, and scholarly jargon, nor to interrupt the narrative flow with endless footnotes. They will crop up where I think they add important context and/or interest and in the very few places where I want to show off (what I believe to be) my original scholarship. I will, however, furnish interested readers with a pretty comprehensive bibliography of primary and secondary sources to get their teeth into. It may just be that some inspired future scholar of Western esotericism stumbles onto the subject for the first time by reading this book. I truly hope so.

My intention is to paint portraits of some of the most remarkable, infamous, and colourful practitioners of magic, recounting their most legendary exploits and reconsidering their reputations, both in the context of their times and from an extra-historical perspective. I hope that an exploration of their lives will reveal some of the beliefs they held and the knowledge and powers they sought to attain, as well as the impact they had on their fellow humans and their place in the history of magic.

The lives of many of the great wizards come down to us in tattered and often contradictory fragments. This is the way it is with legends, particularly those that concern a subject as controversial and divisive as magic. Many of the details will be fictions and embellishments, and I will try, at least in part, to sift fact from fiction. But we should not forget that sometimes the legend, regardless of its veracity, is not only more interesting, but also more revealing, than the unvarnished truth, which can prove to be disappointingly mundane. As Francis Brett Young warns us with regard to the historicity of the Arthurian mythos:

> *Nor pry too deeply, lest you should discover*
> *The bower of Astolat a smokey hut*
> *Of mud and wattle—find the knightliest lover*
> *A braggart, and his lily maid a slut.*

Myths and legends generate archetypes that can often tell us more about the true nature of things than dusty archaeological fragments. So I'll polish up the stories and let them ring, but I promise not to actually invent any details myself.

This book is not in itself a grimoire (the marvellous word for a practical handbook of the Dark Arts), but I will be describing the multifarious magical beliefs and techniques entertained and employed by my chosen wizards. I should probably make a disclaimer at this point: I am not, and never have been, a ceremonial magician myself. I've got a great collection of hats, but none are tall and pointy, nor have I ever waved a magic wand in earnest (don't titter, Potter!). My pet passion is alchemy and, as we shall see, alchemy arises from the same tradition as magic, and many of my wizards were alchemists. My personal interest in the alchemical and magical tradition has been piqued and inspired by a number of personal experiences, which my muchmourned alchemy teacher Manfred Junius referred to as "borderline occult." Religious and occult tradition provided these experiences with context and elucidation, and I will pepper this narrative with accounts of some of them in instances where I think they can shed re-

vealing light. Some of them are very bizarre, but they are all true! I
have witnesses! They also illustrate a very important aspect of magic:
It isn't just something that you can do or that can be done to you by
other beings; it is also something that can happen to you. When you
happen to have a profoundly magical experience, the world changes
forever.

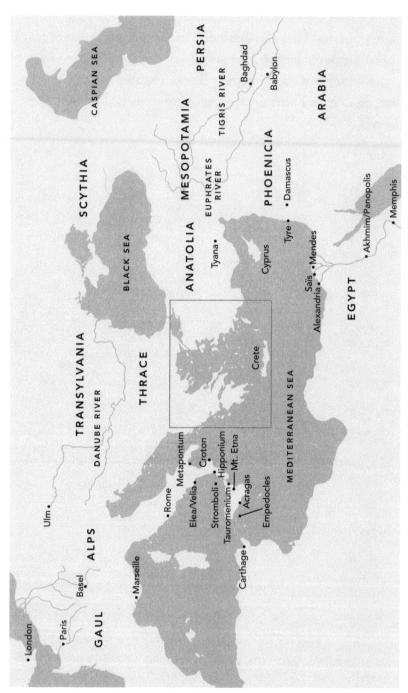

The World of the Great Wizards of Antiquity

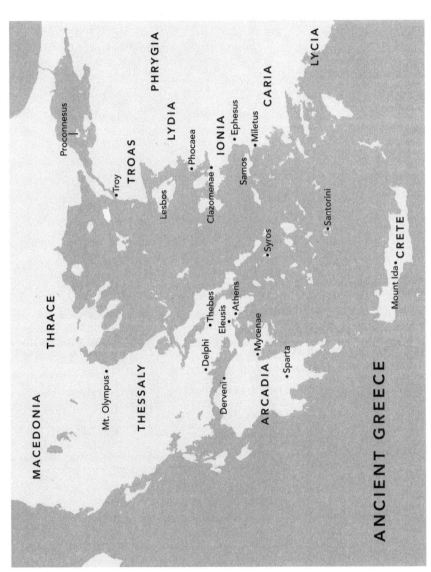

Map of Ancient Greece

INTRODUCTION

It's a funny old business, life, particularly for human beings, cursed or blessed as we are with the ability to contemplate the apparent absurdity of our existence. Trying to make sense of it all has become much more daunting in modern times, now that the old certainties like God, salvation, rebirth, or the promise of eternal life have been not only called into question, but largely rejected by the Academy. Since the "Age of Enlightenment," science has emerged as the arbiter of truth and, in fairness, has achieved dazzling successes in unveiling the physical mechanics of material life, which the inventiveness of technology has exploited to achieve levels of capability that were undreamed of just a few generations ago. Humanity has become a force to be reckoned with, threatened only by itself. For good or ill, we have mastered many of the hows and whats of life; as for the whys and wherefores, however, science is groping in the dark, coming up with speculations that are increasingly metaphysical and bearing ever closer resemblance to ancient traditions of knowledge. The findings of subatomic particle physics are now being applied to speculate on the nature of the outer cosmos in a way that exemplifies the ancient magical axiom, "as above, so below."

The great wizards that this book celebrates are amongst the most famous or notorious of those curious and daring souls who have sought to unravel the meaning of existence, not just through philosophical speculation, but through the exploration and application of techniques designed to provide experiential access to the hidden truths behind the veil of outward forms and the powerful forces that weave the matrix of life. It is the hidden nature of these things and the (often) secret practices used to explore them that give rise to the expression "the occult" (still used by the prurient to titillate and provoke the ignorant), which simply means "that which is hidden" in Latin.

We are not concerned here with the trickery and illusionism of the stage magician, but rather what might instead be termed "real magic"—the performing of wonders that science cannot account for. To attempt a concise definition, real magic can be said to consist of the influencing of things (i.e., events, people, animals, objects, or natural phenomena) by supernatural means. Magic also defines the ability to perform such feats, the means (techniques or agencies) employed, the beliefs of the practitioner, and, to a certain extent, the supernatural *per se*.

Practitioners of magic can be called by many names, the most common being magus, mage, magician, adept, sorcerer, wizard, necromancer, thaumaturge, warlock, and witch. Some of these words are interchangeable, while others refer to specific techniques or proclivities.

Spelling

Since most of these words will be cropping up with some regularity, it is worth exploring their meanings and derivations, especially as this often sheds light on how these people and their arts were viewed. I promised I wouldn't be using too many obscure words, but that was foolish of me. Magic is full of splendidly obscure words and it is worth bearing in mind the importance in magic of how words sound and how they are spelled (geddit?) and the opportunities thereby created for (relatively) meaningful word association. The enigmatic and influential twentieth-century French alchemist Fulcanelli makes great mention of *la langue verte* (green language), which he describes as an *argot* that hides esoteric knowledge in plain sight, for example in Gothic architecture (*l'art gothique*). Linguistically, *argot* or *cant* is based on the connections between similar sounding words. Removing the vowels from any word, as in Arabic and Hebrew, reduces them to a sort of phonetic root or *morpheme*. All the words formed from that phonetic morpheme are related. Hence *word* becomes *wrd*, which creates not just *word*, but also *weird* and *ward*. *Cant* suggests *chant, canticle*, the easy rhythm of *canter* and also, intriguingly, *can't* and *cunt*. Good fun and also valid, since even clunky old science concurs that every manifested thing has a unique vibratory signature, a specific sound-form which is, in a magical sense, its true name, that which truly differentiates one thing from another. Ring that bell and it manifests. It has to, since it fundamentally *is* that sound. This is the basis of magic spells and incantations.

The Lost Language

I should at this point mention that according to esoteric lore there was an original language in which every word really did resonate the actual sonic signature of the phenomenon it referred to. The Biblical fable of the Tower of Babel allegorizes the story of how we came to lose this language. The story goes that we tried to build a spiral stairway to heaven and were punished for our hubris by being made to forget the sacred language. The abuse of the sacred language to usurp divine power (i.e., black magic) was the real sin, and ever since then the languages of mankind have become a babble. Modern languages are for the most part just a set of conventions. They only actually mean anything in relationship to other words; they have no absolute value. The true word for lion smells and feels like lion. It conjures all the splendid and terrible qualities with which we associate these awesome beasts. But the word *lion* has no intrinsic meaning at all. If you don't speak English it is just a sound, and not even onomatopoeic like *growl.* So knowledge gleaned through words is not real knowledge as such. Real knowledge consists in the awareness of the laws of nature, the kind of knowing that can be accessed by a powerful, experienced, intelligent animal. But don't let me put you off reading this book! Magic consists in large part of addressing our impoverished position and regaining our former powers. Words play a big part, because although language may be conventional in its intellectual interpretation, the sounds have a certain value. They can still ring a bell and resonate things within us. Anyway, even "fallen" languages are fun. Bible, Babel, babble on.

Wizard

The word *wizard* is derived from Middle English *wys*, meaning "wise." The modern meaning—that is to say the Harry Potter meaning of wizard, as "one with magical power, one proficient in the occult sciences"—did not emerge distinctly until circa 1550, which suggests that wisdom and magic were not clearly differentiated until the late Renaissance. The *-ard* is what etymologists tend to call an "intensifier," as in *drunkard* or *coward*, but is not necessarily pejorative!

Magus/Mage

Mage is the English form of the Latin *magus*, which is the singular of *magi*, as in the wise men, three kings, or Eastern sages that followed the star to Bethlehem. It is of course the root of the words *magic* and *magician*, and refers to a priestly caste of wisdom keepers, first mentioned about 2,600 years ago, whose influence extended as far west and south as Egypt and Ethiopia and as far east and north as Afghanistan and the Black Sea. We will discover much more about the Magi in the pages to come.

Adept

An *adept*—from the Latin *adeptus*, meaning an expert, "one who has attained" or been initiated—was originally used in the Middle Ages to refer to alchemists who had achieved the secret of transmutation. It subsequently became part of the initiatory ranking hierarchy in secret esoteric orders, such as the Golden Dawn. The great Irish poet W. B. Yeats is known to have been initiated as an *Adeptus Major* on his path to high priesthood of the enduringly influential Isis-Urania Temple.

Sorcerer

This term originally meant a "teller of fortunes by lot," as derived from the Old French word *sorcier*, itself derived from the medieval Latin word *sortarius*—a sorter of sorts. By the early fifteenth century it had somehow come to mean a "conjurer of evil spirits," which gives us an idea of the suspicion that surrounded the idea of divination in those very orthodox Christian times. *Sorcery* has, ever since, been associated with black magic.

Necromancer

A *necromancer* is a practitioner of *necromancy*, which originally meant "the art of divination using exhumed corpses," from the Greek word *nekromanteia*—combining *nekros* ("dead body") and *manteia* ("divination, oracle"). It went on to mean "divination through the agency of the spirits of the dead." In the Middle Ages it was misspelled as *nigromancy*, which would mean "divination through the use of the black arts," hence something of an oxymoron. The correct spelling was established in the mid-sixteenth century. In *The Lord of the Rings*, the necromancer Sauron is so-called because of his control of the "Ringwraiths," the spirits of dead men. This connotes the more common understanding of the term these days. Necromancy was one of the seven forbidden arts of Renaissance magic, along with *geomancy, pyromancy*, and various other *-mancies*.

Kabbalist

A kabbalist (also cabbalist) is a student or practitioner of an esoteric system of magic/philosophy called (the) Kabbalah (also Cabbala,

Qabbalah, QBL), which is of Jewish origin and has been one of the most important constituents of the Western magical tradition since the early Renaissance. The original Hebrew word means "reception, received lore, tradition," the tradition being a mystical interpretation of the Torah (Old Testament) based on the significance of numbers and letters. The seventeenth-century derivation *cabal* has come to mean "secret group," with sinister, conspiratorial connotations.

Hermeticist

The patron spirit of Western magic is a Graeco-Egyptian man-god called Hermes Trismegistus, a tricksy character we will come to know intimately in the second volume of the Great Wizards of History series. Hermeticists are practitioners of magical arts specifically linked to the teachings of Hermes, which included alchemy and astrology from the outset and later came to include other arts, such as tarot and Kabbalah.

Witch

We can safely trace the origins of the word *witch* to Old English *wicce* (female magician, sorceress) which later came to mean "a woman supposed to have dealings with the devil or evil spirits and to be able by their cooperation to perform supernatural acts." *Wicce* is the feminine form of Old English *wicca* (sorcerer, wizard, man who practices witchcraft or magic) from the verb *wiccian* (to practice witchcraft). The word *witch* was not originally gender-specific and beyond Old English the root of the word becomes very hard to pin down. What is certain is that witches had a bad reputation, and were consequently persecuted, as far back as Saxon times in England. The Laws of Alfred (c. 890) state that "women accustomed to receive, (female) enchanters, sorcerers and witches should not be allowed to live." Men have been referred to as witches up until modern times, but the tendency to apply the term exclusively to women led to men being referred to as "he-witches" as early as 1601. The use of the term to refer explicitly to "an ugly, evil old woman" dates back to the early fifteenth century.

Warlock

The use of the word *warlock* to denote the male equivalent of a witch goes back about five hundred years. The Old English *wærloga* (traitor, liar, enemy, devil) is compounded from *wær,* meaning "faith, fidelity; a compact, agreement, covenant," from Proto-Germanic *wera-* (cognates: Old High German *wara* "truth," or "verity," Old Norse *varar* "solemn promise, vow") and *leogan,* "to lie" (modern German *lügen*). The original sense of the word seems therefore to be "traitor to truth, deceiver," hence its later meaning of "one in league with the devil," the devil being the "Great Deceiver."

SECTION 1

PREHISTORIC AND MYTHIC MAGIC

History ain't what it used to be. We used to think of it as the whole story, but now it is more narrowly defined as the study of the past as documented in written records. Prehistory is established by what the archaeological record reveals, but over recent years a new field of history has emerged, known as deep history, which explores the roots of human existence using the findings of such distinct fields as anthropology, genetics, linguistics, and neuroscience.

Anatomically modern humans are now known to have been around for at least 300,000 years. Since our brain capacity has not grown since then we must assume that our earliest human ancestors were no less intelligent than we are today. We are not so much evolving as adapting to the different circumstances that we have created for ourselves. Although human consciousness may have been different, emphasizing the use of different parts of the brain, there is no reason to imagine that we were less sophisticated; our interaction with nature was far more sophisticated on an individual level than that of the average "Westerner" today. It appears, moreover, that our capacity for conceptual and abstract thought was already well-developed at a much earlier stage than hitherto imagined.

CHAPTER 1

THE RETURN OF
THE LION MAN

In late August 1939 archaeological excavations of a cave in southern Germany, conducted under the auspices of Heinrich Himmler's *SS Ahnenerbe* (Ancestral Heritage Institute), were abruptly terminated by the impending outbreak of the Second World War. Several important discoveries had been made there and the Reichsführer-SS had been due to visit the site in person, before his attention was diverted by preparations for the invasion of Poland. On the very last day of the dig, some carved fragments of mammoth ivory were discovered, prompting SS-Sturmbannführer Robert Wetzel, a professor of anatomy in charge of the dig, to write to SS headquarters in Berlin stating that a "significant discovery" had been made. For reasons that remain mysterious, however, several decades were to elapse before the true significance of this discovery was established.

Following the collapse of Nazi Germany, Wetzel's findings found their way into the museum at Ulm, a city on the Danube (and birthplace of Einstein) ten miles upstream from the cave, where they languished unnoticed until 1969, when an inventory inspection conducted by young archaeologist Joachim Hahn uncovered a box containing the fragments of mammoth ivory that had struck Wetzel as significant. Together with a couple of students, Hahn eagerly threw himself into a three-dimensional jigsaw puzzle and swiftly assembled an extraordinary, upright, two-legged carved figurine with both human and animal characteristics.

Hahn was apparently hip enough to have read the avant-garde writer William Burroughs, for he named the headless figure "der Mugwump," after the grotesque creatures Burroughs introduced in his deranged cult novel *The Naked Lunch*.[1] Such reading matter reveals just how different a kettle of fish the bearded, pipe-smoking Hahn was to the Nazi ideologue Wetzel, indicating the extraordinary cultural shift that had taken place in post-war Germany in the space of just one generation.

The mugwump was an archaeological sensation, but proved to be merely the start of a reconstruction process that was to last another forty-four years. Several further digs at the cave, not all of them fruitful, produced another seven hundred mostly tiny fragments, and the conclusive assembly completed at the end of 2013 revealed a standing figure, just over a foot tall, of what appears to be a human with a lion's head, reliably dated as 40,000–43,000 years old, making it the oldest work of figurative art ever discovered anywhere in the world. Let's pause for a second to consider just how old that is in human terms. That's twenty times older than Jesus, ten times older than Stonehenge

---

1 Interestingly "mugwump" is derived from a Native American word meaning "kingpin" or "great chief."

and the Great Pyramid of Giza, and seven times older than the earliest urban civilization in ancient Sumer.

The figurine's antiquity and the astonishing level of artistry it displays have led many academics to suggest that the Lion Man represents *the* peak cultural moment in human history: the arrival of the modern mind. *Ecce Homo!*

What the Lion Man may have meant to its maker is an extraordinarily rich question, but we can safely assume that it had something to do with magic; indeed, various key magical ideas are directly associated with it. Writers often trot out the line that magic is as old as mankind, and if the Lion Man represents the dawn of us as we know us, then it may well be true. So, given his cultural status and the fact that so few people have even heard of him, let's take a close look at the old thing and see what it can tell us about the way we were relating to everything at the dawn of Homo sapiens as a magician.

Who Made the Lion Man?

The great quantity and variety of similarly ancient artefacts found in the vicinity of the Lion Man, including bone flutes and beautiful animal figurines, provide a context that allows us to build an incomplete but reasonably detailed picture of the kind of lifestyle experienced by its makers. The tools and techniques employed by these people provide archaeologists with the means to define their culture, which they have dubbed "Aurignacian," after a site at Aurignac in southwest France.

As our understanding of deep history in Europe circa 40,000 BP[2] develops, the term *Aurignacian* will probably become defunct, but for now it identifies modern humans of the period, who first appeared in eastern Europe and gradually moved westwards along the course of the River Danube and beyond. They were hunter-gatherers identified by their

---

2 BP means "before present" and is widely used amongst archaeologists when referring to the distant past.

advanced tool-making and highly sophisticated figurative art. Their range extended throughout almost all of sub-glacial Europe and appears to have remained culturally consistent in many respects over a period of 15,000–20,000 years.[3] Their numbers seem to have been very small. Indeed, when I met archaeologist Dr. Rob Dinnis on a dig at Kent's Cavern in Southwest England, where the oldest modern human remains in Northern Europe have been found[4] (dated, like the Lion Man, to circa 40,000 BP), he told me that the human population of Britain—at least the part not buried under hundreds of feet of ice—may have numbered no more than forty at the time. They seem to have ranged far and wide, maintaining contact with other groups, and the Lion Man may have made such journeys with them. Some experts believe that the rapid breakthroughs in tool-making technology, after many thousands of years without progress, indicate the appearance of complex and abstract language. Certainly we see the appearance of complex and abstract art, which can only have been created by a brain as modern and developed as those of humans today.

Anatomy

The anatomy of the Lion Man is very curious. The head is certainly leonine, the body is long like a lion's, and the limbs are lion-like, with extremities more like paws than hands. The limbs are articulated like a human's, though, and the creature is standing (or lying) like a human.

The anatomy of the Lion Man allows us not just to recognise its blending of human and leonine characteristics, however, but also to discern precise features that may be suggestive of both its bearing and its function. The figure appears at first glance to be standing, but the configuration of the feet, although less carefully carved and/or

---

3 Which is pretty jaw-dropping if you consider the cultural shift that happened in Germany in the space of just one generation during the period of the Lion Man's rediscovery and re-membering.

4 A piece of jawbone, including teeth, discovered by my kinsman Arthur Ogilvy in 1927.

incomplete, has led some to suggest that the figure is standing on its toes, levitating, or even in flight, but it is also possible that it is floating or lying on its back. A recent academic paper[5] pays close attention to the very precise carving of the ears, which shows that the carver had a clear understanding of how the muscles of a lion's ear work, allowing him or her to indicate that the Lion Man is listening attentively.

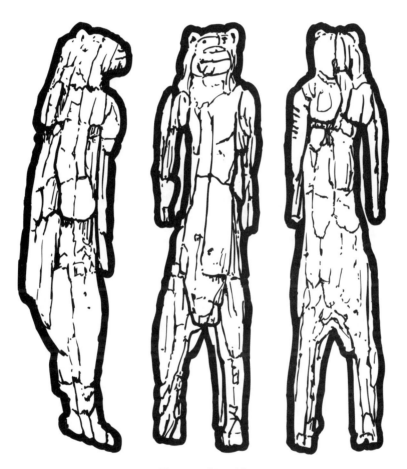

Figure 1: Lion Man

No such study has yet been made of the Lion Man's mouth, but if we are allowed to assume that it was carved with the same degree

---

5 http://www.historiaorl.com/pirsig-wehrberger-the-lion-man/.

of purpose and accuracy as the ears, then we must conclude that the carving of the upper lip as continuous, like a human's, rather than split like a lion's, is both deliberate and suggestive. The mouth is slightly open with one corner cast slightly down and the other slightly up. This not only confers a sense of personality, but it also suggests that the Lion Man is not just listening; it is also talking. What can it tell us?

The Meaning of the Lion Man

What is the Lion Man? Is it simply an extraordinary and powerful piece of art conjured from an individual imagination, or does it have a profound cultural significance shared by the whole tribal group? If so, what did the Lion Man mean to its people? Does it represent a god, a hunting totem, a talking stick, a being encountered in the spirit world, or something else entirely? The search for answers to this enormous question must necessarily be speculative, particularly since our knowledge of human culture at such a vast historical remove is so sparse.

We can thank archaeology for the discovery and reassemblage of the thousand-plus pieces of mammoth ivory to which time had reduced the figurine. The astonishing development of various scientific dating techniques has allowed the accurate dating of the piece to circa 41,000 BC, effectively more than doubling the age that archaeologists might reasonably have guessed at when it was first discovered in 1939. Another far smaller lion-man figure, also carved from mammoth ivory and of similar antiquity, was discovered in another cave in the same region, which is certainly suggestive of a profound cultural significance associated with lions.

Does the Lion Man's talking mouth suggest that its makers invested it with oracular powers? If the Lion Man was used as an oracle, either directly or through the mediation of a shamanistic medium, to help its makers make important decisions, it would certainly have played a very significant role in the life of its people. Analysis of the ivory fragments that make up the Lion Man indicates that the figurine was much handled over its lifetime, lending weight to the idea that it might have been used as a talking stick, such as are still used by traditional aboriginal tribes and even taken up by the Boy Scouts movement in the twentieth century. Talking sticks represent tribal democracy, allowing whoever is holding the stick to state their opinion on matters of shared concern. A talking stick that has been used for generations bears witness to tribal history, and Lion Man's maker may have spent many of the hundreds of hours that it took to carve it relating the tribe's history and ideas to the emerging totem. From a shamanic perspective, the Lion Man would thus resonate the tribe's entire wisdom tradition, affording it oracular powers that could be tuned into in prayerful, contemplative, or shamanic trance states.

Gender Blender?

Prior to the dating of the Lion Man, some of the oldest known figurative works of art were the so-called *Venus*[6] figurines, one of which is the Venus of Hohle Fels, believed to be the oldest representation of the human form, which was discovered in a cave just a few miles further up the Danube valley from the Lion Man's cave. Dated at 35–40,000 years old, it is a classic female fertility figure, squat and round with exaggerated hips, buttocks, and breasts. Also carved from mammoth ivory, instead of a head it has just a short, narrow stump with a hole bored in it, presumably so that it could be worn as a pendant. The figurine, and others like it found in Europe and Siberia, encouraged the idea, particularly popular with New Age feminists, that our ancestors lived in matriarchal tribal groups where Mother Earth, fertility, and child-bearing were honoured above all else and women ruled the roost. The arrival of the almost phallic-shaped Lion Man threatened to undermine the matriarchal myth, and the figurine's gender was hotly disputed, with the lack of mane, prominence of the belly button and the triangular pudendum claimed as suggestive

---

6 This appellation has become controversial because it has its origins in "the Hotten-tot Venus," a name under which a black African woman called Sarah Baartman was exhibited in freak shows in early nineteenth century Europe. Her large breasts and enormous buttocks were supposed by white Europeans (often mockingly) to be a perfect expression of a "savage" black African ideal of feminine beauty.

of femininity. Indeed, from the 1980s until just a few years ago, the figurine became something of a feminist icon, triumphantly renamed the Lion Lady. It was then established that male European cave lions lacked distinctive manes, and the discovery of more fragments and the figurine's final reassembly in 2012 and 2013 seem to have settled the dispute in favour of a masculine sex, although it may be that a certain androgyny was intended by its maker.

I recently stumbled across an ancient leonine deity that sheds a very interesting light on the Lion Man. Originally depicted as a lion standing upright, he is an *apotropaion* (protective totem) called Bez[7] and he is the guardian angel/demon of all things connected with maternity—pregnant women, fertility, suckling infants, and the home. His job is to protect the maternal home from all malign influences, including disease, evil spirits, and the "evil eye" (the projection of harmful thoughts by ill-wishers), the former usually agents of the latter. He first appeared nearly five thousand years ago in Old Kingdom Egypt, although some authorities think he may have originated elsewhere and possibly much earlier. Certainly, he appears to have no connection to the more familiar Egyptian pantheon that includes Isis, Set, Osiris, and Thoth. He gradually morphed from a standing lion to a dwarfish human figure wearing a lion skin, and sometimes a priapic ithyphallic figure similar to the Roman wine god Bacchus. He became increasingly associated with music, dance, and sexual pleasure and may even have been used as a sex toy. Essentially, he represents the honouring and protection of the feminine mysteries, particularly in relation to sex, fertility, and motherhood. He was also very much a domestic figure, kept in the house. There were no temples dedicated to him and he was never central to any form of hierarchical religion, but his popularity grew and he travelled (back?) into Europe and the Middle East. Intriguingly Bez is immortalized in the name of

---

7 More commonly spelled *Bes*, but as the "s" is pronounced as a "z," this spelling makes more sense.

the Mediterranean island of Ibiza, synonymous to many with music, dance, and pleasure. It was named after him by Phoenician colonisers in 654 BC.[8]

It is possible that the Lion Man served the same functions, although maybe not exclusively, as Bez. The miniature Lion Man discovered in the Hohle Fels cave near to the Venus figurine was also apparently designed to be worn as a pendant. The Lion Man and Venus figurines were clearly used by the same tribe at the same point in history when the human population was very low—maybe around 30,000 in the whole of Western Europe. With no need to defend themselves against other tribes, except for the odd family spat, and with everyone in each tribal unit knowing each other intimately,[9] only the most natural of hierarchies would have pertained. At this early point in our history we appear to have been honouring the masculine and feminine principles equally. One was begetter and protector, the other bearer and nurturer. We can but speculate on how sex was managed, but the only taboo vital to genetic fitness would have been incest. It is safe to assume, however, that the extraordinarily successful evolution of the species could not have been possible without a natural selection at play that instinctively avoided incest, probably on a biological level through the production of pheromones that attract those less closely related, while repelling near kin. At this stage of the game we are (mercifully) a long, long way from Freud...[10] The irony is that the species' reproductive success would eventually result in population increases that in turn

---

8 I wonder if that original Madchester raver, Bez, member of the seminal Happy Mondays and himself synonymous with music, dance, and pleasure, is aware that his favourite island is named after him. He'll no doubt be back at Glastonbury Festival this year with "Bez's Acid House," so I'll have the chance to ask him...

9 "Dunbar's Number" posits the ideal number of tribal members as 150 with an upper limit of 250.

10 Instinctive incest avoidance ensured the success of the species. From a Darwinian perspective: the closer to nature, the more natural the selection. The further from nature, the closer to Freudian complexes.

would engender competition, division, and war, all of which tend to result in the marginalisation of women.

So if, like Bez, the Lion Man is a protective totem, what is he protecting the women from, if the men already see themselves as defenders of femininity? Well, one clue is in the figurine itself. The greatest threat to man's emergence as the dominant species would have been that perfect predator, the King of the Beasts: the lion.

Animal Magic

Archaeologists and anthropologists agree that our Ice Age ancestors used magical techniques to improve their prowess as hunters. A common belief amongst hunter-gatherers is that by eating the flesh of an animal, they form a soul-bond with the species. This connection is enhanced by the ritual wearing of animal skins and jewellery made from teeth and bones. This kind of magic is called *sympathetic magic*, because it helps foster a sense of kinship between hunter and prey. By identifying with your prey, you can understand it more intimately, helping swing the odds of success in your favour. Cave paintings of prey animals and lions may have served a similar purpose.

Therianthropy

Depictions of beings that combine human and animal features are very rare in Ice Age art. The stunning Chauvet cave paintings discovered in southern France in 1994, also attributed to the Aurignacians, include a remarkable figure, the so-called "Venus and the Sorcerer," which depicts the pubic area and thighs of a female human. One of the thighs also forms the front leg of a bison, but the bison figure was superimposed later and the image is less clearly a deliberate hybrid than the Lion Man.

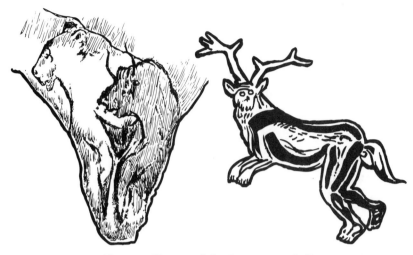

Figure 2: Venus and the Sorcerer art (left)
Figure 3: Sorcerer of Les Trois Frères (right)

The famous "Sorcerer of Les Trois Frères," dated to around 15,000 BC, is a cave painting that appears to depict a man wearing the antlers and skin of an elk or deer, with an owl's face and the tail of a fox or wolf. The reason why these two cave paintings are associated with sorcerers is that anthropologists have associated them with the magical art of shape-shifting. Shape-shifting into animal or hybrid form is known as therianthropy. Such abilities are traditionally attributed to shamans or "sorcerers" in various cultures around the world, particularly in Siberia, Africa, and the Americas. European folklore preserves the memory of such traditions in therianthropic tales of werewolves and witches' familiars. Some of our great wizards were believed to have the ability to shape-shift. Merlin is supposed to have been able to turn himself into the fierce little falcon that bears his name, while the great Renaissance wizard Cornelius Agrippa had a great black dog that could act as its master's doppelganger.

Meetings with Remarkable Insects

My own experiences of shape-shifting extend beyond the occasional hallucinatory sensation of assuming another form. While travelling in South America in 1988 I met a *curandero* [11] called Valentino in Otavalo, Ecuador, who assured me that he could cure the recently diagnosed arthritis in my right knee in a week. I was in continuous pain, and bearing in mind that the last thing my doctor had said to me before I left London was "keep taking the pills and when you get back we'll see how long we can keep you out of a wheelchair for," I figured that this might represent my only chance of avoiding premature disablement. Four days into the cure, Valentino, my girlfriend, Caddy, and I were sitting cross-legged on the king-size bed in our bamboo cabin in the high cloud forest, chanting jungle *icaros*. [12] Feeling comfortably zorbed out, my attention fell on two bright green half-lozenge shapes on the cabin wall behind Valentino.

Just as I noticed that they were symmetrically arranged like a pair of eyes, they suddenly seemed to project a cold, malevolent intelligence that penetrated me to the core. As my chanting faltered, Caddy shuddered with disgust, her attention caught by a large dull-brown beetle scurrying on the blanket between us. She twitched the blanket and the beetle flipped over onto its back, revealing a metallic emerald belly carapace that was exactly the same size, shape, and colour as the two "eyes" on the wall. My first reaction was one of relief. Phew, they weren't eyes after all, just beetles. Then I realised that if they had been beetles they would be holding onto the wall with their legs, exposing not their emerald bellies, only their dull-brown backs. My mind reeled and I looked beseechingly at Valentino. He was observing me curiously, but calmly said "grab the beetle, go to the door, throw the beetle out, and come back to the bed." I immediately did exactly as he

---

11   Traditional healer.

12   Traditional Amazonian healing songs.

said and looked to him again, completely flabbergasted, but hoping he could shed some light on the anomaly. "Sometimes," he said with a raised eyebrow, "a *brujo*[13] may choose to enter a space in the form of an insect, in order to disrupt the energy or simply to observe the scene."

"Like a fly on the wall," I said, a dawning sense of realisation allowing me to speak at last.

"Precisely so," said Valentino. I hadn't even mentioned the eyes.

Chavín de Huántar: The Lair of the Jaguar

This incident helped make sense of another meeting with a remarkable insect I'd had just a few weeks earlier. We had visited Chavín de Huántar, a remarkable archaeological site 10,000 feet up in the Peruvian Andes, at the confluence of two tributaries of the mighty River Marañón, whose waters joined the Amazon, eventually spilling into the Atlantic Ocean thousands of miles to the east. Built out of blocks of pink granite and black sandstone, the three-thousand-year-old Old Temple houses within its labyrinthine, many-chambered interior a bizarrely carved granite megalith—the *Lanzón*—depicting a terrifying, highly stylized jaguar-man with snakes for hair. The exterior was studded with ghoulish gargoyles, some feline, some human, and as we arrived at the site in the company of two travelling companions, we were importuned by a couple of small boys trying to sell us little soapstone copies of the gargoyles.

I persuaded them instead to cut us some pieces of San Pedro, a ubiquitous hallucinogenic cactus that the ancient inhabitants appear to have revered, given the carved depictions of the plant on the walls of the complex.

---

13 Maleficent sorcerer.

Figure 4: Jaguar Deity

The interior of the building was very cunningly constructed, with water channels tapped from the river, designed, it seems, to mimic the growling or roaring of a jaguar, the apex feline predator of the Americas and apparently the central deity of the Chavín civilization, which covered a good part of the coast-to-mountain area of Peru at the time of the biblical David and Solomon. The carving on the *Lanzón* is so stylized that I found it hard to visualize the entity it is supposed to represent, but a bas-relief (figure 4) clearly represents the same entity: an anthropomorphic figure bristling with fangs, claws, and snakes, brandishing a dripping San Pedro cactus. Was it a shape-shifting jaguar shaman, a jaguar god, or death personified? No one knew for sure.

We emerged from the disorientating gloom of the Old Temple and there were the young hustlers waiting for us with four nice lengths of freshly cut San Pedro. We decided to head down to the coast to brew it up. The air was too cold and thin so high in the mountains and we were all feeling a bit queasy from *siroche*—altitude sickness. The rains had come in and we caught the last bus down to the coast, a terrifying experience at night down precipitous crumbling roads with two blatantly drunk drivers. Arriving safely, miraculously, in the warm morning sunshine of a little coastal town, we bought a large aluminium cooking pot and various other supplies and hitched a ride on a donkey cart up the narrow oasis hugging a river that was starting to swell with the mountain rains we had escaped.

The donkey cart dropped us off at the edge of a granite desert with a granite hill topped by the remains of what appeared to be a huge, crumbling granite fortress.[14] We made camp under the shade of two great trees, whose heavily-leaved branches hung to the ground, forming a tent-like space around them. We made a fire, cut the San Pedro into thin slices, and started to brew it up in water. We boiled it for several hours, by which time night had fallen precipitously, plunging the outside world into blackness. Our travelling companions were a couple of surfers: John from Cornwall and Len, a full-blood Maori, who wore an ancient tribal whalebone pendant around his neck. John and Caddy decided to pass on the San Pedro, so Len and I embarked on our journey alone. The San Pedro soup had boiled down to a thin, slimy consistency and tasted unbelievably foul. We choked down as much of it as we could stand and waited. And waited. Caddy and John had fallen asleep. Nothing. Eventually we decided to have a look outside. We parted the curtain of branches and stepped out into a night of such total darkness that we couldn't even see each other's faces.

---

14 Thanks to Google Earth, I now know that our camp was on the northern side of Sechín Alto, a vast Chavín architectural complex dating back over 5,000 years.

We were amazed. No stars, no lights, no nothing; and none of the phosphene visuals that we were expecting from the San Pedro.

Suddenly we heard a sound close by that made us jump. It was a very low, challenging, guttural, masculine, animal-like noise. Alarmed, Len and I tried to identify the animal, if such it was. Horse? No. Donkey? No. Bull? No. Umm… jaguar? Suddenly we heard it again. This time the sound was right next to me and a hideous vision flashed like lightning in my mind.

"Shit, did you see that?" gasped Len.

"A crook-backed stick man with a square head, green lozenge eyes, and red fangs," I blurted.

"Same!" squeaked Len. We clung to each other like Scoob and Shaggy. But then there was nothing, just the thick, breathy blackness.

A profound strangeness had settled on us though, and after a while, we each started perceiving shadowy figures going about some strange business, not as if they were there with us, but as if we were watching some ancient black-and-white film projected onto a screen by a light too pale to let us clearly make out the action. We each had an awful feeling of dread and the sense that the shadowy figures were bent on something evil. We were becoming convinced that the San Pedro was showing us what really went on inside the Old Temple at Chavín. The priests seemed to be using San Pedro to generate a state of such terror in their victims that they were able to steal their souls at the moment that they tore out their hearts and impaled them on the lozenge-shaped megalith in the Old Temple. A sacrificial terror torture cult! We had to stop comparing notes. It was too appalling.

We retreated back behind the curtain, stoked up the fire, and crawled into our sleeping bags. I prayed for sleep to rescue me from the ghastly horrors in my mind, but no such release came. All was hideous, pointless, soul-destroying horror. I could hear Len, tossing, turning, and groaning, but could offer him no comfort. In the midst of my despair I suddenly noticed a little light come in through the curtain on the other side of the fire, flashing gently. Flash-flash,

flash-flash. A firefly. But it was blue! As I questioned its blueness, I was gently engulfed by a blue wave of the deepest, most comforting, redeeming bliss, lifting me out of the abyss of my despair and bearing me lovingly to the Land of Nod where good children are safe and sound forever. The last thing I knew was Len sighing with the same profoundly grateful relief.

We awoke at the same moment. Morning sun was shining through the curtains. John and Caddy were quietly busying about, making breakfast and brewing up coffee, oblivious of the horrors of the night. Len and I looked into each other's eyes, both seeing a mixture of wonder, awe, and relief. All was well. "Did you see the blue firefly?" asked Len.

What *was* the blue firefly? I can only speculate. There is one species of blue firefly, the Blue Ghost (*Phausis reticulata*), but it is confined to the eastern and central United States and it just glows, but doesn't flash. Twelve years later I encountered a little swarm of blue fireflies during an alchemy seminar with Manfred Junius in northern Bohemia, Czech Republic. It was in the walled garden of Roztěž Castle, former hunting lodge of the splendid Count Sporck, the founder of Czech Freemasonry. At dusk on a damp Summer Solstice evening I was looking for firewood to build a Solstice bonfire. I came through the rickety old door and suddenly there was a blue firefly a few yards away. I was amazed by its miraculously familiar flashing blueness, and suddenly there was a fantasy of them[15] flitting and flashing just a couple of feet in front of me. They were the nearest thing to a traditional Victorian flower fairy that I have ever seen, although, in truth, that was more the way I felt them, as it was too dark to see anything of their bodies other than their amazing, gently flashing blue lights. I sensed a wonder and delight in them that touched me so deeply that I burst into tears on the spot. My memory is slightly hazy at this point, but I think that after maybe less than a minute they faded and disappeared. I went

---

15 I hereby propose that the collective noun for a bunch of fairies be a "fantasy."

back to the lobby of the castle and asked the gate keeper, in German, about the fireflies. He said that fireflies only appear at the end of a long hot summer. This was late June after a cold, wet spring and dismal early summer, so I could not have seen any fireflies. As for blue ones! He laughed and looked at me as if I were stoned, deranged, or having him on. I was certainly neither the former nor the latter.

As for the crook-backed thing that had so spooked Len and me at Sechin Alto, who knows? When Caddy and I met Valentino in Ecuador a few weeks later, he was appalled that I could have been so foolish as to ingest such a powerful and unpredictable *planta de poder* (power plant) as San Pedro without a guide, particularly specimens gathered from Chavín de Huántar. We concluded my arthritis cure with a San Pedro session that was entirely different from my Chavín experience. Deep in the night, Valentino had fallen asleep in his hammock, tired of the Scottish folk songs that I was singing with clannish gusto. The candles on the altar sputtered and flared occasionally as small moths sacrificed themselves to the flames. I looked up at the rafter of the spacious hut and spotted the largest grasshopper I had ever seen. It was at least six inches long, with a head the size of a crab apple, and it gazed down on me balefully. I recalled the "fly-on-the-wall" incident a few days earlier, but I was feeling so strong and ecstatic that I didn't feel at all spooked. I did, however, entertain the thought that it might be acting as the eyes and ears of some brujo, so I stared back at it and engaged it in psychic warfare. My technique was unsophisticated, but confident, and I found myself projecting that old English hooligan taunt: "If you think you're hard enough!" I had to laugh, and at that moment the grasshopper hurled itself at the largest candle, bursting into flames and splashing hot wax all over the altar. The crackling and spitting were loud enough to waken Valentino, who roused himself in time to prevent his entire altar from going up in flames. Having brought everything under control, he gazed at me levelly and pronounced, "Now I see you are cured." And I was. Nearly thirty years later I'm still not in a wheelchair and I have no problem with my right knee.

Cat People

My suspicion that the jaguar priests of Chavín were conducting a terror cult was sustained by what I later found out about the infamous Leopard Society of West Africa, who terrorized people into believing in the reality of shape-shifting were-leopards by dressing in leopard skins and murdering people with brutal false claws. This terrifying cannibal cult was not extirpated until the mid-twentieth century, and, so a firsthand witness has told me, survives in some aspects even to this day. Lion-man murders have also been committed. In 1948, three women and four men were executed for their part in the "lion-men murders" in the Singida district of Tanganyika. The perpetrators had dressed in lion skins and murdered more than forty natives in ritual slayings that left wounds on their victims resembling the marks of a lion's claws.

My old friend Mike Jay, intrigued by my Chavín adventures, visited Chavín de Huántar himself a few years later. The piece he wrote, *Enter the Jaguar*,[16] has been published in various journals and remains probably the best English language overview of what may really have been going on there. He convincingly demonstrates that Chavín de Huántar was probably the centre of a psychedelic initiatory cult using DMT, the most powerful plant psychedelic in the world, in addition to San Pedro. The chambers in the temple were for incubating those to be initiated, creating the kind of sensory deprivation which would have been an ideal prelude for the DMT-fuelled encounter with the Lanzón entity at the heart of the labyrinth. The sense of feline transformation under the influence of DMT remains a common element of South American DMT shamanism, and I can attest from my own

---

16 First published in *Strange Attractor Journal, Volume 2* (2005), more recently in *Entheogens and the Development of Culture* (2013).

recent experience that the manifestation can appear extremely real. Far from losing my soul, my belief in its existence was powerfully affirmed.

The Catholic priests of the Spanish conquistadors believed that the frightening imagery of the pre-conquest civilizations proved that they were enslaved by devils, but perhaps in the case of Chavín de Huántar, at least, the gargoyles serve to protect the sacred sanctuary just as they do on Catholic cathedrals. An alien visitor might also find the sacred image of the deity at the heart of the cathedral no less cruel and barbaric than the jaguar totem of Chavín. One of the things that helped Mike unravel the mysteries of Chavín as far as he has was an understanding of the context in which the mystery traditions of Ancient Greece manifested and flourished around the same time. The Mysteries are central to the Western esoteric tradition, and, as we shall see, one of their central deities also has a penchant for dressing up in the skins of ferocious felines.

The Lion Man has many descendants, it seems, but there are still more clues to be derived from his earliest known manifestation before we pick up later traces of his legacy.

Theriomorphism

Theriomorphism, as opposed to therianthropy or shape-shifting, confers the status of a deity onto an animal. This probably began with ancestor worship; many ancient peoples identified particular animals as ancestor figures. Animal gods are often half-human hybrids, usually combining an animal head with a human body, as in the ancient Egyptian pantheon. Like the Lion Man, the ferocious Egyptian warrior goddess Sekhmet is depicted with a lion's head and a human body, often crowned with a sun disk, which identifies her as a solar goddess. The same goes fors Bastet, originally an Egyptian warrior lioness, but later depicted with the head of a cat. Both these feline goddesses were revered as protectors of the faithful and of the kingdom. And then there is Bez, of course, our little lion man guardian of all things maternal. A possibly even older lion-man deity than Bez is Narasimha ("lion-man"), described in the Upanishads of the Indian Vedic tradition as the god of knowledge and the Lord of Brahma, the creator god. He is associated with heat and fire and sometimes depicted with a sun-like mane. Other solar gods associated with lions include Ra, Mithras,[17] and Yaghuth, while in Christianity Jesus is called the Lion of Judah, the same epithet Rastafarians apply to His Imperial Majesty Haile Selassie, King of Kings, Emperor of Ethiopia, represented as a crowned lion. In astrology, the zodiac sign of Leo is ruled by the Sun, whose symbol is $\odot$, resembling a golden lion's eye in bright sunlight. The symbol for gold is also $\odot$.

In alchemy, the lion corresponds to both the Sun and gold. The primary symbol of the Philosophers' Stone, the agent that transmutes base metal into gold, is the Red Lion, which happens to be the most common pub name in Britain. The earliest known stamped gold coins feature a lion's head, while colour photography, revealing the full spectrum of colours made visible by sunlight, was enabled through the use of gold chloride. The lion Aslan in the Narnia series incorporates all these correspondences.

Star Lore

At least as far back as the third millennium BC[18] the Sumerians associated the constellation they called the lion with the sun, and Leo remains ruled by the sun in contemporary astrology. But just how far back in time can we find evidence for animal-related star lore? Some very interesting recent research by Dr. Michael Rappenglück of the

---

17 As Chronos leontocephalus ("lion-headed time"), Mithras (or Aion) is depicted as a lion-headed man, often with wings. In this form, he represents eternity. For the great psychologist C. G. Jung (1875–1961) it represented death/rebirth. Interestingly, I recently came across a depiction of a lion-headed Tibetan deity called Simhamukha, which I immediately recognized from a picture on Valentino's altar in Ecuador.

18 http://www.ancient-wisdom.com/zodiac.htm.

University of Munich suggests that some of the cave paintings of Lascaux (circa 17,000 BP) are pictorial images of constellations, a prime example being a depiction of a bull/aurochs incorporating the constellation of Taurus with the Seven Sisters of the Pleiades above its withers. A panel in the cave of La-Tête-du-Lion (circa 21,000 BP) also features a painted bull/aurochs with seven dots. At both sites, the bull's eye marks the position of Aldebaran, the primary star in the Taurus constellation. French researcher Chantal Jègues-Wolkiewiez has produced compelling evidence to suggest that the whole gallery of paintings in the Great Hall of Lascaux represents an ice age star map,[19] depicting the night sky as it would have appeared to the artists some 17,000 years ago, suggesting a continuity of pictorial astronomical associations going back much further than previously thought.

Figure 5: Lascaux cave painting

19 http://news.bbc.co.uk/1/hi/sci/tech/871930.stm.

Interestingly, the name "seven sisters" has been used for the Pleiades in the languages of many ancient cultures, as far apart as Australia, North America, and Siberia, suggesting an ancient common origin at least as old as the Lion Man, unless the aboriginal Australians coincidentally just happened to choose the same name.[20] At Chavín de Huántar, the temple of the Jaguar Man, there are many indications of the cultural importance of astronomy, including a large stone with seven concavities configured like the Pleiades.

Apart from the merging of lion and human anatomical characteristics, the Lion Man has one other distinct feature: there are seven parallel lines carved into its left arm. There are many possible explanations for what these could signify, but if the number seven is in itself significant, then it is possible that they represent the Pleiades. Intriguingly, there is a well-established New Age myth generated by many well-known channellers such as Murry Hope, which claims that the ancestors of humanity are inter-galactic lion beings that colonised the Pleiades. Easy though such claims are to dismiss, it is nevertheless interesting that such an idea should surface and find wide acceptance amongst New Agers just at the time when the Lion Man was being re-membered. I first came across the idea of cosmic lion beings at the same time that I was researching the Lion Man, while on a walk with my friend Sabrina in crop circle country in Wiltshire, England. A somewhat eccentric fellow greeted us as we emerged from our car and insisted on telling us a long and garbled tale. We humoured him, while obliging him to maintain our brisk walking pace, and when we reached the summit of the hill we paused, allowing him to catch his breath and, eventually, reach his punch line, which involved a personal encounter with an alien being with a lion's head! A few days later, Sabrina reported that there was an exhibition in a gallery in nearby Glastonbury that featured several portraits of lion-headed angelic entities. Previewing it

---

20 Cf. Munya Andrews, *Seven Sisters of the Pleiades: Stories from Around the World*, Spinifex Press, 2004.

online, the quality of the art did not strike me as especially inspired, so I resisted the urge to visit the gallery and question the artist. That may have been a missed opportunity, but when exploring the esoteric it is easy to get lost if you follow every white rabbit down every hole…

The Magnificent Seven

Another significant seven to consider, perhaps the most significant seven of all (along with the seven colours of the rainbow and the seven notes of a musical octave[21]) are the seven "wandering stars" visible to the human eye. These wanderers are the visible bodies of our solar system that the ancients observed in an endless dance against the backdrop of the fixed stars. The seven wanderers account for one of our constant time cycles, the seven days of the week—Satur(n)day, Sunday, Mo(o)nday, etc.—as well as the pantheons of such diverse cultures as Chaldean, ancient Greek, Hindu, Norse, Mayan, and Roman, after which the planets are still named in Latin tongues.[22] The Lion Man's makers no doubt experienced a mythic relationship with the night skies that had developed over many thousands of years. Joining the star dots to make pictures and weaving myths out of them is a universal, fundamentally human trait and I have spent many nighttime hours on my back beneath stars throbbing with mysterious stories, meanings, and connections. The heavens, as the devil's doctor Paracelsus the Great might have said, are an open book for those with the eyes to read it.

---

21 The word *octave* refers to the number eight, the eighth note being the repetition of the first note at a higher octave.

22 In English, the names of some of the planetary days have been supplanted by Norse/Germanic gods, such as Odin/Woden for Wednesday, instead of Mercredi. As we will eventually discover, there are direct connections between Odin/Woden and Hermes/Mercury, just as the thunderbolt-wielding Thor replaced his counterpart Zeus/Jove/Jupiter.

There is no reason to believe that the Aurignacians did not imbue the wanderers with personalities and even deify them as later cultures did. It may even be that they identified themselves with the wanderers, recognising a connection with their nomadic hunter-gatherer lifestyle. They may even have mapped the planets' movements against the skyscape of the stars upon a mythologised landscape below.

As Above, So Below

One lion man associated with the sun and the number seven is an ancient Vedic deity depicted with seven rays emanating from its crown and described by the great esoteric religious syncretist Helena Blavatsky as the "man-lion Singha…the Solar lion…the emblem of the Sun and the Solar cycle."[23] Given the endlessly observable phenomenon of the wanderers, only those who doubt that the Aurignacians had a fully developed consciousness would deny that the Lion Man could be an anthropomorphic solar deity, the embodiment of the sun or the solar system as a whole. With its human attributes, the Lion Man may even represent an astonishingly early example of the ancient magical notion of the microcosm, which sees man as embodying the whole of the universe, the macrocosm in miniature. This notion is exemplified in the famous "Emerald Tablet of Hermes Trismegistus," an Egyptian alchemical allegory concerning "the operation of the Sun," which may be a mere two thousand years old, but possibly echoes a primordial wisdom tradition that may be even older than the Lion Man. Isaac Newton's translation reads, "That which is below is like that which is above & that which is above is like that which is below…"[24]

The idea that the earth mirrors the heavens is found in many traditions and civilisations other than the ancient Egyptians, including the Mayans and the aboriginal Australians. Graham Hancock's

---

23 Blavatsky, 1888.

24 We now know that Newton was obsessed with alchemy; cf. Dobbs, 1975.

bestselling *Heaven's Mirror* explores this idea in detail. There is considerable evidence to suggest that the ancient Egyptians were not just conscientious observers of the heavens, but that they understood the precession of the equinoxes and actually built many of their monuments, such as the pyramids at Giza, to reflect the alignments of certain constellations at certain specific points in history. The Mayans and Australian aboriginal tribes were aware of the "Great Year," as a full processional cycle is known. Indeed it appears to be central to many of the world's great myth traditions. A Great Year lasts about 25,800 years, which happens to be the same amount of time that separates the Lion Man from the Lascaux cave paintings.

The question, then, is whether our early Aurignacian ancestors were sufficiently intelligent, observant, and imaginative to make the same associations that we find expressed in much later cultures with combined sun-lion-human-planetary imagery. The answer, according to such experts as Dr. Jill Cook, Head of Prehistory at the British Museum, is an emphatic "yes!" The ability to conceive imaginary abstract concepts and express them in art indicates the activity of what Dr. Cook describes as "a complex super brain like our own, with a well-developed pre-frontal cortex powering the capacity to communicate ideas in speech and art." [25]

It seems clear from the evidence that has emerged in recent decades that the people of the Lion Man were as human as we are. This should shift the pernicious perception that our ancestors of the time were lumbering cavemen dragging their women around by the hair. We were clearly sensitive, creative, expressive people who had mastered the art of tribe and, having identified with the lion as an ancestral totem possibly many thousands of years before, were in the process of taking the lion's crown and wearing it ourselves.

---

25 Jill Cook, *Ice Age Art: Arrival of the Modern Mind*, British Museum Press, 2013.

CHAPTER 2

ORPHEUS AND THE MAGIC OF MUSIC

The great Renaissance magi Marsilio Ficino and Pico della Mirandola helped establish the idea of the *Prisci Theologi* ("original theologians"), a line of adepts stretching back into deep history who carried the perennial flame of a primordial wisdom tradition that was, they insisted, concordant with the accepted teachings of the Catholic Church. As mentioned before, this Golden Chain of illuminated masters included various characters both historical and legendary, such as Enoch, Abraham, Noah, Zoroaster, Moses, Hermes Trismegistus, the Brahmins, the Druids, David, Solomon, Pythagoras, Plato, the Sibyls, and Jesus. Most such roll calls quoted by authorities through the centuries are shorter than this, but one character who is invariably included, usually placed between Solomon and Pythagoras, is Orpheus.

Ancient Greek Superhero

Like all "classically educated" children, I first encountered the magical musician Orpheus when reading the epic Greek superhero myth of Jason and the Argonauts and their quest for the Golden Fleece. Orpheus was one of the Argonauts, the crew of the mighty ship Argo, whose number included other great mythic heroes like Hercules, Theseus,[26] Bellerophon,[27] and the heavenly twins Castor and Pollux. I realise now that I must have been particularly drawn to the story because at the time I first read it, aged nine, my father was coincidentally serving a "roving commission" aboard the Royal Navy frigate HMS *Argonaut*, which kept him away at sea—like Odysseus on his odyssey—for nearly a year. I compensated for his absence by immersing myself in tales of seafaring heroes battling forces so monstrous and extraordinary that my imagination was permanently inflamed. Fifty years later I am still teasing out the secrets hidden beneath the surfaces of these wild stories. Because these myths are expressions of fundamental relationships, they operate on a magical level, so it is worth sifting through them for the gold they contain.

The name Orpheus chimes with Greek *orphne*, meaning "darkness (of night)"and *orphanos*, "fatherless, orphan"; the Proto-Indo-European root *orbh-* means "to separate"; a school nickname for Orpheus might be *Orifice*, or *Orful*, or *Orsome* if he was popular. Orpheus's superpower was the ability to enchant any living thing, even the elements, through the captivating power and beauty of his singing and lyre playing. He is often depicted surrounded by wild animals in thrall to his music.

The classical Greek poet Pindar tells us that he inherited his innate love of music from his mother Calliope, the greatest of the Muses (from whom the word *music* is derived) and was taught by his brother Linus, the legendary inventor of melody and rhythm. It was Apollo that gave Orpheus the lyre that he in turn had been given by its inventor Hermes,

---

26 Slayer of the snake-haired Gorgon Medusa.

27 Slayer of the Chimera.

who had charmed his way out of trouble and into the eternal company of the gods of Mount Olympus through the enchanting power of his music. The words *enchant* and *charm* come from the same verbal root (meaning *song*) that also gives us the word *incantation*, demonstrating that music and song are fundamentally magical devices.

Orpheus's magical musical exploits as an Argonaut included conjuring the wind to propel the good ship Argo through the waves, stilling the fearsome Clashing Rocks of the Bosphorus, and plunging the guardian dragon of the Golden Fleece into a sleep deep enough for Jason to steal it. Aside from such marvellous adventures, Orpheus will always be best remembered for his doomed attempt to save his wife, Eurydice, from the Underworld.

It was not until exploring the history of Western esotericism, however, that I realised that Orpheus held a position of importance and influence in the ancient Greek world and beyond that raised him above all the other mortals immortalised in classical mythology. A mystery cult known as Orphism was established in his name and the cosmological and theological "Orphic" literature ascribed to him had a significant influence on both Plato and Pythagoras. His name, if not his cult, survived the Dark Ages that followed the fall of the classical world, and he was rediscovered and championed by Renaissance mages such as Pico and Ficino. Ficino translated the *Hymns of Orpheus* and played them on a lyre, becoming known himself as "the Second Orpheus." As a result, Orpheus became one of the great muses of the late Renaissance, a highbrow subject for art, literature, and music. His most enduring presence has been on stage, especially in opera. Following Ficino's translation of the *Hymns of Orpheus*, his friend Poliziano wrote a play called *Orfeo* that was a forerunner of opera, being at least half sung, and envisioned as a rebirth of classical Greek tragedy. It was staged at Carnevale in 1474 with an ingenious set designed by Leonardo da Vinci.

The earliest opera whose music has survived is Jacopo Peri's *Eurydice*, first performed in Florence in 1600. Seven years later Monteverdi wrote opera's first acknowledged masterpiece *L'Orpheo* and since then there have been over seventy operas based on Orphic themes, including three this century. Orpheus was a principle muse of the Romantics and has inspired numerous plays, ballets, and films, notably *Black Orpheus* (1959) and Jean Cocteau's *Orphée* (1950).

The End of the World: The Late Bronze Age Collapse

Before we explore the cultural archaeology of Orpheus and Orphism, let's see what historical and religious context we can place Orpheus in. This is always difficult with early Greek history, not just because so many differing accounts by so many different authors have miraculously survived the millennia. On a topographical level, we have the findings of archaeology to help identify the most concrete stories. A good example of this is the discovery of the ruins of Troy in 1868, which demolished the fashionable Enlightenment opinion that Troy was a mythical place spun from the imagination of Homer along with all the other fabulous nonsense. We now know that at least nine different Troys existed between 3000 BC and 500 AD, all of which—apart from the first, presumably—arose phoenix-like from the ruins of their predecessor. The Troy of Homer's *Iliad* is believed to have been the one known to archaeologists as Troy VIIa, which fell to Achilles and the Greeks around 1183 BC, a hundred years after its legendary construction by Poseidon, Apollo, and Aeacus.

Archaeology has also come to our aid in sifting fact from fable in Plato's histories. There's still no sign of Atlantis, but the wars he refers to in the *Timaeus* and *Critias* are identified by historians as part of the "Late Bronze Age Collapse," a cataclysmic period between 1200 and 1150 BC when Levantine civilization[28] was obliterated by a perfect storm of volcanic eruptions, climate change, drought, famine, earthquakes, invasions, internal disruption, and plague. We remember this cataclysm in the cautionary tales of Atlantis, Sodom, and Gomorrah. It is now clear that the level of civilization that had been achieved, as evidenced by the ruins of countless cities from Greece to Syria down

---

28 Mycenean Greek civilization and the Hittite Empire of Anatolia (Turkey) in particular.

to the Nile, was highly advanced. We know that the trade routes that became known as the Silk Road predate the collapse, linking Greece with all the lands to the east as far as China and Mongolia, allowing for a flow not just of exotic goods, but also exotic ideas. The collapse stalled all that, resulting in major depopulation and a near total loss of literacy, precipitating the Greek Dark Ages that persisted for three hundred years or more. In parts of Anatolia[29] the cultural high-water mark was not reached again for a thousand years.

A coherent script known as Linear B was deciphered from inscriptions and tablets found on Crete and mainland Greece by two English linguists in the early 1950s. They established that the language behind it was Mycenaean Greek, but Linear B did not survive the Greek Dark Ages and it was not replaced with the Greek alphabet until the late ninth or early eighth century BC. Most of the familiar Greek gods and goddesses are named in Linear B, showing that the Greek religion survived the disaster, but with only Homer and Hesiod's compilations of pre-collapse Greek myth/legend/history to go on, there is no knowing how much tradition was lost forever.

The post-traumatic stress following the collapse of Mycenaean civilization must have been as emotionally and psychologically devastating as it was culturally. Greek civilization was all but wiped out. The impression I get from my research is that even the horrors and aftermath of the Second World War may not be comparable. Not only was the death toll probably far higher—perhaps 40–70 percent of the population—but there was no one to pick up the pieces the way the winning side did in 1945. There was no winning side. There were small pockets of traumatised people clinging to life, hiding out in the hills from brutal bands of desperate killers who gradually exterminated each other or died of starvation. There was nothing left; no books, no writing, little tradition, and after a few generations, few cultural memories. As Plato writes in *Critias*, the Greeks forgot their heritage "because for many generations the survivors of that destruction died and made

---

29 Modern Turkey.

no sign." [30] The writings of Homer appear in this context to have been almost miraculously produced. They were written in a completely new script for which a new alphabet had been adapted from the Phoenician one just a few decades earlier, possibly by a single person, possibly by Homer himself,[31] the old one having been completely lost and forgotten.

Alexander the Great considered Homer's epics to be the epitome of Greek genius, and indeed they seem to have been the one thing that carried over the germ of the rich culture that had blossomed before the holocaust. Greek civilization had to start again, pretty much from scratch, and it kicked off with a couple of epic sagas that had presumably survived in oral tradition, which provided Greece with a cultural identity, and which remain, along with the Bible, amongst the most influential literature ever written, at least from a Western perspective.

The Origins of Orpheus

We first hear of "famous Orpheus" at the dawn of the so-called Classical Period,[32] when ancient Greece had emerged from its dark age

---

30 Plato, *Critias*, Benjamin Jowett translation, 1860s.

31 The writings attributed to Homer may actually have been written by several different people, as some scholars believe is the case with Shakespeare's works.

32 Spanning the period between the fall of the last Athenian tyrant in 510 BC and the death of Alexander the Great in 323 BC.

and city-states like Athens, Sparta, Corinth, and Thebes were becoming powerful enough to resist the might of the Persian Empire, eventually securing their independence through such famous victories as Marathon and Salamis. The classical Greece of Plato, Socrates, Aristotle, Sophocles, and Democritus had an enormous influence on the Romans, whose empire eventually subsumed it. It later had a similar influence on Islam, through which it entered Christendom, thus bringing an end to the European dark ages and laying the foundations of Western civilization. Western politics, philosophy, art, science, theatre, and literature are all in great part derived from this period of Greek history. Western civilization has therefore tended to pride itself on its pristine European pedigree, uncontaminated by outside influences, despite the fact that Plato himself acknowledges the Greeks' cultural inferiority to ancient Egypt. In *Critias*, Plato relates his forbear Solon's experience when visiting the temple of the ancient goddess Neith at Saïs in the Nile Delta. The priests tell him that Neith and Athena, patron goddess of Athens, are one and the same and that their two cities were once closely related. When Solon tries to tell them about the history of Athens, one of the priests says "O Solon, Solon, you Hellenes [Greeks] are but children," and tells him that the Greeks are completely ignorant of ancient tradition as a result of all the "many destructions of mankind arising out of many causes." Such historical statements have traditionally been dismissed by scholars as having no foundation in truth, but the discoveries made by earth scientists and archaeologists in recent decades are increasingly supportive of their veracity, which makes the rest of the priest's remarks to Solon all the more interesting.[33]

In Virgil's classic version of the story of Orpheus, our hero fails to save his dead wife, Eurydice, from the Underworld, despite having enchanted the seven-headed hellhound Cerberus and the king and queen of the Underworld, Hades and Persephone. Afterwards, he

---

33 See Appendix 1.

wanders the land disconsolately until torn apart by furious Maenads, devotees of the man-god Dionysus, who himself was mythically dismembered. Their stories have also come down to us, like that of the Lion Man, in scattered fragments, and the scholarly process of re-collecting them correctly has taken twists and turns over the last two centuries as new bits have been exhumed from the far-flung graves of the longtime dead.

The historical Orpheus, if he ever existed, is said by both Diodorus[34] and Apollodorus[35] to have been born in Thrace in the far north of the Greek world, where the cult of Dionysus was said to have (re)surfaced out of the old earth mystery cults of the late Palaeolithic era. As Diodorus writes:

> *He was the son of Oeagrus, a Thracian by birth, and in culture and song-music and poesy he far surpassed all men of whom we have a record; for he composed a poem which was an object of wonder and excelled in its melody when it was sung. And his fame grew to such a degree that men believed that with his music he held a spell over both the wild beasts and the trees. And after he had devoted his entire time to his education and had learned whatever the myths had to say about the gods, he journeyed to Egypt, where he further increased his knowledge and so became the greatest man among the Greeks both for his knowledge of the gods and for their rites, as well as for his poems and songs.[36]*

He also took part in the expedition of the Argonauts and was so distraught at the tragic death of his wife that he dared the impossible in his attempt to rescue her from Hades; in this exploit he resembled Dionysus, for the myths relate that "Dionysus brought up his mother Semelê from Hades, and that, sharing with her his own immortality, he changed her name to Thyonê."

---

34 Diodorus Siculus wrote a massive universal history during the first century BC.

35 Now more correctly known as Pseudo-Apollodorus (first or second century AD), his *Bibliotheca* is considered the most important mythographical source work.

36 Diodurus, *Volume 4*, Book 25, Section 2–3.

Elsewhere Diodorus writes that Dionysus gave the kingdom of Thrace to Orpheus's grandfather Charops "and instructed him in the secret rites connected with the initiations; and Oeagrus...then took over both the kingdom and the initiatory rites which were handed down in the mysteries, the rites which afterwards Orpheus,...who was the superior of all men in natural gifts and education, learned from his father; Orpheus also made many changes in the practices and for that reason the rites which had been established by Dionysus were also called *Orphic.*" [37]

Dionysus: Ecstatic Lord of the Dance

It is impossible to understand the significance of Orpheus without first trying to get to grips with Dionysus. Dionysus is a deeply mysterious divinity. Indeed in one aspect he represents the old earth mysteries; the Green Man personified; the chthonic force of nature that erupts unstoppably in spring; germinating and proliferating like a writhing green vine that attains its fullest growth before flowering, cross-pollinating, withering, and dying; spending its last energy into the precious, potent seed that falls into the dark, receptive, subterranean soil whence its

37 Diodorus, 3, 65, 6.

sire first sprung, there to abide in nurturing darkness until the quicken-
ing force should spring again in the endless cycle of eternal becoming
and dying.

The fruit borne by this serpentine vine is the grape and Dionysus
is credited with introducing wine wherever he travels, which is far and
wide. Dionysus is an exotic, beautiful, androgynous stranger clad in
killer cat skins,[38] arriving like a triumphant, conquering hero from Elsewhere, astride a leopard or in a golden chariot drawn by lions or tigers,
always holding his strange magic wand, the *thyrsus*. His retinue, or *thi-
asos*, is no less exotic, resembling something out of an R-rated Narnia:
nymphs, centaurs, priapic satyrs, fauns, and other magical beasts cavort
lewdly in his wake, playing music, drinking wine, singing "hey babe,
take a walk on the wild side," his Maenads in dithyrambs,[39] arching
and gyrating in ecstatic enthusiasm,[40] legs akimbo, heads thrown back,
ready to be mounted by the divine spirit of the gorgeous god.[41]

Dionysus is a half-human Olympian god (his father being Zeus
and his mother Semele, a mortal) and he gets just a few mentions in
the earliest Greek writings by Homer and Hesiod. We know that his
cult in Greece predated the Greek dark ages, however, because Dionysus appears on Linear B inscriptions, confirming that he was not
a comparatively recent foreign import at the start of the classical period, as some scholars liked to think. In the so-called Homeric Hymns
(seventh century BC) he is celebrated with eighty lines, which ranks
him fifth behind Hermes, Apollo, Demeter, and Aphrodite. In one of

---

38 Usually panther. The Greek word for *panther* is not specific to any genus of the big
   cats and can mean lion, leopard, tiger, or, in ancient times, any super scary big beast
   apart from a dragon.

39 An archaic expression; to be "in dithyrambs" literally means to be ecstatically
   chanting hymns of praise to Dionysus. Frequently used by my parents to denote a
   highly loquacious state of over-enthusiasm.

40 *Enthousiazein* means to be inspired or possessed by a god in Greek.

41 This classic pose for divine possession is depicted on ancient Greek pottery and still
   seen amongst dancing devotees of voodoo/vodou.

the hymns, he turns into a lion to free himself from pirates, while another alludes to the mystery of his birth by insisting that he was not born in Naxos, Dracanum, Icarus, or by the river Alpheus, but on Mount Nysa, which is not much help, since the location of Mount Nysa has variously been cited as Arabia, Ethiopia, Egypt, Babylon, the Red Sea, Thrace, Thessaly, India, Libya, Lydia, Macedonia, Naxos, Syria, and somewhere near Pangaios (a mythical island south of Arabia). Homer and Diadorus opt for somewhere "between Phoenicia and the Nile," while Arrian, the generally reliable Roman biographer of Alexander the Great, says that when Alexander invaded the Indus valley in 327 and 326 BC, he came upon a town called Nysa that the locals insisted was dedicated to the god Dionysus, and as such was to be treated with respect. Alexander was so impressed to be following in the fabled footsteps of Dionysus that he granted the town's wish to be left unharmed and free.

Diodorus relates that Dionysus conquered the entire world apart from Britain and Ethiopia, whereupon he returned with the gift of wine.

Dionysus is the very definition of exotic[42] and therefore the least Greek of the Olympians. He also has many different names and epithets. The latter, which refer to aspects and characteristics of the god, include, among many, many others: "The Wild One," "The Dancer," "The Saviour," "Bringer of Many Joys," "The Healer," "The Liberator," and, fittingly, "The Many-Named One." The fact that so many places across the entire world known to the ancient Greeks were variously cited as the birthplace of Dionysus gives an indication of just how universal his cult may once have been, even if under the guise of different names.

Alternative names and other gods with whom he was often conflated include Liber, Phanês, Zagreus, and Sabazius. There is even a Sri Lankan divinity called Skanda-Murukan, whose cult is still celebrated at

---

42 From the Greek *exotikos:* "foreign," literally "from the outside."

Kataragama,[43] and who has been associated with Dionysus for at least two thousand years. Dionysus's exoticism has had him compared by scholars to foreign gods, particularly Hindu Shiva and Egyptian Osiris. Shiva is an ambivalent god of ecstasy presiding over death and rebirth. *Shiva Nataraja* is the symbolic depiction of Shiva as Lord of the Dance and patron of actors and the dramatic arts.

As for Bacchus, it is generally thought that it is just the Roman name for Dionysus, but according to Diodorus:

> *Many epithets … have been given him by men, who have found the occasions from which they arose in the practices and customs which have become associated with him. So, for instance, he has been called Baccheius from the bacchic bands of women who accompanied him, Lenaeus from the custom of treading the clusters of grapes in a wine-tub (lenos), and Bromius from the thunder (bromos) which attended his birth; likewise for a similar reason he has been called Pyrigenes ("Born-of-Fire").*[44]

So Bacchus comes from *bacchic*, not the other way around. Indeed the word *bacchic* appears in Greek texts dating back to at least the fifth century BC, centuries before the cult of Bacchus/Dionysus reached Rome. It appears to refer, as Diodorus suggests, to a type of "practice and custom," or rather a state of being—*bakkheia*—and therefore has a meaning that is not exclusively identified with Dionysus. The root of the word is obscure, but it may be related to "Vakchos," from the same root as Latin *vox* meaning "voice, cry, call," which makes me think that those in a state of bakkheia may commonly be ululating or "speaking in tongues."

Apart from all his many names, Dionysus is also distinguished by being twice or even thrice-born. Here's how:

His mother Semele is so beautiful that Zeus is smitten and courts her in the guise of many animals to convince her of his divinity, until

---

43   Cf. http://kataragama.org/research/dionysus.htm.

44   Diodorus, 4, 5, 1.

she falls for his charms and conceives. Zeus's wife Hera finds out, and to get revenge, disguises herself as an old woman. Winning Semele's confidence, Hera sows doubt in her mind about her lover's true identity. When he returns, Semele easily persuades the besotted god to promise the granting of a wish. Demanding that he reveal himself in his real form, she refuses to back down and forces Zeus to reveal himself in all his lightning-wreathed glory. Poor Semele is incinerated on the spot. Zeus is aghast, but is quick-thinking enough to rescue his unborn son from his mother's ashes and stitch him into his own thigh, where he gestates till birth. This theogenesis confers immortality on the infant, who is then handed over to Hermes to be raised far away from the vengeful eye of Hera. Dionysus eventually rescues his mother from the Underworld and raises her to Olympus as an immortal.

Another tradition, which continues to give scholars a lot of headaches, is that of a deity called Zagreus, who was merged with Dionysus at some stage in antiquity (probably sixth or seventh century BC). Zagreus himself is a fairly shady character and could possibly be an Underworld version of Zeus; he is the consort of Gaia, the mother earth goddess. The Zagreus myth (whether earlier or later then the Dionysus tradition, or simply from elsewhere, is very hard to ascertain) adds elements that appear to be key factors in the Orphic tradition. This time Dionysus is initially engendered by Zeus coupling, in the form of a serpent, with Persephone, queen of the Underworld, or alternatively with her mother Demeter.[45] Again, Hera is jealous and persuades the Titans to kill him. Distracting the boy with a mirror and toys, they seize him, dismember him, and eat him. Alerted by the smell of burning flesh, Athena arrives in time to save his heart, which Zeus then uses to inseminate Semele in order that he be reborn. Olympiodorus, the last pagan Platonist of Alexandria, uses alchemical imagery to explain what happened next: "Zeus, angered by

---

45 Diodorus writes: "The ancient poets and writers of myths spoke of Demeter as Gê
    Meter (Earth Mother)." Diodorus, 3, 62, 1.

the deed, blasts them (the Titans) with his thunderbolts, and from the sublimate of the vapours that rise from them comes the matter from which men are created." [46] Thus mankind is descended from the Titans, who themselves contained the dismembered god, making us both damned and divine.

The Birth of Music

The specific name of a song or hymn to Dionysus is a *dithyramb*, which chimes phonetically with both rhythm and drum. In the rural Dionysia it is clear that the use of musical instruments was a crucial factor in generating the ecstatic states of the dancers. Voodoo drumming still works in precisely the same way today and there is no reason to suppose that it was something new in ancient Greece. After all, ancient Greece isn't all that ancient. Compared to the time of the Lion Man, forty-odd thousand years ago, ancient Greece is modern. Recognising, responding to, and generating rhythms is something Homo sapiens has specialised in since it found its own identity, differentiating itself from its nearest hominin predecessor. One of our specialisations was a lighter, lither frame, capable of running all day, but only with coordinated rhythmic breathing.

Drumming starts with tapping, clapping, the pounding of feet on the earth. It's as ancient as we are. Rhythm is in our blood, circulating to the beat of the heart; but one art form that appeared as if out of nowhere around the same time as the Lion Man was lyrical music. Lyrical music, meaning music that expresses complex feelings, as opposed to purely rhythmic music, requires instruments capable of making individual notes. In European myth, the first such instrument to appear was the lyre,[47] and this may be historically true, since the Aurignacians would certainly have picked up on the twang made by stretched and twisted gut strings and sinews that we know they used

---

46 Westerink.

47 The word *lyrical* comes from Greek *lyrikos* meaning "singing to the lyre."

for sewing. No remains of anything resembling a lyre from the period have been found, but some of the oldest instruments ever discovered, as old even as the Lion Man, have been found in the same region of Germany, in the form of flutes made from swan and vulture bones, and even, most laboriously, mammoth ivory.

The way the flutes are made indicates that their makers clearly understood how their sound is influenced by the positioning and size of the holes and the length and diameter of the bone. So the prototype for Orpheus, the shamanic musician whose music has magical powers and can even charm the lords of the Underworld, probably existed forty thousand years before the ancient Greek hero. The Aurignacian flutes represent a technological breakthrough, just as their stone tools do. Earlier musical technology, such as drums and maybe stringed instruments, obviously goes back much further. In fact, drumming probably predates Homo sapiens. Any hominin that made stone tools, however basic, will have recognized the patterns that can be made with rhythmic tapping, and if clapping and toe tapping were already being enjoyed along with singing, then you've got people making music. Early twentieth century field recordings of chain gangs in the American South are testimony to the phenomenon of how people working together breaking rocks naturally fall into a shared percussive rhythm and spontaneously break into song, typically through call and response. The development of instrument making may have gone hand in hand with many other shared practical tasks, such as preparing hides and making pipes for fire bellows and other uses. Blowing through bones and hollow stems quickly leads to the discovery of musical pipes, and making holes in the right places is only a matter of time and adaptation.

From the esoteric perspective, sound is not just the very basis of magic, it is the prime mover of Creation itself. In the beginning, there was the Word. The Word is the *logos*, the verb which *reverberates* upon the "dark waters" of the void to generate order out of chaos: Time, form, and space; the matrix of manifestation. Our very blood, flesh, and bone are essentially vibrations ordered by the law that governs all Creation: harmony. One of my alchemy teachers, Jean Dubuis, founder of *Les Philosophes de la Nature*, shared this very revealing analogy with regard to Harmony:

> Harmony exists in all realms, but we can get a clear idea of it in the realm of music. If we play a sequence of notes on the piano, we notice that some notes, even though they are different seem to have analogies between them.
>
> If we start with a G, each time we strike the higher note of G, we notice that each note is recognizable as such; but the G evolves. The number of vibrations per second (384 for the G) is characteristic of each note. If we double the number of vibrations, we obtain a new G.
>
> Let us imagine a keyboard that is long, so long it extends infinitely. With each new octave, the number of vibrations doubles: after five successive Gs we no longer hear anything (certain individuals can perceive as far as the sixth or seventh G). If we could build a piano fitting this description, the vibrations would eventually disturb the radio, then television, then radar. The next note would produce heat and after the forty-second G there would be a red light. Then, there would be no sound, nor light. A C would create hydrogen, an A would create oxygen. If we make a chord with these two notes we would obtain water.
>
> All created things are but a chord of notes on the cosmic keyboard. If we made the same chord in the audible realm, we could have an idea of the vibrations and this would be the true name of its manifestation into the language of the Lost Word. G is the note which corresponds to the red light. A sound containing the same numbers as C and A would be the true name of water.[48]

Moses pronounced the true name of water in the desert and it immediately appeared. It had to. Moses had made the sound that literally *is* water. In the Abrahamic tradition, Adam is given the task of

---

48 Jean Dubuis: *Spagyrics, Volume 1*, translated by Brigitte Donvez, Triad Publishing, USA, 1987. Quoted with permission. All Dubuis's courses on alchemy, Kabbalah, and esoteric wisdom are freely available to download at archive.org.

naming all the animals. The esoteric understanding of this is that the creative consciousness which humanity was given, the "Adamic" consciousness, brings the animals into being—literally breathes life into them—by pronouncing their true names, which is to say uttering the extraordinarily complex but unique sonic signatures that represent their materially manifest forms. This is pure magic, but it requires the use of the original language of Creation, which is considered to be lost. Once, we all spoke the original language and were in harmony with nature. The languages spoken by the peoples of the earth today are for the most part purely conventional. Words can only be explained in relationship to other words. They no longer are in themselves the things of which they speak. The Lost Word is at once Harmony, Power, and Knowledge, and Love. It has been and remains the holy grail for many of the greatest wizards, some of whom have rediscovered it within themselves. Orpheus is clearly one of these.

Jean Dubuis believed that the only language that retained a connection to the primordial language was Hebrew, and for that reason he was a practising kabbalist as well as alchemist. The ancient Egyptian magician-priests recognized the magical poverty of mere words, as a passage from the so-called Hermetic writings clearly states:

> The very quality of speech and the (sound) of Egyptian words have in themselves the energy of the object they speak of. Therefore, my king, in so far as you have the power (who are all powerful), keep the discourse uninterpreted, lest mysteries of such greatness come to the Greeks, lest the extravagant, flaccid and (as it were) dandified Greek idiom extinguish something stately and concise, the energetic idiom of usage. For the Greeks have empty speeches, O king, that are energetic only in what they demonstrate, and this is the philosophy of the Greeks, an inane foolosophy of speeches. We, by contrast, use not speeches but sounds that are full of action." [49]

Music can communicate ideas and evoke feelings that define both the soul and spirit of humanity in ways that even our highly developed

---

49 Copenhaver.

(if fallen) languages struggle with today. Music can also trigger the release of endorphins in the brain, stimulating group experiences ranging from the pleasurable and bonding, to the ecstatic, visionary, and religious. Music is fundamentally magicalm and in the hands of shamanic master musicians like Orpheus it played a key role in both the inner and outer rites of Dionysus. The use of the flute, in particular, was associated with healing and purifying the soul.

The Dionysia and Bacchanalia

Modern Western culture remembers Dionysus for the drama festivals held in his honour. The *Dionysia* were annual festivals held in Athens from the sixth century BC. It was here that Greek tragedy was born: highly stylized dramatic performances of aspiring human lives destroyed by their own hubris or by fickle fate. The use of music and a chorus articulating emotional response caught the audience up in the pathos of the situation, allowing them to empathise with the tragedy. This had the cathartic effect of allowing them to release their own pent up emotions in a way that was both empowering and uplifting, thereby achieving the trick of resurrecting a sense of dignity and compassion by exposing the apparent meaningless nature of life. The Dionysia produced the first great heroes of theatre. The tragedies of Sophocles and Euripedes are still performed today, while the word *thespian* is derived from Thespis, an actor and playwright who wrote and performed in the first Dionysian tragedy.

The roots of the Dionysia are far more Bacchanalian, however.[50] The so-called rural Dionysia were bawdy wine festivals where everyone was encouraged to let their hair down—even slaves—and soberness and propriety were frowned upon in a reversal of standard mores, similar to the Feast of Fools, presided over by the Lord of Mis-

---

50 The word *Bacchanalian*, after Bacchus (or bacchic), the Roman name for Dionysus, is synonymous with libertine orgies. The word *libertine* itself comes from Liber, a native Roman god of wine and fertility. Lady Liberty, of New York City statue fame, was his wife.

rule in medieval Europe. Women carried *phalloi*[51] in baskets as symbols of the god, in processions in which people dressed up in animal skins and vegetation to look like nymphs and satyrs and put on plays and held dancing competitions. But even the rural Dionysia were tame versions of the wild rites of the god, which were infamous for driving women into wanton frenzies of lust and crazed bestiality, running amok in the countryside, tearing creatures or even babies apart in wild abandon.

There is a problem getting to the bottom of the Dionysian rites, because everything that history has to tell about them was written down by civilized men, not wild women. We therefore see them through a lens ground and polished by all the civilities that are associated with Apollo, the bright, blonde, rational, lyre-playing counterpart of Dionysus; perhaps as much a patron deity of Athens as Athena herself. His virtues inspired the development of architecture, law, order, formal art, and philosophical principles founded on reason. In a word: civilization. The generally received impression of Apollo represents clarity, harmony, the soaring spirit's quest for eternal truth, and the purest light. Dionysus rules over the primal urges, the convulsive, yearning soul, the things that intrude on our dreams.

According to Ovid and Plutarch,[52] some of the Maenads were civilized women who attempted to resist the siren call of Dionysus but were driven insane trying to repress their wild, natural femininity, resulting in a pathological inversion of maternal feelings. There may well be something in this, given that women in Athenian society were restricted to domestic roles, while it had become *de rigueur* for older men to take young male lovers as part of their education.

Being the antithesis of all things Apollonian, Dionysus was initially resisted by the Athenian authorities. Some accounts state that the reason why phalloi were carried in the Dionysian processions was

51 Dildos or other phallic symbols.

52 Influential Greek essayist and biographer who lived c. AD 46–AD 120.

as a reminder that when the Athenians rejected the gift of a statue of Dionysus their men were struck down by a mysterious malady of the genitals, which was only cured when the statue was accepted and the god's cult enshrined.

On a social and political level it made sense for the Athenian authorities to tolerate the cult of Dionysus, as it provided an outlet for the frustrations of those disenfranchised by the civic hierarchy—women, slaves, and the poor. The point of the revelries was to surrender oneself to the godhead, to lose oneself completely. This was more appealing to those who had the least to lose. The greater the self-importance and sense of status, the more threatening Dionysus appeared.

Vicious Bacchic Orgy Cult

The Roman version of the Dionysia was known as the Bacchanalia. In true Roman style, the Bacchanalia became increasingly decadent and orgiastic until, according to the great Roman historian Livy, the situation got so out of hand that the authorities had to clamp down on them in 186 BC. A former initiate and prostitute called Hispala Faecenia gave evidence to a Roman consul that a priestess of Bacchus called Paculla Annia had perverted the rite, turning it from a women-only daytime affair to a regular nocturnal orgy open to all social classes, ages, and sexes. The cult mushroomed in size, attracting all sorts, including many highly placed citizens. Hispala Faecenia claimed that homosexuality, drunken sexual violence, rape, theft, and even murder were rife.

The morally conservative Livy may well have exaggerated and sensationalised the situation, but the fact is that the Senate took these allegations seriously enough to convene a special meeting, whose findings and edicts, under the name *Senatus consultum de Bacchanalibus*, have been preserved to this day. The cult was banned, on pain of death, throughout Italy, except in a very restricted form under the direct control of the Senate. More sensationally, as a result of rewards being offered to informants, thousands of people were arrested—seven thousand according to Livy—the majority of whom were executed. The cult survived in its reduced form and even regained something of its former popularity during the reign of Julius Caesar, when Mark Anthony was an enthusiastic devotee.

The Mysteries of Eleusis

The criminally debauched Bacchanalia described by Livy are far removed from the powerful but formalized tragedies performed at the city Dionysia in Athens, and even further removed from the solemn, dignified, and entirely venerable ethos of the Eleusinian Mysteries, with which Dionysus was also identified.

The Mysteries of Eleusis, near Athens, represented the greatest known mystery cult of the ancient world and came under the direct protection of Athens. It is tempting in our iconoclastic world to think of Eleusis as an arm of the Athenian state, the equivalent of the Church in the Holy Roman Empire, maintaining a rigid state-approved orthodoxy, but it survived many collapses and convulsions of the state over an extraordinarily long period.

Deliberate mystification is certainly the stock-in-trade of charlatans and false cults, but the fact is that details on the specifics of the inner rites of the Mysteries are very scanty. Since humans are so notoriously bad at keeping secrets, it is astonishing to note that the inner rites of the greatest known mystery cult of the ancient world, the Eleusinian Mysteries, were seldom publicly revealed or profaned, despite the fact that over a period of nearly two thousand years millions of people were initiated; from queens and emperors to beggars and slaves. What could have given the cult such power?

Modern researchers familiar with ethnobotany have suggested that a powerful magic potion may account for the extraordinarily consistent effectiveness of the rites over a span of time that saw successive empires rise and crumble into dust. There is good evidence for this theory.

Magic Potion

At Eleusis, a sacramental brew known as *kykeon* was drunk by initiates. In the wake of the psychedelic revolution of the 1960s, various enthusiasts suggested that kykeon may have had "entheogenic"[53] properties, as at Chavín de Huántar. Attempts have been made by some of the greatest pharmaceutical chemists, such as the saintly Albert Hofmann, discoverer of LSD, and Alexander Shulgin, discoverer of ecstasy (MDMA), to reproduce the kykeon potion of Eleusis using various types of magic mushroom and other ingredients such as ergot, a parasitic fungus that grows on cereal grains, which would have been very neat as the mysteries revolved around the story of Demeter the corn goddess and her daughter Kore, who was raped by Hades and carried away to the Underworld. Zeus negotiated her release because Demeter's grief and fury were laying waste to the land, but Kore was tricked into having to return to the Underworld where she remains as Persephone for four months of the year, her absence corresponding with winter and return with spring.

Ergot is both poisonous and psychedelic. If enough of it is ingested, it causes ergotism, commonly known as St. Anthony's Fire, a horrifying disease that can cause delirium and mania as well as grotesque physical symptoms such as gangrene. This makes ergot a problematic contender as an Eleusinian entheogen. Hofmann derived LSD from ergot while seeking treatments for circulation and respiratory disorders, but he was using highly advanced chemistry. There may have been another ingredient that inhibits the toxic effects of ergot, but this may be overstretching the imagination.

Nevertheless, there was something so compelling about the Dionysian mysteries that by the sixth century BC they appear to have been incorporated into the cult at Eleusis; and it is Orpheus the mu-

---

53 Meaning "that which manifests the divine within." This is now the preferred term amongst many ethnobotanists and psychonauts for plants that tend to induce spiritual/religious experiences.

sical magician who is credited with bringing about that chemical wedding. It may be that the use of Dionysus's wine helped make the Eleusinian potion more effective—alcohol is, after all, a more effective solvent than water for extracting the powerful alkaloids from entheogenic plants—or it may just be that Orpheus had (re)discovered the secret behind that strange magic wand that Dionysus is nearly always depicted carrying: the thyrsus.

Magic Wand

The thyrsus is of ancient but mysterious origin. It is a staff, traditionally a giant fennel stalk, topped by a pinecone and tied with a ribbon. Osiris, the dismembered Egyptian god-king, who has much in common with Dionysus, also carried a thyrsus, which was sometimes entwined by serpents like the caduceus of Hermes. The pinecone has always been considered a phallic symbol, but there is circumstantial evidence to suggest that it may have meant much more than this to adepts such as Orpheus. In the esoteric lore of Freemasonry, an initiatory secret society, the pinecone symbolises the pineal gland, so-named because it closely resembles a tiny pinecone. The pineal is located at the geometrical centre of the brain, where the left and right brain meet.

Inner Eye

René Descartes, often dubbed the father of modern Western philosophy, described the pineal gland as "the seat of the soul" and the nexus between the body and the mind, which is not far from the traditional esoteric understanding of it as the "third eye," which regulates spiritual illumination. In actual fact, the frontal part of the pineal has the residual structure of an eye, and in some animals it is light-sensitive.[54] The pineal gland regulates the secretion of melatonin, which affects brain chemistry in ways that are still not entirely understood

54 See Lucas et al: "Regulation of the mammalian pineal by non-rod, non-cone, ocular photoreceptors." *Science*, 1999 Apr 16; 284 (5413): 505–7.

by conventional science. Its main function is to help modulate sleeping patterns. Fittingly, given the Dionysian connection, melatonin is stimulated by darkness and inhibited by light.

A controversial, but tantalizing theory has recently proposed that another substance produced in the pineal gland is DMT, the mind-blowing *entheogen* used with San Pedro at Chavín de Huántar. DMT is naturally produced in the bodies of mammals and occurs in hundreds of plants, some of which are common in Europe. In order to be effective when orally ingested, another plant that allows absorption in the digestive tract needs to be added to the mix. An "old world" plant that perfectly fits the bill is Syrian rue, which has been used as an incense and medicine since time immemorial. The natives of hundreds of different tribes in Amazonia worked out the equivalent "new world" ingredients for just such a brew, known as *ayahuasca* or *yagé*, so it is feasible that a cunning herbalist created a similar potion to add some serious clout to Dionysus's sacramental wine. If Orpheus did deliver such a potion to enhance the kykeon, or if the potion originated with him, then it is hardly surprising that, as some scholars claim, the initiation offered at Eleusis was into the mysteries of Orphism, which focussed on the most fundamental realities of life, death, and the afterlife.

Life After Death

In the mainstream religion of ancient Greece no great emphasis was placed on the afterlife. There was no great distinction between good or evil either. It was generally believed that, regardless of your doings on earth, when you died your "shade" or ghost would descend into the murky Underworld ruled by Hades and Persephone, where it would have a listless, barely conscious existence. Only those beloved by the gods could hope for a better outcome in the Elysian Fields, the Isles of the Blessed, where the lifestyle was a whole lot better. Elysium was a very elite club reserved for demigods and mythic heroes, but its membership gradually expanded to include military heroes, civic worthies, and the odd saint. The mysteries, however, promised far greater possibilities and it is Orpheus that takes us behind its veil of secrecy.

The Orphic rites appear to be closely related to the version of Dionysus's multiple birth and death story, which includes his death at the hands of the Titans. The *sparagmos* (dismemberment, "tearing apart") and subsequent *omophagia* (eating of the raw, dismembered flesh) become key ritual elements, while the *anthropogeny* (engendering of humanity) from the murderous Titans unites us in guilt. Born of the Titans' remains, all humans contain the essence of the consumed Dionysus on the one hand, but on the other are tainted by their sin and doomed to be trapped in flesh and endlessly reborn, unless they become conscious of the true nature of their condition and make their peace with God.

Which god? Well, despite the apparent polytheism of ancient Greece, their great philosophers started reasoning towards an idea of a supreme "first cause" during the classical period, and in the remarkable Derveni Papyrus—the oldest European manuscript ever discovered, which was found in burnt fragments in a grave in southern Greece in 1962—we find an attempt to unify all the gods into one supreme deity. The unnamed author, writing around the time of Plato (circa 400 BC) is attempting, rather like me right now, to unravel the meaning of a (probably fifth century BC) poem attributed to Orpheus and insisting that it be understood allegorically. Much of the text concerns an attempt to unravel Orpheus's "riddling" ideas of the true nature of Zeus, concluding that Orpheus believes all the deities simply act as servants of the will of Zeus, whose name after all simply means "god," as in Latin "deus." The Orphic poem declares: "Zeus is head, Zeus is centre, all things are from Zeus."

The Orphic literature introduces apparently dualistic elements foreign to traditional Greek religion, such as the idea that the body is a prison trapping the essentially divine and immortal soul, which is liberated upon death, but doomed to endless reincarnation unless eventually redeemed through piety, self-purification, and love of God.

In light of this, Dionysus's status as the son of god fathered on a mortal woman draws parallels with Christ, which is augmented by another parallel between omophagia and the symbolic eating of the flesh of Christ in the Eucharist, while the sparagmos that both he and Orpheus suffer is highly reminiscent of the classic "shaman's death" experience of being mercilessly dismembered by anthropomorphic but alien entities. I have experienced such a symbolic death myself and it was all too horrifyingly real at the time. Paradoxically, such an experience ultimately reveals that not all aspects of the self can be killed; for such a death can lead to the encounter with the immortal soul in the presence of the Absolute, or something authoritatively representing it—in my experience an unfathomably profound being in the form of a huge black panther. Nothing in that experience told me to keep silent about it, but classical writers had to be careful not to be too specific.

In extolling the Mysteries, the poet Pindar (517–438 BC) refers to a singular God in a way that sounds positively monotheistic:

> Blessed is he who hath seen these things before he goeth beneath the hollow earth; for he understandeth the end of mortal life, and the beginning of a new life given of God.[55]

Plato frequently has his great teacher Socrates refer, as a believer, to "god" as such, and he was sentenced to death for not according sufficient reverence to the gods of the state.

In Plato's *Phaedrus*, Socrates describes his experience of initiation:

> ...we following in the train of Zeus, and others in that of some other god, were initiated into that which is rightly called the most blessed of mysteries, which we celebrated in a state of perfection, when we were without experience of the evils which awaited us in the time to come,

---

55 Quoted by Clement of Alexandria in *Miscellanea, 3. 3.*

being permitted as initiates to the sight of perfect and simple and calm
and happy apparitions, which we saw in the pure light, being ourselves
pure and not entombed in this which we carry about with us and call
the body, in which we are imprisoned like an oyster in its shell.[56]

Plato was certainly an initiate, at least at this "entry level," and gives us various insights into his understanding of the Mysteries while being careful not to break the code of silence regarding specifics.

It seems to me that liberation from the fear of death through knowledge of the immortality of the soul is precisely what the Orphic Mysteries are supposed to have delivered through initiation. That the Orphic, Dionysiac, and Eleusinian Mysteries were all the same or very similar is something I would tentatively affirm. It seems fitting, however, that we have so little written evidence to go on. Words can never adequately describe an experience as ineffable as the encounter with soul. The irony is that the attempt to rationalize the nature of reality through the use of language appears to have been inspired, at least in part, by such indescribable experiences. The author of the Derveni Papyrus is at pains to point out that the Orphic retellings of the myth of Dionysus's (multiple) lives and deaths should be understood allegorically and the additions and changes to the traditional Greek cosmogony reveal a symbolic ontology that was already influencing the emergence of both metaphysics and theoretical physics in the writings of Plato, his contemporaries, and his successors.

The Death of Orpheus

The danger with trying to define the sublime is that such philosophizing, in the face of its own ignorance, has a tendency to try to explain away that which it doesn't understand. There is always the danger of sophistry: the use of clever but specious arguments designed to

---

56 Plato, *Phaedrus 250b-250c* from *Plato in Twelve Volumes, Vol. 9,* translated by Harold
    N. Fowler. Cambridge, MA, Harvard University Press; London, William Heine-
    mann Ltd. 1925.

make a writer appear wise, when he is actually being trite. In light of the Derveni Papyrus, it is interesting to note what Plato puts in the mouth of Protagoras:

> Now I tell you that sophistry is an ancient art, and those men of an-
> cient times who practised it, fearing the odium it involved, disguised it
> in a decent dress, sometimes of poetry, as in the case of Homer, Hesiod,
> and Simonides sometimes of mystic rites and soothsayings, as did Or-
> pheus, Musaeus and their sects; and music was the disguise employed
> by your own Agathocles, a great sophist, Pythocleides of Ceos, and
> many more.[57]

The miraculous Orpheus is accused by the divine Plato (albeit in-directly) of sophistry! Is his crime the attempt to mystify or demy-stify? Presumably the former. Elsewhere Plato has someone accuse Orpheus of cowardice; of sneaking into Hades to try to steal back his love rather than dying for it. Diogenes Laërtius is also critical:

> And thus did philosophy rise among the Greeks and indeed its very
> name shows that it has no connection with the barbarians. But those
> who attribute its origin to them, introduce Orpheus the Thracian, and
> say that he was a philosopher, and the most ancient one of all. But if
> one ought to call a man who has said such things about the gods as he
> has said, a philosopher, I do not know what name one ought to give to
> him who has not scrupled to attribute all sorts of human feelings to
> the gods, and even such discreditable actions as are but rarely spoken
> of among men; and tradition relates that he was murdered by women;
> but there is an inscription at Dium in Macedonia, saying that he was
> killed by lightning, and it runs thus:
>
>> Here the bard buried by the Muses lies,
>> The Thracian Orpheus of the golden lyre;

---

57 Plato, *Protagoras 316* from *Plato in Twelve Volumes, Vol. 3*, translated by W. R. M. Lamb. Cambridge, MA, Harvard University Press; London, William Heinemann Ltd. 1967.

> *Whom mighty Jove, the Sovereign of the skies,*
> *Removed from earth by his dread lightning's fire.*[58]

Why was he killed by the Maenads or by Jove/Zeus? What was his crime?

Diogenes goes on to recount that Zeus struck him down with a thunderbolt for revealing the mysteries of the gods to mortal men and the Derveni Papyrus confirms that the Orphic poems were analysed by the early Greek philosophers in order to look behind the veil of myth. This rationalizing process led eventually to the development of science, which has indeed revealed many of the mysteries of the gods. So in that respect Orpheus is guilty, by association at least.

As for being torn apart by the furious Maenads, Aeschylus's lost tragedy *Bassarides* recounts that they killed him for betraying Dionysus and abandoning his rites in favour of Apollo, who had given him his lyre and taught him how to play it. A year before publishing his great dissertation on the dichotomy of the Apollonian and Dionysian, *The Birth of Tragedy*, Nietzsche wrote a short piece titled "On Music and Words," in which he insisted that music is a primary expression of the essence of everything. The lyre inspires lyrical poetry, which gives birth to the art of tragedy. For Nietzsche, Aeschylus and Sophocles represent the epitome of tragedy at its purest. After them, playwrights such as Euripides start introducing morality and rationalism, undermining the very foundation of tragedy, which is the creation of pathos and empathy. Reason and ethics introduce judgmental elements, which distance the audience from the suffering of the protagonists, thus upsetting the balance of the Apollonian and the Dionysian in favour of the former. For Nietzsche, art is identification; the subjective experience of the titanic experience of life, while reason is dispassionate objectivity, the antithesis of art. European culture has since been dominated by the triumph of Apollo over Dionysus, of spirit over soul, which has suppressed art, myth, magic, and nature.

---

58 Diogenes, Book 1, Preface.

The first century AD Roman poet Ovid provides a different account of Orpheus's death at the tearing hands of the Maenads, relating that after failing to rescue Eurydice, Orpheus became a homosexual: "he was the first of the Thracians to transfer his love to young boys, and enjoy their brief springtime, and early flowering, this side of manhood." [59] This is not an invention of Ovid's; it is attested in a poem by the classical poet Phanocles, who says the women killed him "because he was the first to reveal male loves among the Thracians and did not recommend love of women." [60] Hell hath no fury like a Maenad scorned it seems, and when a band of them came upon him in the woods, they attacked him with such fury that even the magical power of his music was unable to protect him.

For Phanocles, the story does not end there. The avenged Maenads nailed Orpheus's head onto his tortoiseshell lyre and threw it into the sea where it floated to the "holy isle of Lesbos," and was enshrined: "And even now, the Lesbian women pay reparations to the dead Orpheus because of that sin." [61] Lesbos is associated in the modern mind with female homosexuality as a result of it being the place where the great female poet Sappho lived in late antiquity. Sadly, little of her poetry has survived, and while most of the remaining fragments consist of love poetry addressed to women, there is little evidence that Lesbos was specifically associated with lesbianism in Phanocles's time. Nevertheless, there is no escaping the fact that this final element in the mythic tragedy of Orpheus is, in the context of his supposed homosexuality, suggestive now of a polarisation of the sexes. Pederasty was a significant factor in the orientation of the classical Greek philosophers from Socrates onwards. The masculine human form is idealised and glorified in classical statuary, and the erection of tower-

---

59 A. S. Kline's translation: *Metamorphoses*, USA: Borders Classics, 2004.

60 Translation by S. Burges Watson, *Living Poets* (Durham, 2014), https://livingpoets .dur.ac.uk/w/Phanocles,_fragment_1_Powell?oldid=2551.

61 See footnote 60.

ing temples represents a further movement away from the grottoes, caves, and fissures of the chthonic, feminine mysteries. The sacred and hidden is exposed to the mercilessly bright Apollonian light of a self-regarding rationalism, while the wild, natural impulses that drive the uninhibited urge to lose oneself in ecstatic sacred union with the Dionysian other descends into the licentious, pornographic horrors of the Roman Bacchanals.

The consequences of the triumph of Apollo over Dionysus reverberate throughout the planet to this day. The human story can be viewed as the greatest Greek tragedy of all, and in this respect, the Orphic mythos in all its paradoxical complexity continues to exemplify the dynamic tension between opposing forces, the drama of the struggle for supremacy between nature and civilisation; the rational and the intuitive; left brain, right brain; masculine, feminine; light and dark; the Apollonian and the Dionysian.

SECTION 2

THE PRE-SOCRATIC
SORCERERS OF
ANCIENT GREECE

The tragedy of Orpheus was not entirely in vain. He may have failed to rescue Eurydice from Hades, but he did discover a treasure beyond compare during his shamanic journeying between the realms of the living and the dead; and this time he was able to return with it and share it with those able to recognize it for what it was. The treasure was something that we call the soul; something quite distinct from the pale ghosts that resided in Hades; something that not only did not die, but was reborn into another body countless times; something that recognized itself outside the body as the true self; that could, if it avoided forgetfulness and proceeded correctly after death, even be reborn with the memory of its previous life intact.

From the early nineteenth century, archaeologists started discovering inscribed gold tablets amongst grave goods in classical-era tombs in Greece and Italy. They fall into two groups: those written in the first person, which seem to be words that the dead should speak upon arriving in Hades, and those consisting of instructions for what the dead should do when arriving there. These tablets were generally believed to be Orphic, until scholarly revisionism made it more fashionable to dismiss Orphism as a fanciful literary creation and identify the tablets as "Pythagorean." The discovery of the Derveni Papyrus appeared to have quashed that theory once and for all, but, as we shall see, the distinctions between Orphic and Pythagorean are murky. Probably the most interesting of the gold "death passports," discovered at the site of ancient Hipponium in southern Calabria reads thus:

> *This is sacred to Memory: when you are about to die, you will find yourself at the House of Hades; on the right there is a spring, by which stands a pale cypress. Descending there, the souls of the dead seek refreshment. Do not even approach this spring; beyond you will find cool water flowing from the Pool of Memory; there are guards before it, who will ask you with cool penetration, what you seek from the shades of murky Hades. Say: "I am a son of earth and star-filled Heaven, I am dry with thirst and dying; but give me swiftly cool water flowing from the Pool of Memory." And they will take pity on you by the will of the Queen of the Underworld, and they will give you water to drink from the Pool of Memory; and then you will go on the great Sacred Way, along which the other famed initiates and bacchants make their way.*[62]

---

62 First translated from the Greek by Giovanni Pugliese Carratelli in *"Studi sulla Calabria Antica,"* in: *La Parola del Passato, fasc. CLIV-CLV, vol. XXIX, page 111, Napoli 1974.* This English translation is by Hugh Bowden from *Mystery Cults of the Ancient World,* US: Princeton University Press, 2010, p. 148.

CHAPTER 3

PROPHETS, CAVES, AND SAGES

THE MAKING OF A MAN-GOD

One of the most famed initiates who ever lived appears to have drunk from the sweet waters of *Mnemosyne*, the Pool of Memory, since he was able to remember a whole series of previous incarnations. He called this "transmigration" of his soul *metempsychosis*, and two and a half millennia after this particular incarnation Brewer's wildly popular *Dictionary of Phrase and Fable*[63] confidently related that:

---

63 "Revised and updated" edition, 1894. Latest edition still in print.

He distinctly recollected having occupied other human forms before his birth at Samos: (1) He was Æthalides, son of Mercury [Hermes]; (2) Euphorbos the Phrygian, son of Panthoos, in which form he ran Patroclos through with a lance, leaving Hector to dispatch the hateful friend of Achilles; (3) Hermotimos, the prophet of Clazomenae; and (4) a fisherman. To prove his Phrygian existence he was taken to the temple of Hera, in Argos, and asked to point out the shield of the son of Panthoos, which he did without hesitation.

The man in question is Pythagoras, a name familiar to schoolchildren the world over for hundreds if not thousands of years as the (imagined) father of geometry and mathematics. He is popularly believed to have been a vegetarian; an expert on the soul, ethics, and religion; a musical theorist and astronomer—in short, the ultimate philosopher. Indeed, some say, the first person to call himself such, and the founder of an extraordinarily influential school of philosophy.

Pythagoras is the first of our wizards who we can claim confidently to have been a real historical person. We know without doubt that his ideas had a decisive impact on the development of science and philosophy, although, as the great classical scholar Walter Burkert has noted, "There is not a single detail in the life of Pythagoras that is not contradicted."[64] Fortunately, as Burkert also notes, "it is possible, from a more or less critical selection of the data, to construct a plausible account." My plausible account, based principally on the oldest sources, goes like this:

---

64 Burkert, Walter: *Weisheit und Wissenschaft: Studien zu Pythagoras, Philolaos und Platon.* Nürnberg: Hans Carl, 1962. Author's translation.

Pythagoras: The Mathemagician

Pythagoras was born around 570 BC on the Aegean island of Samos. His mother was said to have been from an old established Samian family, while his father was a dealer and/or engraver of gems [65] from the Phoenician city of Tyre in modern Lebanon. The Phoenicians seem to have survived the late Bronze Age collapse better than the Greeks, or at least to have bounced back more quickly, and were the greatest seafarers and colonisers in Europe at the time, with city states dotted all around the Mediterranean littoral, including Carthage, which went on to establish a great empire of its own. Tyre was the hub of the Phoenician world and very cosmopolitan, with merchants, travellers, craftsmen, and specialists from all over North Africa, southern Europe, and Asia Minor, including Egypt, Babylon, Sheba, and Ethiopia. Pythagoras would therefore have inherited the broadest cultural

---

65 Some engraved gems are considered amongst the greatest works of art produced in Bronze Age Europe. The exquisite detail of the so-called Pylos Combat agate sealstone, discovered in 2015, is so fine that it can only be fully appreciated with a microscope.

horizons from his father, while his mother is said to have come from one of the most aristocratic families on Samos.

As a youth Pythagoras accompanied his father on trading trips and is specifically said to have studied under scholars from Syria while on a visit to Tyre. He was also said to have spent years in Egypt and Babylon, becoming acquainted with all the wisdom of the East, prior to which he was a pupil of such famous Greek sages as Pherekydes, who was believed to have been the first to write philosophically in prose.

Legendary Teachers

Pherekydes is known to this day to have inhabited two caves on the island of Syros, where his summer cave remains a popular tourist attraction. The sole surviving fragments of prose attributed to him constitute a cosmogony,[66] which was probably titled *Pentemychos* ("The Five Recesses"), although some sources claim it was called *Heptamychos* ("The Seven Recesses"). His pet subject, however, was metempsychosis, as Porphyry, an important third-century Neoplatonist, suggests:

> *Pherekydes of Syros, speaks of cavities, pits, caves, openings and gates, and through these speaks in riddles of the becoming and goings of souls.*[67]

---

66 A cosmogony is a theory or story about the origins of life or the universe. Many such creation stories were written during the Archaic and Classical Greek periods.

67 Porphyry, *De Antro Nympharum*.

Pherekydes was believed to be the first Greek to teach of the immortality of souls and to have reached this understanding without a teacher. The latter is possible; the former most unlikely, since the immortality of the soul was a central understanding of the Orphic Mysteries, whose roots are much earlier. And, of course, Pythagoras had demonstrated the reality of metempsychosis in two of his previous incarnations. Maybe Pherekydes was the first to teach it openly, which, if he had discovered it for himself, he would have been free to do, having made no vow of secrecy.

Pythagoras then went on to study under Thales and Anaximander in nearby Miletus. Thales was one of the Seven Sages of Greece and is considered the father of Greek philosophy and, by some, the father of science. He claimed that everything in nature derives from the same prime matter, the nature of which he tried to define. This remains a goal of both alchemy and quantum physics. He was an engineer by trade and the first person to apply deductive reasoning to geometry by deriving four corollaries to his own theorem, making him the earliest person to have a mathematical theorem named after him. As an astronomer, he described the position of the constellation Ursa Minor, suggesting that it might serve as a guide for navigation at sea. He calculated the duration of the year and the timings of the equinoxes and solstices and is attributed with the first observation of the Hyades and with calculating the position of the Pleiades. Remarkably, he is widely credited with predicting the solar eclipse of May 28, 585 BC, that brought the Battle of Halys to a halt, resulting in a lasting peace.

Pythagoras was also taught by Thales's pupil Anaximander, who was as groundbreaking a polymath as his master. In geometry he introduced the idea of the *gnomon* [68]; in geography he contributed a very useful map of the world; in astronomy, he made an interesting attempt to describe the movements of celestial bodies in relation to the Earth; and his idea of an indefinite principle (*apeiron*) that preceded

---

68 Initially the upright part of a sundial, used for measuring intervals of time.

the elements as the limitless indefinable source of all things contributed to the development of both theoretical physics and Platonic metaphysics. Anaximander's apeiron has been resuscitated in quantum mechanics as a name for Werner Heisenberg's mooted primordial substance.[69] Apart from his scientific contributions, Anaximander is credited with predicting an earthquake in Sparta and successfully persuading the inhabitants of Lacedaemon to evacuate their city. The earthquake struck the next day as predicted and devastated the city.

Judging by the reputations of these teachers, Pythagoras clearly received a most impressive education, but we can only speculate at the means by which this education was transmitted. We have a conditioned image of balding, bearded sages clad in off-the-shoulder flowing robes loftily intoning their intellectual insights while obedient pupils dutifully take notes, but it seems unlikely that the transmission was so prosaically academic. Indeed, the founding of Plato's famous academy in Athens lay nearly two hundred years in the future. The site of the academy, however, already existed as a sacred grove of olive trees dedicated to Athena, the goddess of wisdom. Situated just outside the city walls of Athens, her cult had been honoured there since pre-collapse Bronze Age times. The teaching of wisdom in the days of Pythagoras was a sacred act; the imparting of sacred truths. Those selected to be initiated would have been a chosen few, qualified by social status or recognized as precocious minds ready to receive. The fact that Pherekydes is credited as the first person to have waxed on (what we would now call) philosophical subjects in prose suggests that pupils may have been traditionally addressed, at least in part, in verse. A teacher may have been a bard, a poet who understood the

---

69 Modern physics postulates four fundamental forces (gravitational, electromagnetic, strong nuclear, and weak nuclear), which can be equated without too much of a stretch with the four interacting elements of classical Greek thought (Fire, Water, Earth, and Air). Plato named a fifth, indefinite element that infused all things as æther. Medieval alchemists named a similar substance "the Quintessence." In modern physics this term is being used for a hypothetical form of dark energy; a fifth fundamental force.

sacred power of words to affect the receptive mind of the neophyte. Sacred truth is, after all, necessarily poetic. Such magical, incantatory instruction would then give way to dialogue between teacher and pupil, the former helping the latter to find his way through asking the right questions in order to reach the understanding or realization of a truth.

Or something like that, perhaps. But what about instruction regarding metempsychosis? At what stage are we to imagine that Pythagoras became aware of his previous incarnations? Was Pherekydes's teaching on the subject designed to help a person remember such things or simply to help contextualize such memories? We live in a culture that no longer agrees that such a thing as a soul really exists; indeed it is fashionable to agree that the idea of a soul that has an existence independent of the body is a dualist absurdity. This is only true from the perspective of Gilbert Ryle's "ghost-in-the-machine" argument, which itself depends on the idea of "mind" being directly equated with "soul" and being in some way substantial. From the esoteric perspective (which is not the same as the "Cartesian rationalism" Ryle is wrangling with) the soul falls into that alchemical category of "thing that is not a thing." [70] As we have already seen, however, the idea of an immortal soul as opposed to a ghostly shade was an equally esoteric idea at the time of Pythagoras.

Porphyry's association of Pherekyde's "pits and caves" and caves with "the becomings and deceases of souls" gives us a clue as to how knowledge of the soul could be gained. Pherekydes's caves were not just allegorical. As we have seen, he was in the habit of living in them, and Pythagoras was to become well known for his affinity with caves, as we will discover after having first considered the rest of his education.

---

70 It may have a subtle sheath, a container of sorts independent of the body, but the soul itself is entirely intangible.

Journeys to the East

Porphyry quotes Antiphon (fifth century BC) from "his book on illustrious Virtuous Men":

> *Pythagoras, desiring to become acquainted with the institutions of Egyptian priests, and diligently endeavouring to participate therein, requested the Tyrant Polycrates to write to Amasis, the King of Egypt, his friend and former host, to procure him initiation. Coming to Amasis, he was given letters to the priests; of Heliopolis, who sent him on to those of Memphis, on the pretence that they were the more ancient. On the same pretence, he was sent on from Memphis to Diospolis. From fear of the King the latter priests dared not make excuses; but thinking that he would desist from his purpose as result of great difficulties, enjoined on him very hard precepts, entirely different from the institutions of the Greeks. These he performed so readily that he won their admiration, and they permitted him to sacrifice to the Gods, and to acquaint himself with all their sciences, a favour theretofore never granted to a foreigner.*[71]

All his biographers concur that Pythagoras visited Egypt, and, in addition to Antiphon's account, other sources say he was afforded deeper and deeper access into the Egyptian mysteries under the high priests Oenuphis and Sechnuphis and the so-called "archprophet" Soches. Iamblichus records that he spent twenty-two years of assiduous study in Egypt before being captured by the invading soldiers of the Persian Emperor Cambyses II and taken in captivity to Babylon.[72]

Although Cambyses II did successfully invade Egypt in 525 BC (with the help of Polycrates, who had turned against his former allies), and Babylon was in Persian hands following his father Cyrus's

---

71 Porphyry, *Life of Pythagoras*, translated by Kenneth Sylvan Guthrie, 1920

72 Iamblichus (c. 245–c. 325 AD) was a Syrian philosopher and theurgist; usually described as a "Neoplatonist," he might, more accurately be called a Neopythagorean. He wrote an important *Life of Pythagoras* that is generally dismissed as fanciful by scholars, but resonates with me.

conquest fourteen years earlier, there is no evidence that captives were taken to Babylon in the way the Israelites had been, for example, after the fall of Jerusalem to Nebuchadnezzar some eighty years earlier. Nevertheless, it is quite possible Pythagoras visited the city, which was a famous centre of "oriental wisdom" such as those held by the Magi priests of Zoroastrianism, the legendary Chaldean astrologers,[73] and the Jewish mystics. Porphyry tells us that Pythagoras met a certain Zabratas (or Zaratas) there "by whom he was purified from the pollutions of this past life, and taught the things which a virtuous man ought to be free."[74] In fact, even if Pythagoras hadn't visited Babylon, his later biographers would have required him to have done so. The Greeks seem to have had a curious relationship with foreign wisdom and magic. They were fascinated by it and suspicious of it in equal measure. Some contemporary commentators complained that Greek cities were teeming with diviners and augurers of every hue— soothsayers, astrologers, fake Magi, and bacchoi—all claiming special powers learned in Egypt or Babylon or somewhere else exotic. The Greeks loved their own folklore, myths, and gods, but since magic is by its very nature exotic, real magic had to be from elsewhere. The prevalence of such "low magic" practitioners inevitably led to the scorning of magic by the more learned and sophisticated Greeks, which itself contributed to the rise in rationalism that characterizes the classical era.

Therefore Pythagoras could not have been as astonishingly knowledgeable, wise, and impressive as he obviously was without having studied in places like Egypt with the highest priests and sages. Or could he? His Greek teachers clearly gave him an impressive start in most of the subjects that he would become such a legendary authority on. Iamblichus tells us that he was initiated into the mysteries by the

---

73 Some claim he learned much from "Zaratas the Chaldean," who is sometimes conflated with Zoroaster, which is chronologically impossible.

74 Porphyry, *Life of Pythagoras*, translated by Kenneth Sylvan Guthrie, 1920

Orphic priest Aglaophamus at Leibethra, where the Muses are said to have buried the remains of Orpheus. A more substantiated tradition says that he was instructed in "moral doctrines" and "much else" by the Delphic Oracle Themistoclea. Who or what was the Delphic Oracle? Well, this mysterious institution played such an important role in the ancient Mediterranean world that it will be worth exploring it in some detail to add context to the life of Pythagoras, whose birth the oracle is said to have prophesied.[75]

The Delphic Oracle

The sanctuary of Apollo at Delphi on the slopes of Mount Parnassus in southwest Greece was home for over 1,200 years to the most famous oracle in ancient Europe. The Delphic Oracle exerted considerable influence throughout the Greek world, and was traditionally consulted before such major undertakings as wars, alliances, and the founding of colonies. According to the painstaking scholarship of Joseph Fontenrose, between 535 and 615 of the oracle's statements are known to have survived since classical times, of which over half are said to be accurate historically.

---

75 This will be the first of several long digressions, during which we will learn many remarkable things and encounter many remarkable characters before returning to Pythagoras himself.

The Pythia: Python Priestess of Delphi

Traditionally a virgin,[76] the oracle was the High Priestess of Apollo, a prophetess who performed the role of a medium, seated upon a tripod in a cave-like recess below the temple, giving answers to those who sought her prophetic advice. She held the title of Pythia, named after the monstrous serpent Python that had originally presided over the oracular cult of the primordial earth goddess, before being slain by the arrows of Apollo, who then established his own cult on the same spot. At least that is the simplest way of telling it. Trying to untangle the origins of Delphi is like wrestling with Python itself, who keeps shape-shifting like a transgender protean chimera, switching names, appearance, allegiance, and attributes. *He* morphs into a *she*, from Python to Typhon, to the snake-woman Delphyne[77] or Echidna, from dragoness to dragon and even into Dionysus, at least by implication. Dionysus and Apollo all tied up again. At what stage Dionysus became attached to the oracle is not clear, but Leicester Holland, writing in 1933, has some very interesting things to say on the matter:

> *In modern times the tripod itself has been a matter of much discussion, some believing that there were two at Delphi, one the mantic tripod of the Pythian priestess, the other the funeral tripod of Dionysus. For Clement of Alexandria thus relates a current myth: "The Titans, they who tore him to pieces, place a bowl (lebes) upon a tripod, and casting the limbs of Dionysus into it, boil them down; then piercing them with spits they hold them over Hephaistos ... Zeus the*

---

76 It is recorded that the oracle was always a virgin until one was raped, whereafter celibate older women were chosen, usually from the local population. Social standing does not appear to have been important.

77 Delphyne is said by Apollonius of Rhodes to have been appointed guardian by her earth goddess mother, Gaia. Her name is derived from *Delphys*, "womb." Delphi could also be named after Delphinios, an epithet for Apollo in dolphin form, in which guise the Homeric hymn to Pythian Apollo declares he arrived at Delphi bearing Cretan priests on his back.

Thunderer discomforts the Titans and entrusts the limbs of Dionysus to his son Apollo, for burial. In obedience to Zeus, Apollo carries the mutilated corpse to Parnassus and lays it to rest." Arnobius repeats the story of the luring away of Dionysus by the Titans, in order to tear him to pieces and cook him in a pot; and of the Titans being cast into Tartarus by the thunderbolts of Zeus. It is quite possible that he copies directly from Clement, but he does not mention the entombment at Delphi. *The Etymologicum Magnum* says: "The Titans tore apart the limbs of Dionysus, cast them into a lebes and gave them to Apollo. This was set upon the tripod by the brother." That this savage legend was not purely a Christian concoction is attested by Tzetzes, who gives the following clear and definite statement: "Together with Apollo, Dionysus was also worshipped in the innermost part of the temple at Delphi, as follows: The Titans cast into a lebes and gave to Apollo the limbs of his brother which they had torn apart, and he set it up upon the tripod, as Kallimnachus (c. 256 B.C.) says. And Euphorion (c. 235 B.C.) says they cast the divine Bacchus into fire above a bowl. We can be reasonably certain from this, that at least as far back as the early third century it was believed that the bones of Dionysus lay in a bowl on a tripod in the Temple at Delphi. That this notion was widespread and persistent is shown by the definition of Servius; "Cortina, the place from which the oracle is given, because the heart (cor) of the seer is kept there."[78]

I was more familiar with the idea that it was the remains of Python that were kept in a bowl above the tripod, so Holland's findings suggest a conflation of Dionysus with the chthonic serpent/dragon. One of the myths relates that Zeus took the form of a serpent when fathering Dionysus and the same animal is one of Dionysus's many familiars, so on the surface the slaying of Python/Dionysus looks like a classic case of a cult takeover demonising the incumbent, overpow-

---

78 Leicester Holland: "The Mantic Mechanism at Delphi." *American Journal of Archaeology.* 37 (2): 204–214, 1933.

ering it, and then using its power. The slaying of the dragon by the radiant hero is echoed in the stories of Perseus and Andromeda, St. Michael versus Satan, and George and the Dragon. Plutarch, however, confirms that Dionysus was as highly regarded at Delphi as Apollo himself and that for three months a year Dionysus presided over the oracle, while Apollo wintered in his original home of Hyperborea.

According to the Homeric Hymn to Pythian Apollo,[79] the *radiant one* had been searching far and wide for just the right location for his oracle, and the sanctuary guarded by Python didn't just have a great location with streams and groves and a stunning view: it was the centre of the earth. Legend tells that Zeus sent two eagles flying from opposite ends of the earth, and where they crossed in the sky, he dropped a stone, and where the stone landed was the centre of the earth. That stone was called the *omphalos* ("belly button") and the same stone still stands in the ruins at Delphi, having once stood in the *adyton*[80] where the Pythia sat in a cauldron upon a bronze tripod placed above natural rock fissures, from which intoxicating vapours rose up that allowed her to achieve a state of mind in which Apollo, Dionysus, or their *daimons*[81] could speak through her and answer the questions put to her by those seeking her advice. These visitors include a parade of many of the most famous names in Greek and Roman history, including the (proverbially "as rich as") Croesus, the Emperor Nero, Alexander the Great, and Pythagoras himself.

---

79 Now believed to have been written around the time of the birth of Pythagoras: 580–570 BC.

80 The adyton was a small cell or recess below the temple where the prophetic process took place.

81 A daimon is a spirit belonging to almost anything—a god, a human, an animal, a planet, a river, or even an elemental force. It is not the thing itself, rather an interactive mode of its being.

The Testimony of Plutarch, Pythian Priest

The highly influential Greek writer Plutarch (c. 46 AD–120 AD),[82] who spent the last thirty years of his life as a temple priest at Delphi, has some very interesting things to say about the operations of the Pythia and how the "exhalation" of the intoxicating vapours had become unreliable:

> As for my part, I believe the exhalation itself which comes out of the ground is not always of the same kind, being at one time slack, and at another strong and vigorous; and the truth of that experiment which I use to prove it is attested by several strangers, and by all those which serve in the temple. For the room where those do wait who come for answers from the oracle is sometimes—though not often and at certain stated times, but as it were by chance—filled with such a flagrant odor and scent, that no perfumes in the world can exceed it, and this arises, as it were, out of a spring, from the sanctuary of the temple. And this proceeds very likely from its heat or some other power or faculty which is in it; and if peradventure this seems to any body an unlikely thing, such a one will, however, allow that the prophetess Pythia hath that part of the soul unto which this wind and blast of inspiration approacheth moved by variety of passions and affections, sometimes after one sort and sometimes another, and that she is not always in the same mood and temper, like a fixed and immutable harmony which the least alteration or change of such and such proportions destroys. For there are several vexations and passions, which agitate bodies and slide into the soul, that she perceives, but more that she does not, in which case it would be better that she should tarry away and not present herself to this divine inspiration, as not being clean and void of perturbations, like an instrument of music exquisitely made, but at present in disorder and out of tune. For wine does not

---

82 Plutarch was much quoted by Shakespeare and long accepted as a reliable authority. He is the principal biographical source regarding the lives of many historical persons, including Alexander.

at all times alike surprise the drunkard, neither does the sound of the flute always affect in the same manner him who dances to it. For the same persons are sometimes more and sometimes less transported beyond themselves, and more or less inebriated, according to the present disposition of their bodies. But especially the imaginative part of the soul is subject to change and sympathize together with the body, as is apparent from dreams; for sometimes we are mightily troubled with many and confused visions in our dreams, and at other times there is a perfect calm, undisturbed by any such images or ideas.

When therefore the imaginative part of the soul and the prophetic blast or exhalation have a sort of harmony and proportion with each other, so as the one, as it were in the nature of a medicament, may operate upon the other, then happens that enthusiasm or divine fury which is discernible in prophets and inspired persons. And, on the contrary, when the proportion is lost, there can be no prophetical inspiration, or only such as is as good as none; for then it is a forced fury, not a natural one, but violent and turbulent, such as we have seen to have happened in the prophetess Pythia who is lately deceased. For certain pilgrims being come for an answer from the oracle, it is said the sacrifice endured the first effusion without stirring or moving a jot, which made the priests, out of an excess of zeal, to continue to pour on more, till the beast was almost drowned with cold water; but what happened hereupon to the prophetess Pythia? She went down into the hole against her will; but at the first words which she uttered, she plainly showed by the hoarseness of her voice that she was not able to bear up against so strong an inspiration (like a ship under sail, oppressed with too much wind), but was possessed with a dumb and evil spirit. Finally, being horribly disordered and running with dreadful screeches towards the door to get out, she threw herself violently on the ground, so that not only the pilgrims fled for fear, but also the high priest Nicander and the other priests and religious which were there present; who entering within a while took her up, being out of her senses; and indeed she lived but few days after. For these reasons it is that Pythia is obliged to keep her body pure and clean from the company of men, there being no stranger permitted to converse with her. And before she goes to the oracle, they are used by certain marks to examine whether she be fit or no, believing that the God certainly knows when her body is disposed and fit to receive, without endangering her person, this enthusiastical inspiration. For the force and virtue of this exhalation does not move all sorts of persons, nor the same persons in like manner, nor as much at one time as at another; but it only gives beginning, and, as it were, kindles those spirits which are prepared and fitted to receive its influence. Now this exhalation is certainly divine and celestial, but yet not incorruptible and immortal, nor proof against the eternity of time, which subdues all things below the moon, as our doctrine teaches—and, as some say, all things above it, which, weary and in despair as regards eternity and infinity, are apt to be suddenly renewed and changed.[83]

Despite the authority of such a credible witness as Plutarch, later Enlightenment scholars came to suspect that since all forms of divination are impossible and therefore bogus, the whole set up at Delphi must have been a scam; another example of an invented religious tradition designed to fleece the gullible. So it seems you can fool the most significant people all over the eastern Mediterranean world for well over a millennium, but you can't fool sturdy, sound-minded rationalists. They can only be fooled by themselves.

The Rational Desecration and Scientific Restoration of the Temple

From 1892, a series of French archaeologists examined the ruined site and found no fissures in the rocks and concluded that there could therefore have been no intoxicating vapours to account for the Pythia's trances, deliriums, and oracular utterances. In 1904 a French scholar called Oppé concluded that since there were no fissures, and

---

83 Plutarch, Vol. 4, 1878.

since no natural gas could account for the Pythia's oracular powers, the testimony of countless writers over the centuries could be dismissed as the reports of hoodwinked fools. His opinion was shared by all reputable scholars thenceforth, and in 1950 the academic Pierre Amandry, who had dedicated his career to investigating Delphi and led many excavations there on behalf of the French School of Athens, further claimed that gaseous emissions were not even possible in a non-volcanic zone such as Delphi.

And that would have been that. Debunked, end of story. Delphi? Load of old nonsense; smoke and mirrors. Then fate intervened when, in the 1980s, a geologist called de Boer, an earth sciences professor at Wesleyan University in Connecticut, started working for the Greek government on the seismicity and tectonic setting of the Corinth Rift zone in order to assess the region's suitability for building nuclear reactors. His main work was searching out hidden faults and judging the likelihood of tremors and earthquakes.

By chance, heavy tourist traffic had prompted the government to carve in the hills east of Delphi a wide spot in the road where buses could turn around, exposing what de Boer described as "a beautiful fault." It looked young and active, so he traced it for days on foot, moving east to west over miles of mountainous, thorny terrain. The fault was plainly visible, rising as much as thirty feet. West of Delphi, he found that it linked up to a known fault. In the middle, however, it was hidden by rocky debris. Yet the fault appeared to run right under the temple.

"At that time I took a good look at previous and newly exposed segments of the Delphi fault and discovered another fault intersecting it," de Boer explained. "Following the fault traces brought me to their covered intersection below the Sanctuary. I had read Plutarch and the Greek stories, and I started thinking, 'Hey, this could have been the fracture along which these fumes rose.'"[84] Not being familiar with the archaeological literature, he assumed that someone else must have made the same observation years earlier and come to the same conclusion. He had no idea that the idea of fumes and fractures had been debunked decades earlier.

A few years later another lucky thing happened. While visiting a Roman ruin in Portugal in 1995, he met Dr. John R. Hale, an archaeologist from the University of Louisville, who was studying the Portuguese site. At sunset, over a bottle of wine, the geologist began telling the archaeologist of the Delphi fault.

"I said, 'There is no such fault,'" Dr. Hale recalled. But de Boer convinced him otherwise. Hale realised that this opened up many of the possibilities that had previously been debunked. "He told me that the majority of archaeologists did not believe in the ancient descriptions of fissure and rising fumes that influenced the Pythia," de Boer related. "I challenged him to come with me to Greece and he accepted."

Within a year, the two men had travelled to Greece to resurvey the fault at Delphi and study the regional maps of Greek geologists. These revealed that the underlying rock stratum was bituminous limestone containing up to 20 percent blackish oils. No volcanic activity was required; simple geological action could heat the bitumen sufficiently to release petrochemicals into the ground water beneath the sanctuary; and various petrochemicals have psychoactive effects. Things were looking promising.

During a second field trip in 1998 they discovered another fault heading north-south that intersected the original east-west one just below the sanctuary and proved to be aligned with a series of ancient dry and modern wet springs, one directly beneath the temple. The dry springs were coated with a mineral called travertine, which de

---

84   All quotations regarding this story are taken from Geological Society of America (*Geology*, 29, 8), as cited in "The Ancients Were Right—Delphi Was a Gas!" Science-Daily, 7 August 2001.

Boer recognized as an intriguing sign. When hot water seeps through limestone, it leaches out calcium carbonate that stays in solution until it rises to the surface and cools quickly. The calcium carbonate can then precipitate to form rocky layers of travertine, which can trap other substances contained in the water.

Increasingly excited, the two men won permission from the Greek authorities to sample the travertine and added Dr. Jeffrey P. Chanton, a geochemist at Florida State University, to the team. In the United States, he analyzed the travertine samples gathered from dry springs near the temple, finding methane and ethane. Each can produce altered mental states. But a better candidate suddenly occurred to de Boer.

"A small light went off in my mind," he recalled. Perhaps, he speculated, ethylene had been there as well. Ethylene is significantly less stable than ethane and methane, so it was not surprising that none was to be found in the travertine samples. Yet ethylene has more potent psychoactive effects than ethane, methane, or even nitrous oxide.

To find out if ethylene might have been part of the heady vapour mix, Chanton would have to go to Greece and test the waters of the springs that still ran beneath the temple. He went on his own, and the rest of the team waited on tenterhooks for news. After several days, Chanton finally called. He had found ethylene, as well as methane and ethane. To confirm that ethylene could generate the dissociative states of consciousness apparently attained by the Pythia, the team invited toxicologist Dr. Henry A. Spiller, director of the Kentucky Regional Poison Center, to join and help with the pharmacological analysis.

"There's a fair amount of data on the effects of ethylene," Dr. Spiller said. "In the first stages, it produces disembodied euphoria, an altered mental status, and a pleasant sensation. It's what street people would call getting high. The greater the dose, the deeper you go." Once a person stops breathing ethylene, he added, the effects wear off quickly.

Ethylene has never caught on as a street drug, so the data on its effects is not actually as extensive as Spiller suggests. However, if the effects are similar to its very close cousin ether,[85] then, as any reader of Hunter S. Thompson's *Fear and Loathing in Las Vegas* may recall, they can be pretty spectacular. In this context it may be instructive to quote the experience of the famous Dr. Oliver Wendell Holmes of Harvard Medical School 150 years ago:

> *I once inhaled a pretty full dose of ether, with the determination to put on record, at the earliest moment of regaining consciousness, the thought I should find uppermost in my mind. The mighty music of the triumphal march into nothingness reverberated through my brain, and filled me with a sense of infinite possibilities, which made me an archangel for a moment. The veil of eternity was lifted. The one great truth which underlies all human experience and is the key to all the mysteries that philosophy has sought in vain to solve, flashed upon me in a sudden revelation. Henceforth all was clear: a few words had lifted my intelligence to the level of the knowledge of a cherubim. As my natural condition returned, I remembered my resolution; and, staggering to my desk, I wrote, in ill-shaped, straggling characters, the all-embracing truth still glimmering in my consciousness. The words were these (children may smile; the wise ponder): "A strong smell of turpentine prevails throughout."* [86]

The Pythia's utterances were not always as prosaic as Holmes's, but they needed to be more helpful. If the "disembodied euphoria" of ethylene could match such a state of ecstasy it is easy to imagine that with practise, dedication, and perhaps rather profounder levels of

---

85 Diethyl ether is produced as a by-product of the vapour-phase hydration of ethylene to make ethanol. If this were to occur naturally then ether may have been part of the gas cocktail inhaled by the Pythia.

86 Oliver Wendell Holmes, *Mechanism in Thought and Morals*, Phi Beta Kappa address. Cambridge MA: Harvard University, June 29, 1870 (Boston: J.R. Osgood and Company, 1871).

sincerity, that an oracle could achieve a state of prophetic awareness, particularly if she was channelling an oracular deity such as Apollo or Dionysus. It seemed as if de Boer and Hall had indeed solved the enigmatic riddle of the Delphic Oracle once and for all.

Their findings were published to wide interest and support amongst the scientific and academic communities, with positive reports in many journals, including *Geology, Clinical Toxicology, Nature, National Geographic,* and newspapers such as *New York Times.* There have been a couple of challenges to their findings, but for now the legend enjoys official scientific sanction, and scholarly doubt amongst classicists about the thesis has given way to wide acceptance and praise. It also ties in with Plutarch's recounting of how the site was originally discovered when a goatherd noticed the effects on his goats of fumes emanating from cracks in the rock, and also tallies with his statement that there was a strong, sweet smell when the vapours were intense—ethylene has a sweet smell. Legend also recounts that after the death of Python, its rotting corpse (the root of python means "to rot") gave off a strong odour. It may be that in earlier times, other gases, such as sulphur dioxide (classic rotten egg "stink-bomb" smell), were also part of the mix.

It's not all about brain chemistry though. Psychoactive substances affect brain chemistry, which affects consciousness, but for the mystic, chemistry is not consciousness *per se.* Even the ethylene theory is unsatisfactorily reductive as an explanation for the Pythia's prophesying ability. With or without significant quantities of, say, ethylene,[87] when the Pythia descended into the adyton, she was preparing herself to be receptive, allowing a suggestible state in which she was open to impressions from behind the veil of what we take to be "normal" reality. In letting the spirit take her, allowing the voices to speak in her head, whether those voices belong to Apollo, Dionysus, or their daimons,

---

87 Chewing laurel leaves and even snake venom have also been proposed as potential entheogens.

she is acting as a psychic, a medium, an intermediary between the worlds. We will come to consider just what mediumship is all about later in the series when dealing with the extraordinarily widespread craze of *spiritualism* that emerged in the nineteenth century.

The achievement of the success of the ethylene theory is to restore some dignity to the fallen reputation of Delphi in these cynical and materialist times. An idea of just how far respect for both the Pythia and ancient Greek religion had fallen can be gauged from the fact that visitors to Delphi, at least until recently, were frequently told by their guides that the Pythia were poor, helpless women, drugged and exploited by a corrupt and rapacious priesthood,[88] an idea grotesquely mirrored in the recent film *300*. Such a jaundiced view has never been supported by the evidence and may reflect the decadence of modern thinking more than ancient practice. The balance of power between priesthood and Pythia is bound to have varied over the centuries, according to the personalities and dynamics involved, and no doubt some of the Pythia were better at their job than others; some spoke their prophesies and answers in poetic dactylic hexameters, while others might need interpreting, at least on occasions, by their priestly attendants; but to deny the likelihood that some, if not most, of the Pythia were gifted, charismatic, powerful women is to risk being misogynistic as well as cynical. Moreover, Fontenrose's exhaustive examination of all the known surviving proclamations of the oracle supports the Reverend James Gardner's summation of its influence:

---

88 A recent visitor reported the following: "Our guide explained that the priests were actually like a giant network of spies, in that they had eyes and ears all around the land; they knew what was going on in the world, and hence could give solid advice. While the drugged Oracle screeched on, the priest could write whatever he wanted. Generally, what they wanted was to give wise advice that would maintain the peace (and thus keep Delphi safe), so the information from espionage was key in creating this."

See: https://www.aroundtheworldl.com/2012/04/18/scandalous-facts-behind-the-oracle-of-delphi-in-greece/.

Its responses revealed many a tyrant and foretold his fate. Through its means many an unhappy being was saved from destruction and many a perplexed mortal guided in the right way. It encouraged useful institutions, and promoted the progress of useful discoveries. Its moral influence was on the side of virtue, and its political influence in favour of the advancement of civil liberty.[89]

The fact that Pythagoras is said to have been instructed in "moral doctrines" and "much else" by the Pythia Themistoclea,[90] even if untrue, is an indication of Delphi's high standing in the fourth century BC as well as the third century AD.

The connection between Pythagoras and Delphi is as much circumstantial as historical. His name alone connected him with the oracle, while Iamblichus has a very interesting tale to tell. He says that authorities such as Epimenides (a contemporary, of whom we will soon learn more), Xenocrates, and Eudoxus (both fourth century BC) claim that Apollo physically fathered Pythagoras. Iamblichus is at pains to disagree with them, however, saying that what really happened was that on a visit to Delphi to consult the oracle regarding his commercial ventures, the Pythia told his father that his wife would bear them a wonder-child of surpassing wisdom and beauty, whereupon he changed his wife's name from Parthenis ("virginal") to Pythais. When their son was duly born, they named him Pythagoras, meaning "announced by the Pythia." Iamblichus was insistent that Pythagoras should be considered divine because of his virtues and conduct, not because he was the physical son of Apollo, declaring that his body was not divine, only his soul, which "was sent down to men." The parallels with the birth of Jesus are impossible to overlook. There

---

89 Gardner, 1858, Vol 1, p. 688. As a Christian priest, the good rev's words go some small way to right the wrongs of Christian suppression of the sanctuary, which was finally closed down in 381 AD.

90 An assertion of Aristoxenus (fourth century BC) cited by Diogenes Laërtius (third century AD). Porphyry asserts that Pythagoras claimed as much himself.

is further evidence that Pythagoras was considered at least a demi-god by those who came after him, and Aristotle is widely quoted[91] as reporting that, according to his followers, "there are three kinds of rational living creatures; gods, men and beings like Pythagoras." Pythagoras was to become closely identified with Apollo, but before that came to pass a few more elements had to fall into place.

One of the key moral dictums of Delphi was the famous inscription over the entrance of the Temple of Apollo: "Know Thyself." This maxim is also attributed to Pythagoras's teacher Thales, and is perhaps the most important instruction any aspiring initiate could be given. If, as Pythagoras taught his followers, we all have an immortal soul that is ultimately divine in nature, then to know ourselves is to understand everything that connects us with and separates us from the Absolute. To know yourself, therefore, is to know the Truth; to be Truth; to be Divinity. That's a lot to know, and even a genius like Pythagoras who could remember his previous incarnations would need instruction as to how such knowledge might best be acquired.

---

91 By Iamblichus amongst others.

CHAPTER 4

PLAGUE⸱BUSTERS, SKYWALKERS, AND TIME⸱TRAVELLERS

As we have already seen, Pythagoras was not the only famous Greek sage at large at the time. There were certain people whose apparently magical abilities and exploits had made them famous throughout the Greek world, and it seems Pythagoras was on a mission to connect with many of them in his quest for divine knowledge. One of these extraordinary people was said to have acquired his magical powers while lost to the world in a deep cave, which must have made him of particular interest to Pythagoras.

Epimenides: The Tattooed Cave Prophet

Possibly at the suggestion of Themistoclea, Pythagoras travelled to Crete to meet the legendary tattooed prophet, seer, and "purification priest" Epimenides.[92] The most famous story about Epimenides is essentially the same as that of *Rip Van Winkle*. As a young shepherd, Epimenides was searching for a lost sheep in the mountains, when he came across a cave where he lay down to rest. When he awoke, he returned to his village and could find no one he recognised. He eventually found his brother, who had become an old man, while Epimenides himself was unaged. The brother told him that he had disappeared fifty-six (some say forty) years before. The cave in which Epimenides had fallen asleep turned out to have been Zeus's sacred cave and during his sleep he met and conversed with the gods, including Aletheia (truth) and Dike (justice), whose qualities he exemplified ever afterwards, together with such newfound powers as prophecy, plague-busting, and catharsis.[93] He became known to the Greeks as *theophilistatos*, "the most beloved of the gods," was said to have lived

---

92 Presumably the same Epimenides who stated, according to Iamblichus, that Pythagoras was sired by Apollo.

93 The Greek word *catharsis* originally referred to the purging of "spiritual maladies that are vexatious to the soul" or psychological confusion.

for 157, 199, or even 299 years, and achieved such a superhuman reputation while alive that he was worshipped as a god after his death.

His fame was such that the Delphic Oracle advised Plato's forbear
Solon the Athenian to send for him to cure the city of a plague, which
he duly did. Again sheep come into the story, for Epimenides had
some sheep brought to the Areopagus (the "Rock of Ares") above the
city and told the Athenians to help him observe the sheep and mark
the spots where they lay down to sleep. On those spots, sacrifices were
made to the unknown local divinity, which was deemed responsible
for the plague. Altars dedicated to *Agnosto Theo*, "An Unknown God,"
became a feature in Athens thereafter and are mentioned by the likes
of Apollonius of Tyana and St. Paul.

According to Plutarch, Empimenides founded various sacred build-
ings, curbed some of the more "severe and barbarous ceremonies
which the women usually practiced," and generally made the citizens
"more submissive to justice and more inclined to harmony." Plato recalls that Epimenides reassured the Athenians that the Persian invasion
they feared would not happen within ten years and would fail in its
aims. His visit established a long-standing alliance between Athens and
Crete.

One of the most remarkable things I have discovered about Epimenides is that his tattooed skin is supposed to have been flayed from
his body following his death and preserved on display at the court of
the ruling "Ephors" in Sparta. There is a lot of strangeness to chew
over here. For a start, it seems that tattooing was very unusual in the
Greek world at the time; it was only used to mark slaves and crimi-
nals. It was therefore associated with barbarians, such as Thracians[94]
and Scythians. Herodotus happily shares with us the Scythians' habit
of scalping ("The way a Scythian skins a head is as follows..."[95]), but

---

94 *The Greek Anthology* (7.10.1–3), compiled and translated by W. R. Paton, 1917.

95 Herodotus: *The Histories*, 4, 64. Translated by Robin Waterfield, London: Oxford
University Press, 1998.

ritually flaying a whole body and preserving the skin is an extremely
unusual thing anywhere and otherwise unheard of in ancient Greece,
as far as I can tell.[96] Epimenides was certainly a significant figure in
Sparta, having purified a plague there and correctly prophesied on
their behalf. Most of the prophesies foretold defeats and disasters
for them, however, and it has even been suggested that the Spartans
killed him after capturing him on a military campaign against the Cretans. The Spartans had a reputation for fierce warrior zeal, but they
were not barbarians, and anyway, why would they want his skin? It
must have something to do specifically with the tattoos themselves.
Some sources say the tattoos were "grammata" (writings); they may
have been his own poetry, possibly oracles or, as some have suggested,
they may have been magical symbols or initiation marks—proofs
of shamanic attainments as/or passwords to the Underworld/other
worlds. For the latter to be true, Epimenides must have been working
with ritual ideas inherited from Central Asian shamanism, for which
I can only find one piece of evidence, in the form of a visiting Asian
shaman, who is about to enter the story. A more prosaic, but also interesting, solution to this strange business, is the possibility that there
was at some time an oracle or sorcery book in circulation called "Epimenides Skin." The term became proverbial for mysterious, oracular,
or magical writing, and if vellum was used, which is very like cured
human skin, it may just account for this oddity.

Epimenides wrote many works (including the earliest *Argonau-
tica* [97]), none of which have survived. He was famed for his profound
knowledge of herbal medicine and magic, and subsisted on such a
meagre diet of herbs that he never had to evacuate his bowels. One
source says he ate a pill made up of mallow and asphodel, two herbs

---

96 The only other incidence I have come across is a single mention of Pherekydes's
    skin also being preserved by the Spartans, but that might be a mistaken conflation
    with Epimenides.

97 It was something of a rite of passage for Greek writers to compose a history of the
    voyages of the Argonauts.

highly valued in the famous vegetarian diet that Pythagoras is said to have recommended or imposed upon his followers. The idea was that the lighter and more natural the diet, the more the body's hold on the soul was loosened, allowing closer communion with the Divine. As an annual faster myself I can certainly attest that I become much more "spiritual," or rather soulful, after a few days fasting. One's centre of attention seems to move from the head to the heart, and the mind is calmed, becoming more contemplative and understanding. The gods themselves were believed by Pythagoreans to subsist on essence alone, which is why sweet-smelling incense and spices were burned in their honour. An altar at Delos, said to be the one most revered by Pythagoras, which forbade animal sacrifices and consisted only of cereals, herbs, and spices, may well have been inaugurated by Epimenides, who was also revered for curing that city of a plague.

It may well be that Pythagoras learned much of his dietary and herbal lore from Epimenides. What is a matter of record is that his host took him down into the cave where Zeus was born on Mount Ida. It is fair to assume that he initiated him into the mysteries of Cretan Zeus. Porphyry confirms the visit to Crete, but doesn't mention Epimenides at this point. He recounts the following:

> *Going to Crete, Pythagoras besought initiation from the priests of Morgos, one of the Idaean Dactyls, by whom he was purified with the meteoritic thunder-stone. In the morning he lay stretched upon his face by the seaside; at night, he lay beside a river, crowned with a black lamb's woolen wreath. Descending into the Idaean cave, wrapped in black wool, he stayed there twenty-seven days, according to custom; he sacrificed to Zeus, and saw the throne which there is yearly made for him. On Zeus's tomb, Pythagoras inscribed an epigram, "Pythagoras to Zeus," which begins: "Zeus deceased here lies, whom men call Jove."* [98]

---

98 Porphyry, *Life of Pythagoras*, 17.

The tomb of Zeus inspired one of Epimenides's famous sayings, which is quoted by St. Paul in his epistle to Titus (1:12): "It is said by one of themselves, a prophet of their own - 'Always liars and beasts are the Cretans, and inwardly sluggish.'" The original saying is intriguingly reminiscent of St. Paul's Christianity:

They fashioned a tomb for you, holy and high one,
Cretans, always liars, evil beasts, idle bellies.
But you are not dead: you live and abide forever,
For in you we live and move and have our being.[99]

Porphyry mentions the "Idaean Dactyls," and they are definitely worth a mention here. The Dactyls are mysterious subterranean "spirit men" that were set by Rhea, the mother of Zeus, to guard the infant god in his cave from his infanticidal father, Kronos. Their name means fingers, and they came into being as Rhea clawed and kneaded the earth from the pain of giving birth to Zeus. The Dactyls are associated with the magical art of metallurgy, mathematics, and music, a combination that makes sense when one considers that the striking of bronze discs of different sizes create different harmonics. They are credited with the discovery of iron and the focus of ancient warrior initiation rites.[100]

Zeus was believed throughout the Greek world to have been born in Crete, but it was only in Crete that he was worshipped as an eternal youth, who was killed and descended into the Underworld. There his cult had such close parallels with Dionysus that he is often referred to as Zeus-Dionysus by scholars. He also has close affinities with the Egyptian god Osiris and like him (and later Jesus Christ) was believed to have suffered a violent death, whereupon he became a judge of the dead.

---

99 Callimachus: *Hymns and Epigrams.* Translated by Mair, A. W. & G. R. Loeb Classical Library Volume 129. London: William Heinemann, 1921.

100 Interestingly the *Bibliotheca of Pseudo-Apollodorus* says that the Dactyls were the offspring of Apollo.

To descend into one of this deity's sacred caves with someone like Epimenides is to be initiated into a technique for separating the soul from the body and encountering the deity face to face. The true nature of that encounter remains a mystery to all but those who experience it, but I can say that to experience a god is in a sense to *be* it, because in the moment of encounter, the mortal human is completely displaced, while the soul is deeply impressed; and the impressions received leave their mark. This is why prophets are supposed to shine, why saints are depicted with halos. Pythagoras was said to have shone like the sun. And in ancient Greece this radiant inner light was the outward sign of special abilities conferred by close encounters with a particular divine being.

Given the special abilities associated with Epimenides, and later with Pythagoras, could it be that the deity encountered deep in the Stygian darkness of the Idaean cave was not Zeus-Dionysus, but Apollo? At first this seems to make no sense. For a start, how can a masculine Olympian sky god, the god of light, be found in subterranean darkness? Surely that is the domain of earthy, chthonic deities such as androgynous Dionysus. And anyway, the cave in question here was sacred to Zeus-Dionysus. But as we have seen, Apollo and Dionysus are closely entwined; they are two sides of the same coin, a sort of yin and yang. Dionysus presides over the endless cycle of life and death, emerging from darkness into the light to possess the ecstatically dancing bodies of those who surrender to him in *enthusiasmos*; while Apollo is a god of light and truth who can only be encountered in utter darkness when utter stillness has been achieved. Where the two gods meet is in their ability to inspire prophecy: they are both oracular deities able to transmit supernatural knowledge and are doors to each other.

Holy Smoke

If utter darkness and stillness are required, then a cave, particularly one guarded by the Dactyls, is the perfect place to encounter Apollo, because the deeper you descend, the greater the sensory deprivation. Darkness, silence. Stilling the senses helps still the mind and the body, and one trained in the art of surrendering all sense of self can become present enough to receive. But the receiver must be beside him- or herself, in the terrific *ekstasis* that can only be achieved in the part of self not subject to endless flux: the soul.

When I first started reading about these ancient Greek sages finding illumination in caves I was struck by the parallels with my own experience. In the mid-1990s I found myself unexpectedly invited by a family of Mexican goat herders to live in a cave near to their mountain rancho in the Sierra Catorce, above the high desert plains of north-central Mexico. When I arrived at the *Cueva de la Leona* ("the lioness's cave") I spotted three specimens of a plant known to some as *Santa Maria*, a vision-inducing plant sacred to Our Lady of Guadelupe, herself a manifestation of the pre-Columbian mother goddess Tonantzin. I dutifully harvested the plants and cured them, and a few days later smoked a pipeful. Deeply chastened and awed by the remarkable experiences that had led me to the cave, my intention was not to relax and get high, but rather to surrender myself in humility to whatever higher apprehension of truth there may be within me or without. I took the smoke deep into my lungs and held it down as I became smaller and smaller and descended deeper and deeper, slowly sinking to the bottom of myself. All sense of descent having ceased, I eventually heard a still, small voice in the darkness say "Thank you." I felt myself expanding upwards and outwards and realized with great wonder that I contained the entire world. Everything was a part of me. This was, as I would later understand, my first experiential encounter with the concept of the "microcosm," a key magical understanding that teaches that the individual contains the whole within itself, as exemplified by the Hermetic maxim: *as above, so below.*

The next day I walked over the mountains to the old mining ghost town to get some supplies and dropped by some friends who ran the *Café Nagual*. Perusing their magical bookshelf, I pulled out a book called *The Practical Handbook of Plant Alchemy*, which initiated a process that now finds me writing these words. I realize this is on a minute ratio of equivalence with Pythagoras and Apollo, but I believe it resonates nevertheless. As for my means of descent...

Herodotus writes about the Scythians enjoying the intoxicating benefits of cannabis incense, and it is hard to imagine that such a significant and useful plant, with its wide range of applications including medicine, textiles, and ritual use, would not have been intimately familiar to the Greek world by the sixth century BC. A major conduit for Scythian ideas into Greece was Thrace, that Greek-speaking territory north of Macedonia where Orpheus and the worship of Dionysus came from. I remember reading this long ago:

> *The sorcerers of these Thracian tribes were known to have burned female cannabis flowers (and other psychoactive plants) as a mystical incense to induce trances. Their special talents were attributed to the "magical heat" produced from burning the cannabis and other herbs, believing that the plants dissolved in the flames, then reassembled themselves inside the person who inhaled the vapours ...*[101]

Mercea Eliade, in his groundbreaking studies of shamanism, mentions the use of "Hemp seeds among the Thracians... and among the Scythians," and refers to an ancient term used to describe certain shamans as *Kapnobatai*: "those who walk in smoke." [102] There is clearly the possibility that cannabis use may have at least been peripheral, if not central to the Dionysian ecstasies and, subsequently, Orphism.

That said, it is not necessary to overstate the case, either for or against, with regard to the role consciousness-altering plants may have played in Greek magic or religion. In India, after all, the ancient science of using techniques such as yoga to achieve a wide variety of

---

101 Sumach, Alexander: *A Treasury of Hashish*, Toronto: Stoneworks Publishing, 1976.

102 Eliade, 1982.

different states of consciousness does not rely on the use of drugs.[103] On the other hand, to dismiss the possibility of the widespread use of entheogenic plants in ancient Greece because of a paucity of hard evidence smacks of prejudice, particularly given that the Pythagoreans were sworn to secrecy regarding their techniques of ecstasy. Regardless of the specific techniques being used in these god-manifesting cave rituals, they remain profoundly fascinating and mysterious precisely because they seem to have been so effective.

The Birth of Chillout

As we have seen with Orpheus and Delphi, the encounter with Dionysus can lead the ardent seeker to the encounter with his brother Apollo. The dissolution of the self presided over by Dionysus prepares the chosen few for the encounter with truth that can only occur in the absence of self-identification. A modern expression of this archetype can be seen in the rave culture that emerged in England in the late 1980s. Enthusiasts of electronic dance music would gather at secret locations, ingest a potion called ecstasy, and "go into dithyrambs" dancing to repetitive rhythms right through the night. Out of this wild raving emerged a completely different form of music more suited to tiring bodies and the arrival of dawn, known as "chillout," that promoted a calmer, more spiritual, but no less ecstatic state. The creators of such music were inspired by a non-rhythmic style known as "ambient," a favourite example of which just happens to be Brian Eno's classic "Apollo." An inner core of ravers also started experimenting with drugs such as DMT, which required the participant to be lying down in a quiet shaded place, such as a "chillout room" attended by initiates. Profound religious or quasi-religious experiences were common, as were encounters with intelligent entities or divinities. The ravers emerged from a hedonistic culture centred around

---

103 Although the otherwise ascetic *sadhus*, followers of Shiva, smoke cannabis as a sacrament.

music and drugs rather than a religious one, but the piety of Orphism was preceded with the hedonistic abandon of the Dionysian revels, so the parallels are obvious and not uninstructive to note.

Writers like the highly engaging but often misleading Camille Paglia insist that in ancient Greece, unlike in Egypt, there was a separation between the earth cults and sky cults.[104] She, along with everyone else, had no idea of the chthonic encounters that the likes of Epimenides and Pythagoras (and others we have yet to meet) were having with radiant Apollo (and even with Zeus himself, the greatest sky god of all) in the depths of sacred caves. Proclus, in reference to the Greek mysteries, says: "The gods assume many forms and change from one to another; now they are manifested in the emission of shapeless light, now they are of human shape, and anon appear in other and different forms." [105] In subterranean Apollo, all the gods and goddesses of Greece merge in the encounter of the divine with the human.

Another legendary, possibly mythical, troglodytic sage, closely associated with both Pythagoras and Apollo, is a character called Zalmoxis. He is variously described as a god, an ancient hero, and a slave or pupil of Pythagoras. Porphyry gives us the latter identification, reporting that "Pythagoras had another youthful disciple from Thrace. Zamolxis was he named because he was born wrapped in a bear's skin, in Thracian called Zalmus. Pythagoras loved him, and instructed him in sublime speculations concerning sacred rites, and the nature of the Gods. Some say this youth was named Thales, and that the barbarians worshipped him as Hercules." [106]

Apollo has been twisting and morphing in this story. He started out as the cool, aloof, rational god of truth, form, harmony, and

---

104 See Paglia, Camille: *Sexual Personae*, Yale University Press, 1990.

105 Mackenzie, 1917. Proclus was a major fifth century Greek Neoplatonist philosopher.

106 Porphyry, 14.

beauty, the lord of the Muses, the egregore [107] of classical Greece in the imagination of my school Classics masters. The antithesis of Dionysus, he seemed sober and orderly, lacking in personality, a square prude compared to the hip, counterculture hedonism of his darker brother. This is the image that has come down to us, but as is becoming clear, Apollo is also a dark horse. We have discovered that he is a god of prophecy, initiation, and the terrifying encounter with truth in the darkness. He is a god of healing, but he is also a plague god. It is not so much that Apollo causes plague, although he can [108]; it is more that wherever Apollo is neglected, disrespected, or absent, plague is likely to break out. And when it does, who ya gonna call? A "purifier" —a healer who has been touched by Apollo.

Pythagoras emerges from the Idaean cave ecstatically inspired; maybe not quite divine as such, but no longer quite human. From this point on he is credited with a wide range of impressive powers, and his legend waxes with stories of him predicting earthquakes, chasing away plagues, stopping hailstorms, calming winds and water, and exercising "absolute dominion over beasts and birds by the power of his voice, or influence of his touch." [109] Arriving in Croton, a thriving Greek city state in Calabria (modern-day Italy), renowned for its advances in medicine, he was shown such reverent attention that he was persuaded to start a school to pass on his knowledge.

Around this time Pythagoras was seen at the Olympic Games, where he had been a boxing champion in his youth, using techniques never seen before. This time he is said to have flashed a naked thigh for all to see. Naked thighs were hard to miss in ancient Greece, particularly at the Olympics, but all were in agreement that Pythagoras's

---

107 *Egregore* is a Greek word for the presiding spirit of any group—e.g., a tribe, nation, family, football club, or company.

108 The first I ever read about Apollo, aged eight, was right at the beginning of Homer's *Iliad*, where he answers the prayer of one of his priests by bringing a plague upon the camp of the Greeks besieging Troy.

109 Iamblichus.

thigh was golden. Everyone saw it. And not just everyone who was there, it seems.

Abaris Aethrobates: The Skywalker

Thousands of miles to the north, a man called Abaris felt the flash of gold and knew that Apollo had landed. He took his golden arrow, the arrow of Apollo, and told it the news, saying "we must find him," and the arrow knew it and could feel him and had to find him. So the two took off together, guided by the magnetic pull, and bore each other thither to the source, barely pausing to eat or sleep.

Who was this Abaris? His legend proved so enduring that the first great encyclopaedia of the modern era, the third edition of the *Encyclopaedia Britannica* (1788–97), gave him his own entry, which reads as follows:

> *Harpocration*[110] *tells us, that the whole earth being infested with a deadly plague, Apollo, upon being consulted, said that the Athenians should offer up prayers on behalf of all other nations; upon which several countries sent ambassadors to Athens, among whom was Abaris the Hyperborean. In this country [ancient Greece] he renewed the alliance between his countrymen and the inhabitants of*

---

110 Valerius Harpocration was a Greek grammarian of Alexandria, probably working in the second century AD, when the Alexandrian libraries were still intact, providing him with a wealth of sources that no longer exist.

the island of Delos. It appears that he also went to Lacedaemon: since, according to some writers, he there built a temple consecrated to Proserpine the Salutary. He wrote a book on Apollo's arrival into the country of the Hyperboreans. ... The fictions and mistakes concerning our Abaris are so infinite: however, it is by all agreed that he travelled quite over Greece and thence into Italy, where he conversed familiarly with Pythagoras, who favoured him beyond all his disciples, by instructing him in his doctrines, especially his thoughts of nature, in a plainer and more compendious method than he did any other. This distinction could not but be very advantageous to Abaris. The Hyperborean, in return, presented the Samian [Pythagoras], as though he equalled Apollo himself in wisdom, with the sacred arrow, on which the Greeks have fabulously related that he sat astride, and flew upon it, through the air, over rivers and lakes, forests and mountains; in like manner as our vulgar still believe, particularly those of the Hebrides, that wizards and witches fly whithersoever they please on their broomsticks. The orator Himerius above mentioned, though one of those who, from the equivocal sense of the word Hyperborean, seem to have mistaken Abaris for a Scythian, yet describes his person accurately, and gives him a very noble character. "They relate (says he) that Abaris the Sage was by nation a Hyperborean, appeared a Grecian in speech, and resembled a Scythian in his habit and appearance. He came to Athens, holding a bow in his hand, having a quiver hanging on his shoulders, his body wrapt up in a plaid, girt about the loins with a gilded belt, and wearing trowsers[111] *reaching from his waist downward." By this it is evident that he was not habited like the Scythians, who were always covered with skins; but appeared in the native garb of an aboriginal Scot. As to what relates to his abilities, Himerius informs us, that "he was affable and pleasant in conversation, in dispatching great affairs secret and industrious,*

---

111 Pythagoras was also famous for wearing trousers, a habit considered very "un-Greek" and associated with "barbarians."

quick-sighted in present exigencies, in preventing future dangers cir-
cumspect, a searcher after wisdom, desirous of friendship, trusting
little to fortune, and having everything trusted to him for his pru-
dence." Neither the Academy nor the Lycaeum could have furnished
a man with fitter qualities to travel so far abroad, and to such wise
nations, about affairs no less arduous than important. And if we fur-
ther attentively consider his moderation in eating, drinking, and the
use of all those things which our natural appetites incessantly crave;
joining the candour and simplicity of his manners with the solidity
and wisdom of his answers, all which we find sufficiently attested: it
must be owned, that the world at that time had few to compare with
Abaris.

By the 1840s, however, rational scepticism had hardened to the
point that the accounts given by all the ancient authorities were dismissed out of hand by the *Dictionary of Greek and Roman Biography and*
Mythology (1849), which declared his historicity as "entirely mythical."
Fortunately, such presumptuous positions are no longer fashionable
in academia, so we will not be considered entirely naive for exploring
the story of Abaris with an open mind. All the ancient sources agree
that the incomparable Abaris was a foreign priest of Apollo, of im-
mense personal charm and amazing abilities, who sought out Pythagoras and gave him the golden arrow he always travelled with. Like
Pythagoras, he clearly made an enormous impression everywhere
he went, making friends and giving prudent advice in perfect Greek,
all while quietly "dispatching great affairs" in a quick-sighted and industrious fashion. As for the amazing abilities, apart from prophecy
and plague-busting and never eating, the most striking is his reported
ability to fly through the air on his arrow, which some said had been
given to him by Apollo. At their meeting Abaris gave Pythagoras the
arrow, declaring him to be the "Hyperborean Apollo" he had been
seeking, and, as if to confirm the truth of this, Pythagoras showed
him his golden thigh. All of this is very extraordinary and of course

very hard to reasonably account for. To try to get a handle on the true significance at play here, it is worth breaking the story down into bite-size chunks for closer consideration.

Hyperborea: The Land Beyond the North Wind

For a start, where on earth is/was Hyperborea? Good question. Hyperborea was a name well known to the Greeks, but there was no consensus as to where it was located, apart from that it lay to the distant north, beyond the Riphaean Mountains. Unfortunately, the mountains themselves were of uncertain location. The earliest Greek accounts suggest the Alps, but they could have been the Caucasus, they could have been further north and east. No one knew for sure, except the people who did know, the travellers, but no one tended to believe them. Pytheas the Phocaean, for example, travelled all the way to Britain and beyond in the fourth century BC. Heading ever north, beyond an island he called Thule, he must have approached the Arctic Circle, describing luminal regions that seemed to him to be the very end of the earth, where "the earth, the sea, and all the elements are held in suspension; a sort of bond, which you can neither walk nor sail upon." He recorded detailed and accurate accounts of his discoveries, but his compatriots scoffed and scorned them. Greek authorities of the Classical Age were not easily convinced. Despite an abiding fondness for their myths and folklore, they prided themselves on having sensible ideas and were suspicious of fabulous tales that were not central to their tradition. It is for precisely this reason that the extraordinary stories surrounding the likes of Abaris, Pythagoras, and Epimenides cast such an enigmatic spell to this day.

Hyperborea was *terra incognita*—"unexplored territory"—a fabulous Golden Age land of eternal spring that lay beyond the north wind Boreas. Its river Eridanos was adorned with swans and lined with poplar trees that wept golden tears of amber. Its people were a blessed, long-lived race, untouched by war, hard toil, and the ravages of old age and disease. They were harmoniously ruled by the three gigantic sons of Boreas, high priests of Apollo who honoured their god in an eternal festival of music, song, and dance; their soaring paeans joined by the sweet song of the circling Hyperborean swans who drew Apollo's golden chariot across the sky when he wintered there every year.

Hyperborea was protected to the south by the bitterly cold and impassable Riphaean Mountains, whose peaks were inhabited by gold-guarding griffins and its valleys by the cyclopean Arimaspoi tribe. Beneath the southern slopes lay Pterophoros, a desolate, frozen desert cursed with eternal winter.

Diodorus describes the account given by the sceptical fourth century BC philosopher Hecataeus of Abdera:

> Hecataeus and certain others say that in the regions beyond the land of the Celts there lies in the ocean an island no smaller than Sicily. This island, is situated in the north and is inhabited by the Hyperboreans, who are called by that name because their home is beyond the point whence the north wind (Boreas) blows; and the island is both fertile and productive of every crop, and since it has an unusually temperate climate it produces two harvests each year. Moreover, the following legend is told concerning it: Leto [112] was born on this island, and for that reason Apollo is honoured among them above all other gods; and the inhabitants are looked upon as priests of Apollo, after a manner, since daily they praise this god continuously in song and honour him exceedingly. And there is also on the island both a magnificent sacred precinct of Apollo and a notable temple which is adorned with many votive offerings and is spherical in shape. Furthermore, a city is there which is sacred to this god, and the majority of its inhabitants are players on the cithara; and these continually play on this instrument in the temple and sing hymns of praise to the god, glorifying his deeds.

---

112 Mother of Apollo, daughter of the Titan Phoebe ("Bright"). Phoebus is one of Apollo's most common epithets.

The Hyperboreans also have a language, we are informed, which is peculiar to them, and are most friendly disposed towards the Greeks, and especially towards the Athenians and the Delians, who have inherited this good-will from most ancient times. The myth also relates that certain Greeks visited the Hyperboreans and left behind them there costly votive offerings bearing inscriptions in Greek letters. And in the same way Abaris, a Hyperborean, came to Greece in ancient times and renewed the good-will and kinship of his people to the Delians. They say also that the moon, as viewed from this island, appears to be but a little distance from the earth and to have upon it prominences, like those of the earth, which are visible to the eye. The account is also given that the god visits the island every nineteen years, the period in which the return of the stars to the same place in the heavens is accomplished; and for this reason the nineteen-year period is called by the Greeks the "year of Meton." At the time of this appearance of the god he both plays on the cithara and dances continuously the night through from the vernal equinox until the rising of the Pleiades, expressing in this manner his delight in his successes. And the kings of this city and the supervisors of the sacred precinct are called Boreadae, since they are descendants of Boreas, and the succession to these positions is always kept in their family.[113]

Abaris the Celt: Druid Priest of Albion

British scholars over the centuries have, of course, been particularly keen to identify this Hyperborean island "beyond the land of the Celts" (Gaul) as Britain, and the "notable, spherical temple" as Stonehenge, while the "magnificent sacred precinct of Apollo" makes me think of Avebury. Patriots from different parts of Britain have sought to claim the splendid Abaris as one of their own, as amusingly enunciated by Godfrey Higgins in the 1830s:

---

113 Diodorus, Book 2.

The Abaris of whom mention has been made, was a very celebrated philosopher of the Hyperboreans. It seems to be pretty well established that he was from the British isles, and much pains have been taken by the authors of the different islands to get possession of him. Every true and loyal Scot is certain that he came from the Hebrides: Mr. Vallencey proves, as clear as the sun at noon, that he was an Irishman. This seems odd to the Welshmen, who are quite certain that he came from Wales; and Mr. Borlase does not fail to secure him for Cornwall. I shall not be rash enough to attempt the decision of this grand question. I am quite content that we have him amongst us. He appears to have been a priest of Apollo, and an Irish or British Celtic Druid.[114]

The Mr. Vallencey mentioned by Higgins attempts to make a case for an Irish character called Abhras, who, he assures us, travelled "to distant parts in quest of knowledge and, after a long time to have returned by way of Scotland, where he remained seven years, bringing a new system of religion. This was opposed by the Fribolgs, in consequence of which a civil war arose, which lasted twenty-seven years before the new religion was established."[115]

By "Fribolgs" Vallencey presumably means the Fir Bolgs, a legendary group of settlers mentioned in the *Lebor Gabála Érenn* (The Book of the Taking of Ireland), whose ancestors left Ireland after a great calamity and went to Greece, where they were enslaved for 230 years before returning (apparently at the same time as the Israelites left Egypt) as conquerors. They in turn are displaced by their ancient relations, the Tuatha Dé Danann, who return from the north having achieved supernatural powers. There are some intriguing matches here, but not enough to make a convincing case, especially since I can't find any further mention of Abhras.

---

114 Godfrey Higgins, *Anacalypsis*, IV, IV. London: Longman, 1836.

115 Vallencey quoted by Higgins.

Bladud the Wolf Lord

Another bold claim is made on behalf of the English city of Bath by the eighteenth century English antiquarian John Wood the Elder. In *An Essay Towards a Description of Bath* he recounts the legend of the mythical founder of Bath, King Bladud, father of Shakespeare's King Lear, telling us that, according to Geoffrey of Monmouth,[116] Bladud was sent by his father to be educated in the liberal arts in Athens. After his father's death he returned, with four philosophers, and founded a university at Stamford in Lincolnshire, which flourished until it was suppressed by Saint Augustine of Canterbury "on account of heresies which were taught there." He ruled for twenty years from 863 BC or 500 BC, in which time he built Kaerbadum or Caervaddon (Bath), creating the hot springs there by the use of magic. He is said to have made or grown a set of wings with the help of necromancy, and it is on such scanty and dubious foundations that Wood conjures up his conviction that Bladud is none other than Abaris Skywalker and that the knowledge he returned from Athens with, and upon which he founded the university, was that which was imparted to him by Pythagoras.

---

116 Best known for popularising the myths of Arthur and Merlin (mid-twelfth century).

Alas, in attempting to fly to (or from) the temple of Apollo in London, he plunged, Icarus-like[117] to his death. The connection with Athens and Apollo is again intriguing but unconvincing, and Wood misses an opportunity when he attempts to explain Bladud's name as meaning something like "star dude," when in fact it means "Wolf Lord," which is much more suggestive, since several of Apollo's epithets connect him with wolves: *Lykeios*, "Wolf-god"; *Lykegenes*, "Wolf-born"; *Lykoktonos*, "Wolf-killer"; the wolf who protects the flocks. Apollo's mother Leto is said to have fled Hyperborea in the form of a she-wolf to escape the murderous jealousy of Hera, and Apollo is associated with werewolf cults in Arcadia.

So John Wood missed a trick here, but lest I leave you with the impression that he was a feckless historian, I should point out that a plan he drew of Stonehenge is considered the most important ever made and his detailed survey of much greater value than that of his celebrated contemporary William Stukely.

It is quite possible that the builders of the Neolithic stone circles worshipped a god that was identical to Apollo. Renowned Stonehenge archaeologist Dennis Price is even convinced that the remains of the lost city of Apollo, referred to by the explorer Pytheas, are situated under King's Barrow Ridge overlooking Stonehenge. It is possible too that the Celtic Druids were influenced by, or shared some of the same knowledge as Pythagoras. Higgins insists that in the Celtic Welsh language the verb *pythagori* means "to explain the system of the universe." This would be fascinating if true, but unfortunately the verb does not appear in the Welsh dictionaries I have consulted. I have, however, found another, perhaps more compelling lead with regard to possibly Pythagorean Druidism.

---

117 Icarus was the son of Daedalus, the architect of the Minotaur's labyrinth in Crete. To escape the island, they fashioned wings from feathers. Icarus soared too close to the sun and the wax that held his feathers in place melted, plunging him to his death.

Zalmoxis: The Subterranean Man-God

St. Hippolytus, writing around 220 AD, intriguingly insists that the person responsible for transmitting to the Celtic Druids their Pythagorean understanding of the cosmos and the soul was an intriguing semi-mythical character called Zalmoxis or Zamolxis [118]:

> And the Celtic Druids investigated to the very highest point the Pythagorean philosophy, after Zamolxis, by birth a Thracian, a servant of Pythagoras, became to them the originator of this discipline. Now, after the death of Pythagoras, Zamolxis, repairing thither, became to them the originator of this philosophy. The Celts esteem these [the Druids] as prophets and seers, on account of their foretelling to them certain (events), from calculations and numbers by the Pythagorean art; on the methods of which very art also we shall not keep silence, since also from these some presumed to introduce heresies; but the Druids resort to magical rites likewise. [119]

Zalmoxis appears to have been an ancestor or hero divinity of the Getae or Dacian people of Northern Thrace, who were affected by a massive migration of Iranian Scythians moving east to west during the first half of the first millennium BC, followed by a second equally large wave of Celts migrating west to east. When Celtic warriors first penetrated these territories, they seem to have mixed with the domestic population and merged many of their cultural traditions. Given this understanding, there is no good reason to argue with Hippolytus's main point, since the western and eastern Celtic tribes were all connected by the great waterways of the Danube and Rhine. Whether Zalmoxis really was directly connected with Pythagoras is doubtful. It may be that his legend accounts for the influx of shamanic influences into Greece via the Iranian Scythians, influencing Orphism

---

118 Esoteric historian Mircea Eliade, who can claim Thracian heritage, calls him Zalmoxis, so I go with that.

119 Hippolytus. *The Refutation of All Heresies,* translated by Rev. J. H. MacMahon, Edinburgh: T. and T. Clark, 1868.

and thence Pythagoras. The influence may also have flowed the other way, and in this regard, it is interesting to note that when Julius Caesar arrived in Gaul he found the Celtic tribes worshipping the classical Graeco-Roman gods, including Apollo. We have little choice but to take Caesar's word for it, because the Celts left no written record of their beliefs. We only have the evidence of Caesar and a couple of other authorities, such as Herodotus.

There is evidence that reincarnation has always been an inherent part of the ancient beliefs held in common among all the Indo-European peoples, including the Celts, the Scythians, and the Germanic tribes.

Classical authors mention a belief in immortality held by the Celts. The Greek ethnographer Posidonius was probably the original source for most of these early references (including the one by Hippolytus quoted above) and equated Celtic doctrine with that of Pythagoras. Caesar used Posidonius as his source when he wrote:

> A lesson which they [the Druids] take particular pains to inculcate is that the soul does not perish, but after death passes from one body to another; they think this is the best incentive to bravery, because it teaches men to disregard the terrors of death.[120]

Diodorus writes:

> The belief of Pythagoras prevails among them [the Gauls], that the souls of men are immortal and that after a prescribed number of years they commence upon a new life, the soul entering into another body.[121]

The Vikings also appear to have believed in reincarnation, for we read in the poetic Edda:

> Sigrun was early dead of sorrow and grief. It was believed in olden times that people were born again, but that is now called old wives' folly. Of Helgi and Sigrun it is said that they were born again; he became Helgi

---

120 Hippolytus, chapter 22.

121 Diodorus, V, 28.

Haddingjaskati, and she Kara the daughter of Halfdan, as is told in the
Lay of Kara, and she was a Valkyrie.[122]

As for Zalmoxis, we know very little about him apart from what
Herodotus has to tell us in his *Histories*, where he says that the Getae
("the bravest and most law-abiding of all Thracians") worshipped Zalmoxis as a god, and goes on to say:

> *For myself, I have been told by the Greeks who dwell beside the Hel-*
> *lespont and Pontus that this Zamolxis was a man who was once a*
> *slave in Samos, his master being Pythagoras, son of Mnesarchus;*
> *presently, after being freed and gaining great wealth, he returned to*
> *his own country. Now the Thracians were a meanly-living and sim-*
> *ple witted folk, but this Zamolxis knew Ionian usages and a fuller*
> *way of life than the Thracian; for he had consorted with Greeks, and*
> *moreover with one of the greatest Greek teachers, Pythagoras; where-*
> *fore he made himself a hall, where he entertained and feasted the*
> *chief among his countrymen, and taught them that neither he nor*
> *his guests nor any of their descendants should ever die, but that they*
> *should go to a place where they would live for ever and have all good*
> *things. While he was doing as I have said and teaching this doctrine,*
> *he was all the while making him an underground chamber. When*
> *this was finished, he vanished from the sight of the Thracians, and*
> *descended into the underground chamber, where he lived for three*
> *years, the Thracians wishing him back and mourning him for dead;*
> *then in the fourth year he appeared to the Thracians, and thus they*
> *came to believe what Zamolxis had told them. Such is the Greek story*
> *about him.*
>
> *I for my part neither put entire faith in this story of Zamolxis and*
> *his underground chamber, nor do I altogether discredit it: but I believe*
> *Zamolxis to have lived long before the time of Pythagoras. Whether*
> *there was ever really a man of the name, or whether Zamolxis is noth-*

---

122   *The Poetic Edda ("Helgakvitha Hundingsbana"),* II, 50, translated from the Icelan-
    dic by Henry Adams Bellows, New York: The American-Scandinavian Founda-
    tion, 1923.

ing but a native god of the Getae, I now bid him farewell. As for the Getae themselves, the people who observe the practices described above, they were now reduced by the Persians, and accompanied the army of Darius. [123]

The relating of Zalmoxis's underground seclusion is intriguing, as is the assertion that he returned north, like Abaris, with the great wealth that he had gained. Ah yes, Abaris. According to that scholarly esoteric sleuth Peter Kingsley, if we really want to know where Abaris came from we need look no further than his name, which simply means "the Avar" in Greek.

Abaris the Avar: Tulku Shaman of the Steppes

The Avars were a nomadic people renowned above all else for their archery. They developed a light bow that could be used with devastating penetration and accuracy while astride a galloping horse. The design was not bettered for thousands of years. A tribe of mysterious origin, they still exist, retaining a tribal identity in parts of Dagestan in the Russian Caucasus. Their territory has ranged far and wide over the centuries. In the European Dark Ages, they had a large kingdom that, at its height, covered most of the land to the west of the Black Sea as far as Austria, and absorbed much of the Byzantine Empire to the south, from which it leeched enormous quantities of gold in exchange for peace. They were eventually defeated by Charlemagne and almost annihilated. But where they were at the time when Abaris and his arrow found Pythagoras is a matter of conjecture. Peter Kingsley, whose extraordinary and groundbreaking research has shone unexpected light on the mystery of Abaris Skywalker, is convinced that the Avars were originally of Mongolian extraction and were ranging the

---

123 Herodotus, The Persian Wars, 4, 93–96. First published in this translation as: *The History of Herodotus of Halicarnassus, A New English Version edited with copious Notes and Appendices by George Rawlinson (trans.)*, London: John Murray, Albermarle Street, 1858.

desert wastelands beyond the Altai Mountains when Abaris set off on his mission.

The earliest sources describe him as a Scythian, which for the ancient Greeks meant someone of eastern appearance of rather vague address: somewhere north of Greece and east of the Black Sea. Kingsley makes an exciting and convincing case for Abaris being essentially a Mongolian shaman and explores the history of Buddhist Tibet back to its indigenous shamanic roots, establishing how the invading monastic culture of Tibet displaced the original shamanic tradition (of which Bön-Po is the last remnant), while appropriating some of its most esoteric treasures. Foremost amongst the latter is the *tulku* tradition. A tulku is a reincarnated soul of an important lineage, such as those of the Dalai Lamas and Karmapas of Tibetan Buddhism. The process whereby the reincarnated soul is recognized and accepted as the legitimate successor is not a precise science, making it all the more remarkable that the tulku system has survived so successfully within Tibetan Buddhism for more than eight hundred years.

In the late 1980s I had the opportunity to get to know a cousin of a very close friend, who, at the age of seven, was recognised as a tulku by the sixteenth Karmapa following a visit to the Monkey Temple in Khatmandhu in 1974. The boy, Ossian Maclise, kept telling his parents that he wanted to go up to the temple, so one day they took him up there, and he caught the attention of some visiting lamas from the Karmapa's seat-in-exile in Rumtek Monastery, Sikkim. There was a recognition between the boy and the monks, and he and his mother were invited to visit Rumtek, where a gradual process unfolded, which resulted in the Karmapa formally recognising Ossian as a tulku of an important Karma Kagyu lineage. Ossian was the original Western "Golden Child," the first of several tulkus to be born to white, Western parents.

His mother Hetty, now dead, whom I also met on a couple of occasions, wrote a fascinating account of Ossian's story, which begins before he was conceived with a visit she made to the Hopi nation in the southwestern United States in 1966. A venerable tribal elder took her out to the desert and showed her an ancient petroglyph, which he explained marked a prophecy that a Purifier would come "wearing a red hat, a red cloak, bringing a red God and that he would make rain. They said they would try to trick him to find out if he was the Purifier. They would tell him that they hadn't had any rain. They never have any rain. And he would make rain because he felt sorry for them." In 1974, the year that he recognized Ossian, the Karmapa visited the Hopi in his full red-hatted regalia and it rained for two days. Hetty's story is a remarkable document, but it has never before appeared in print and is currently marooned on a blog site that could disappear at any moment. I was hoping to reproduce it in full as an appendix, but I have been unable to find anyone attached to Hetty's estate from whom to ask permission. I recommend interested readers track her story down.[124]

In Tibetan Buddhism there are various conventions that help to identify a tulku, but one of the most dependable factors is the ability of a highly conscious soul to recognize another. We don't know how Abaris knew that a tulku of Apollo had manifested in Greece, or how he was precisely drawn to him, but we can maybe hazard some guesses. Some scholars are very uncomfortable with the use of such terms as *shamanism* being applied to the likes of Orpheus, Pythagoras, and Epimenides. Some believe that it has too much of an Asian flavour and that it should only be applied to very specific social roles. For example, it is not correct to describe somebody noted by his or

---

124 The complete version of Hetty's intriguing and colourful tale "Namtar of the Wee Lama Boy" was posted on Hetty's blog: www.phantomlyoracula.com. It now seems to have disappeared, but is reproduced in part here: http://tibetanaltar .blogspot.co.uk/2009/10/tibetan-prophecy-hopi-prophecy.html. If any reader wants the full story, they can contact me: guy.ogilvy@gmail.com.

her community for their ability to travel outside the body as a shaman, unless they are also serving their community by providing messages or assistance from "the other side." But in the case of one of
Pythagoras's previous reincarnations, this is precisely the scenario.

Hermotimus of Clazomenae: The Astral Traveller

Hermotimus of Clazomenae was a sixth century BC sage, noted by
Aristotle for being the first to propose the idea of *psyche* being the primal cause of motion. He was famous for claiming to able to travel far
and wide in his sleep and was able to demonstrate the truth of this
by revealing things he could not otherwise have known and bringing
useful messages and news to his friends and neighbours. He would lie
on the ground and leave his body, sometimes for days at a time, just
like the reports of Siberian and Mongolian shamans.[125] The fact (if
such it be) that Hermotimus was able to do this is not in itself indicative of East Asian shamanic techniques filtering into Greece. On the
contrary, "out of body" experiences or *astral travelling*, as it came to
be called by nineteenth century occultists, can happen spontaneously
to people of any culture at any time. It has happened to me. With

---

125 Unfortunately for Hermotimus, his wife allowed a rival group of sorcerer initiates
     called the Cantharids to kill him while his body lay defenceless on the ground.
     He must have achieved very high standing in his community, however, because a
     sanctuary was consecrated in his honour following his death.

experience and practice the ability can be controlled, and adept practitioners can do it at will.

Hermotimus famously identified *psyche* as the fundamental active force, without which matter is inert. Psyche is usually translated as "mind," but it is also the word almost exclusively used for "soul." In fact, since its literal meaning is connected to the word for "breath," it would be best translated as "spirit," which is derived from the Latin for *breath* (as in re*spiration*). The only one of the Pre-Socratic sorcerers to use a different word for soul or spirit was Empedocles, who we shall come to in due course. Establishing to what extent the likes of Hermotimus distinguished between mind, soul, and spirit is highly problematic, and clear philological definitions do not appear in written form for quite some time to come. This is not to say that these three things are simply intellectual ideas just starting to dawn in the consciousness of a few exceptional human beings struggling to give them verbal expression. From the esoteric perspective, these vehicles of consciousness are eternal principles just waiting to be understood. As such, the maker of the Lion Man had the same opportunity to discover them and differentiate between them as Pythagoras did or we do today. The qualification for experiencing them for what they are is not predicated upon a chain of culturally received ideas, specific techniques, or even the "evolution" of consciousness.[126] The only qualification necessary is the quality of attention that an individual human being is able to bring to bear on the reality of its existence.

It is possible that Hermotimus was initiated into some practical techniques for leaving his body at will, but it seems more likely that he was self-taught. By using his brilliant psyche to pay very close attention to itself he had discovered that it, or at least some aspect of it, had certain abilities that he was able to experience and direct, but which still defy scientific explanation. Precisely what part of his psyche / mind / soul

---

126 A species's capacity for consciousness will grow if its brain capacity increases. Consciousness *per se* does not evolve; it simply is.

was able to leave his body remained a subject of much debate amongst Greek thinkers for centuries, influencing Plato's concept of the soul, which in turn influenced all subsequent European thinkers, also impacting Christianity and Islam. The true nature of consciousness remains elusive, of course, to this day. The only way, it seems, to know the reality of the soul/psyche is not through reading verbal explanations, but to experience it for yourself.

So Hermotimus may be an example of spontaneous shamanic activity in a non-shamanic cultural milieu, but let's not get too caught up in pedantic semantics. If Abaris is an Avar, he comes from a shamanic culture, and yet he is possessed by Apollo and performs the same extraordinary actions, such as plague removal, that others identified as priests of Apollo do in lands thousands of miles away. To be a priest of Apollo you clearly don't need to be Greek, and equally it seems that to be a shaman you do not need to be a classically employed member of an anthropologically approved shamanistic society.

Aristeas of Proconnesus: Time Travelling Shape-Shifter

Harpocration claimed that Abaris wrote a book about the arrival of Apollo in Hyperborea. It would be wonderful to know what that book had to say, but I don't believe it is mentioned anywhere else in the surviving literature. After piecing together the clues, however, it is possible to admit that Apollo may have first been introduced to the Avars by a semi-legendary Greek wonder-worker called Aristeas, who lived at some time in the seventh century BC, around fifty to one hunded years before Abaris and Pythagoras. Our two main biographical sources for Aristeas are Herodotus and Pausanias, from whom we can glean the following:

Aristeas was a high-born citizen of Proconnesus between the Aegean and the Black Sea. One day he went into a shop and dropped down dead. The owner locked up the shop and went to find Aristeas's family. News of his death quickly spread around the town, but was soon contradicted by someone claiming to have spoken to him on the road to Cyzicus. The family, meanwhile, had arrived at the shop to find no sign of him. Having vanished without trace, Aristeas reappeared in Proconnesus seven years later claiming that he had been possessed by Apollo [127] and found himself travelling to the borderlands of Hyperborea. He wrote a famous epic poem about his travels called the *Arimaspea* (from which the Greeks seem to have derived most of their ideas about Hyperborea) before he vanished again. Two hundred and forty years later he reappeared in Metapontum and told its citizens to establish an altar to Apollo, saying that the god had chosen that city over all others in Magna Graecia and that he himself had travelled there with the god in the form of a raven. He then repeated his vanishing trick, whereupon the perplexed Metapontines "sent to Delphi and asked the god what the vision of the man could mean; and the Pythian priestess told them to obey the vision, saying that their fortune would be better. They did as instructed. And now there stands beside the image of Apollo a statue bearing the name

---

127 Interestingly, George Rawlinson translated the original Greek Φοιβόλαμπτος γενόμενος, which literally means "taken by Phoebus" (= Apollo), as "wrapt in a Bacchic fury" (1895).

of Aristeas; a grove of bay-trees surrounds it; the image is set in the marketplace." [128]

Metapontum is the city where Pythagoras spent the last years of his life. Was he the Apollo that Aristeas accompanied there in the form of a raven? Telling too is the fact that in retelling the story of Aristeas's first disappearance, Plutarch substitutes Croton for Cyzicus. Croton, just a hundred miles from Metapontum was the place where Pythagoras was first received as Hyperborean Apollo and where he established his school.

Further delving suggests that Aristeas may not have been the first Greek to introduce Apollo to the Hyperboreans. Legend says that mythic superhero Hercules visited Hyperborea and brought back an olive tree, but more historically Pausanias tells us of a legendary ancient poet from Lucia called Olen who the Delphic Pythia Boeo credits with the introduction of the cult of Apollo on Delos, the birthplace of the god. [129] A lost poem of Olen's celebrates Apollo's first priestess, or handmaiden, a woman called Achaeia who came to Delos from Hyperborea to worship Apollo. Another legendary poet, said to have lived between Olen and Aristeas, was Melanopus of Cyme, who Pausanias and Herodotus both say wrote an ode commemorating a Hyperborean maiden called Opis, who arrived in Delos with an offering "vowed for the birth of Apollo."

So when Harpocration mentions that Abaris "renewed the alliance between his countrymen and the inhabitants of the island of Delos," en route to tracking down Pythagoras, he is referring to a tradition that was already centuries old before Abaris. The tradition also implies, as with Abaris, that rather than being introduced to Apollo by the Greeks, it was the Hyperboreans who picked up on the presence of Apollo and reverently sought him out for themselves. Having established the link, the Hyperboreans continued to send votive of-

---

128 Herodotus, *The Histories*, IV. 13–15.

129 Pausanias, *Histories of Greece*, V, 7.

ferings to Apollo. When the first emissaries bearing these gifts failed
to return, they feared the worst and devised a relay system to deliver
the offerings with the cooperation of all the nations lying between
Hyperborea and Delos. Herodotus provides a detailed account of this
tradition, which rings very true and reports that both Homer and Hesiod wrote of the Hyperboreans, although these references have long
been lost to us.

Apollo's name is not to be found in pre-collapse Mycenaean Linear
B script, although the name Paean appears, which was to become one
of his epithets. Hesiod identifies Paean as a clearly distinct deity, however: "Unless Phoebus Apollo should save him from death, or Paean
himself who knows the remedies for all things." And in the *Iliad*, in
which Apollo plays a leading role, Homer mentions Paean on two occasions as a healing god. So if what Herodotus tells us is essentially
true, then it seems likely that the worship of Apollo was introduced
from outside Greece some time after the Mycenean collapse. It seems
extraordinary then that he should have become so firmly established
in the Olympian pantheon in such a comparatively short period of
time and that Homer should have given him such an influential role
in the *Iliad*, which is set at a time in history when there is no sign of
him in the Greek world.

Apollo, as we know, spent the winter months in Hyperborea, during
which time Dionysus presided over Delphi. It is repeatedly described
as his favourite place and the birthplace of his mother, but when the
ancient writers refer specifically to "Hyperborean Apollo" it is only ever
in the context of Pythagoras and Abaris. It is not clear whether the admirers of Pythagoras in Croton identified him as "Apollo arrived from
Hyperborea" [130] before Abaris tracked him down or afterwards. If it was
before, then it would be all the more remarkable. Either way it is an
extraordinary way to describe a Greek who had never travelled north
at all, let alone to Hyperborea. A key distinction between Greek Apollo

---

130 Diogenes 8, 11.

and Hyperborean Apollo seems to be that the Apollo revered by the Hyperboreans is a shaman god, a god of terror and ecstatic possession and, it seems, a god who is able to incarnate in the flesh as a true demi-god, neither god nor human, but a different category of being, as attested by his devotees in Italy.

CHAPTER 5

THE MAN WITH THE
GOLDEN THIGH

The story of the golden thigh is perhaps the strangest single detail amongst all the legends that surround the life of Pythagoras. Various scholars have explored connections with Demeter, Persephone, and shamanic dismemberment. Burkert states that "the myths tell over and over of the favourite of the great mother being wounded in the thigh, as also of the thigh wounds of those who try to make their way into the underworld. Only he who bears the sign can descend into the pit with impunity. In the same way Pythagoras' golden thigh is the sign of the initiation that makes it possible for him to travel to Hades."[131]

---

131 Burkert, 1972, p. 160.

I suspect it also has to do with the magical qualities of gold, that griffin-guarded substance historically so treasured by the avaricious Avars, who are said to have hoarded thirty-five tons of Byzantine gold, worth the equivalent of 1.7 trillion dollars. It would seem that this was not a new habit, since Iamblichus says that when Abaris met Pythagoras he was planning to return to Hyperborea laden with gold that he had collected for Apollo's temple there—presumably payment made by grateful cities for his services as a purifier. The fact that Abaris's gold was intended for the temple suggests that its chief value lay not in its material worth, but in something less tangible: its purity perhaps. For the ancients, the fact that, alone of all the metals, gold does not corrode or discolour, made it a symbol both of purity and immortality. Gold also confers power and authority in other ways, but we will explore the attractions of gold in greater detail when we get to grips with alchemy, an art in which soul, spirit, immortality, and gold all play central roles.

Perhaps Abaris, while in an Apollonian ecstasy, was holding Apollo's golden arrow at the moment that Pythagoras flashed his golden thigh. The arrow quivered, the arrow knew, and, according to some, the arrow flew, carrying Abaris over every obstacle that separated it from that thigh. For of course the arrow was a magic arrow: it was the very arrow with which Apollo had slain the Cyclops. The one-eyed giant is, at the very least, a metaphor for someone who can only see one way, who can only look out, not in. That means everybody who does not have what my father used to call "that Celtic double-ness of eye," the in-sight that can see right through its mirror self to the awesome, transfixing light of Truth on the other side of darkness. That is the mark Apollo's arrow seeks. That is the mark of "far-flying" Hyperborean Apollo. And when Abaris found Pythagoras he found the mark of the god upon him.

Iamblichus says that Pythagoras was so impressed with the Sky-walker's wisdom that he immediately shared his secret knowledge with him; others say that it was Abaris who taught Pythagoras his secrets. It seems reasonable to conclude that the two had much to share.

Indeed, Peter Kingsley [132] believes Abaris's recognition of Pythagoras as a true tulku of Apollo marks an enormously significant moment in Western history: nothing less than the birth of Western civilization that starts with the Apollination of Pythagoras and finds its apogee in the mathematical rocket science that achieved the Apollo landings on the moon. Abaris and Pythagoras were prophets,[133] they knew the significance of their encounter and the alchemy of their meeting must have produced an astonishingly powerful recognition, the effects of which are still rippling through the world.

The Croton School of Wizardry

According to Iamblichus's chronology, Pythagoras had established his school in Croton by the time Abaris arrived. Porphyry gives the following account of Pythagoras's reception there:

When he reached Italy he stopped at Croton. His presence was that of a free man, tall, graceful in speech and gesture, and in all things else. Dicaearchus relates that the arrival of this great traveller, endowed with all the advantages of nature, and prosperously guided by fortune, produced on the Crotonians so great an impression, that he won the esteem of the elder magistrates, by his many and excellent discourses. They ordered him to exhort the young men, and then to the boys who flocked out of the school to hear him; and lastly to the women, who came together on purpose.

Through this he achieved great reputation, he drew great audiences from the city, not only of men, but also of women, among whom was a specially illustrious person named Theano.[134] He also drew audiences from among the neighbouring barbarians, among whom were

---

132 Kingsley, Peter. A *Story Waiting to Pierce You: Mongolia, Tibet and the Destiny of the Western World*, USA: Golden Sufi Centre, 2010.

133 Abaris was said to have pronounced oracles in all the countries he passed through.

134 A widely referred to but obscure philosopher, sometimes said to be the wife of Pythagoras.

magnates and kings. What he told his audiences cannot be said with certainty, for he enjoined silence upon his hearers. But the following is a matter of general information. He taught that the soul was immortal and that after death it transmigrated into other animated bodies. After certain specified periods, the same events occur again; that nothing was entirely new; that all animated beings were kin, and should be considered as belonging to one great family. Pythagoras was the first one to introduce these teachings into Greece.[135]

As Dicaearchus relates, Pythagoras required his teachings to be kept secret, which has presented us with a thorny question as to what he actually taught. One ancient writer tells us that he turned his home into a temple and built an underground chamber, where he would disappear for extended periods, emerging in an emaciated state in full awareness of what had being going on in the outside world. It is not unreasonable to assume that he initiated others into his technique of incubation, but even legend is silent on the matter. Legend does, however, insist that mathematics was central to his teaching, and Aristotle tells us that: "The so-called Pythagoreans, who were the first to take up mathematics, not only advanced this subject, but saturated with it, they fancied that the principles of mathematics were the principles of all things."[136] The widespread consensus amongst scholars today is that "the first Pythagoreans opened up a new way of thinking about, appreciating and using numbers, representing a watershed and having very long lasting impact. Their profound musical/mathematical discovery was as modern as tomorrow's science news, as timeless as any discovery ever made."[137] Some of his later followers were certainly well-known mathematicians, geometers, and cosmologists, and

---

135   Porphyry, *Life of Pythagoras*, 18, 19.

136   Aristotle, *Metaphysics*.

137   Kitty Ferguson: *Pythagoras: His Lives and the Legacy of a Rational Universe,* London: Icon Books, 2011. Previously published in the USA under a racier title: *The Music Of Pythagoras : How an Ancient Brotherhood Cracked the Code of the Universe and Lit the Path From Antiquity to Outer Space.* New York: Walker, 2008.

it seems that number theory was part of the mix in as much as it revealed meaning at play in the cosmos.

The ten-unit pyramid of the *tetractys*, for example, has been said to represent the whole of Pythagorean metaphysics, and it is certainly up to the job. The numbers one to ten allow us to mathematically construct the physical universe and they also construct the mystical universe, the one that leads us through the four elements, the three principles, the divine duad to the monad, the Absolute. Within the tetractys is also hidden the key to musical ratios, and although in describing the mystical tetractys in such a way I am exceeding what can be said for certain of Pythagoras's own understanding, since Pythagoras was, if nothing else, a man of astonishingly charismatic genius, a "man who knows," I imagine any profound meaning I could possibly find in the tetractys will have been revealed to him. For that must be the point about Pythagoras and what he knew: his knowledge was, as far as he and his contemporaries were concerned, primarily "revealed," the result of divine revelation. It is *gnosis* rather than philosophy. It is much more closely related to Orpheus and shamanism than it is to Socrates and Aristotle; he is more interested in direct experience of Truth than airily showing off his neatly dialectical opinions while eying up handsome boys. That's what my dear old Classics masters did at school, and they were sad-sack sophists, not blazingly transfigured sorcerers.

So we should not be surprised if Pythagoras did not write down his philosophy, or that his followers should be equally reticent; nor that we cannot be certain what he taught with regard to specific subjects. His was not a school for the liberal arts, although I have no doubt that his legacy helped inspire the founding of Plato's Academy and the Lyceum. His school was an initiatory sect, a cult. What else could it be? Pythagoras arrives in Croton and amazes everyone he meets, so everyone wants to meet him. The questions everyone wants to ask are "How do you get to be so amazing?" and "Can you teach me how to be as amazing as you?"

So if he is going to tell it the way it is, he's going to say something along the lines of this: "I have lived many lives in search of truth and I have found it. There's really nothing to it, but it requires great dedication and sincerity and requires you to live a life of frugal austerity and give up everything you thought was true. If you want to be like me, you have to act like me." Having said that, it is clear from the range of scientific views expressed by identifiable Pythagoreans between his time and that of Plato a hundred years later, that his teachings were not dogmatic and binding. Pythagoreanism was not a religion, whose adherents stuck piously to a received orthodoxy; it was a way of opening up the intuitive intellect, a way of allowing the individual seeker to learn how to understand the true nature of things for themselves.

What Pythagoras was offering was a way of life that would nurture the soul and give it the best chance of jumping through all the hoops in Hades so that it could complete its journey as directly as possible. He had plenty of takers, it seems, and the school appears to have been a great success. Details on precisely what he taught and how are very scanty. Rather like the sayings of Buddha and the "Hadith" tradition of Islam that collected the sayings of the Prophet, the Pythagoreans had their *akousmata*—maxims or sayings that were handed down as an oral tradition. A lot of these are very enigmatic, rather like Zen koans, but others give an insight into the way of life that was taught, which was very sincere and reverential, with great attention paid to religious observation. Women were honoured and included in all aspects of life, many of them becoming famed, including Pythagoras's daughter Damo, to whom, according to one tradition, he bequeathed all his writings, which she refused to sell. The Pythagorean life seems to have been designed to inculcate a profoundly meditational sense of sacredness. Silence was venerated, animals were respected as fellow beings and a largely vegetarian diet was encouraged. Pythagoras himself was not the focus of reverence, nor was his way, although religious, a religion in itself. His followers venerated the traditional gods as he did himself.

Iamblichus tells us that the Pythagoreans "very much honoured the memory, abundantly exercised, and paid great attention to it. In learning too, they did not dismiss what they were taught, till they had firmly comprehended the first rudiments of it; and they recalled to their memory what they had daily heard, after the following manner: A Pythagorean never rose from his bed till he had first recollected the transactions of the former day; and he accomplished this by endeavouring to remember what he first said, or heard ... for he endeavoured to resume in his memory all the events of the whole day, and in the very same order in which each of them happened to take place. For there is not anything which is of greater importance with respect to science, experience and wisdom, than the ability of remembering. From these studies therefore it happened that all Italy was filled with philosophers, and this place, which before was unknown, was afterwards on account of Pythagoras called Magna Graecia. Hence also it contained many philosophers, poets, and legislators. For the rhetorical arts, demonstrative reasonings, and the laws written by them, were transferred from Italy to Greece. Those likewise who make mention of physics, adduce as the principal physiologists Empedocles and Parmenides." [138]

Iamblichus's mention of Empedocles and Parmenides as Pythagoreans is supported by recent scholarship and is of great interest in the unfolding of a specifically magical tradition, which we shall come to shortly.

The Pythagoreans became leading figures in Croton at a time when the city was expanding its influence, and the influence it exercised with allied neighbouring cities is marked by the Crotonian coinage used by them. Pythagorean influence established itself in all these other cities and some scholars confidently assert that between 510 and 460 BC Pythagoreanism stood at the centre of Magna-Grecian society.

---

138 Iamblichus, *The Life of Pythagoras*, translated by Thomas Taylor, first published in 1818.

It was not to last, as Porphyry, drawing on many sources, relates:

Pythagoras and his associates were long held in such admiration in Italy, that many cities invited them to undertake their administration. At last, however, they incurred envy, and a conspiracy was formed against them as follows. Cylon,[139] a Crotonian, who in race, nobility and wealth was the most preeminent, was of a severe, violent and tyrannical disposition, and did not scruple to use the multitude of his followers to compass his ends. As he esteemed himself worthy of whatever was best, he considered it his right to be admitted to Pythagorean fellowship. He therefore went to Pythagoras extolled himself, and desired his conversation. Pythagoras, however, who was accustomed to read in human bodies' nature and manners the disposition of the man, bade him depart, and go about his business. Cylon, being of a rough and violent disposition, took it as a great affront, and became furious.

He therefore assembled his friends, began to accuse Pythagoras, and conspired against him and his disciples. Pythagoras then went to Delos, to visit the Syrian Pherekydes, formerly his teacher, who was dangerously sick, to nurse him. Pythagoras's friends then gathered together in the house of Milo the wrestler; and were all stoned and burned when Cylon's followers set the house on fire. Only two escaped, Archippus and Lysis, according to the account of Neanthes. Lysis took refuge in Greece, with Epaminondas, whose teacher he had formerly been.[140]

Polybius (264–146 BC) reports that as a result of the murders in Croton "the leading citizens of each city were destroyed," [141] which supports the idea that Pythagoreans occupied leading positions throughout the region. It also suggests that ill-will towards the Pythagoreans extended beyond one spurned wannabe. Apparently there was another opponent, called Ninon, representing the mob, and it may be that he

---

139 Interesting that Luke Skywalker and the cyborg Cylons in *Battlestar Galactica* should be named after characters in P's life.

140 Porphyry, *Life of Pythagoras*, 55–56.

141 Polybius, *Histories*.

stirred up reactionary populist sentiment against the Pythagoreans by satirizing their conventions and promoting suspicions against them.

Reports vary as to where Pythagoras himself was when the massacre took place, and his biography becomes very hazy thereafter. It is generally agreed that he moved to Metapontum, where he may have died soon after. Alternatively, he may have returned to Croton some time later, but is unlikely to have lived long enough to become, as claimed by some, the teacher of another of our Presocratic sorcerers, Empedocles.

In *A History of Western Philosophy* (1945) Nobel Prize–winner Bertrand Russell claimed that the influence of Pythagoras on Plato and others was so great that he should be considered the most influential of all Western philosophers. Russell was considered a polymath genius, but since he was a staunch atheist materialist, who was determined to lead the "revolt against idealism" and the concept of absolute unity, I cannot help but smile to myself here. There have been plenty of scholars who have not shared Russell's view over the centuries, despite the fact that Plato's successors in the Academy—Speusippus, Xenocrates, and Heraclides—all present Pythagoreanism not just as a precursor of late Platonic metaphysics, but as having anticipated its central theses. Aristotle's pupil Theophrastus also claims that Plato inherited from the Pythagoreans his key metaphysical concept of the One and the Dyad (two), in which (to put it at its driest) the One is the active principle that imposes limit on the indefinite or unlimited Dyad, thereby laying the ground for the orderly construction of the cosmos. Through this influence of the One upon the Dyad, numbers are generated, namely the Decad (ten), which in turn generates all other numbers. The most important of these primordial numbers is the *tetraktys*, numbers one to four, the sum total of which is ten, the Decad. The tetraktys generates the four mathematical dimensions, with the number one corresponding to the point, two to the line, three to the plane, and four to the solid. Much more can be conjured from the tetractys than this, but we will allow our later wizards to elaborate when their turn comes.

There are endless examples of Pythagorean ideas to be found in Plato. In this excerpt from *Phaedo* (33) he has Socrates argue that the body is a constant hindrance to the apprehension of truth. Anyone who has tried meditation will find his words familiar:

> *The body is always breaking in upon us, causing turmoil and confusion in our enquiries, and so amazing us that we are prevented from seeing the truth. It has been proved to us by experience that if we would have pure knowledge of anything we must be quit of the body—the soul in herself must behold things in themselves: and then we shall attain the wisdom which we desire, and of which we say that we are lovers; not while we live, but after death; for if while in company with the body, the soul cannot have pure knowledge, one of two things follows—either knowledge is not to be attained at all, or, if at all, after death. For then, and not till then, the soul will be parted from the body and exist in herself alone. In this present life, I reckon that we make the nearest approach to knowledge when we have the least possible intercourse or communion with the body.* [142]

Plato's understanding of the primacy of knowledge gleaned by the unattached soul should mark him out as an initiate, but he does not allude to the possibilities of freeing the soul from the body while alive; on the contrary, he says that "either knowledge is not to be attained at all, or, if at all, after death." [143] Unless Plato is being careful to honour an initiatory vow of secrecy, it would appear that his/Socrates's opinion of the soul's capacity for consciousness is based on an acceptance of Pythagorean ideas rather than experience. Perhaps "the divine Plato" never tasted his own divinity. His famous cave allegory describes a situation where benighted prisoners confined in a cave

---

142 Plato, Phaedo, 217–228. Trans. Jowett.

143 Plato, *Charmides*, 156d–157a. Trans. Jowett.

have only a shadowy understanding of reality, which they imagine, however, to be complete, until, freed from their bonds, they finally discover how deluded they were. The soul sorcerers discover true knowledge not by ascending from darkness up into the light, but by descending into the darkness to find a deeper truth within. Had Plato experienced the illuminating encounter with shining Apollo or the Queen of the Underworld in the utter stillness and darkness of a cave, then I very much doubt he would have invented such an allegory. It seems sacrilege to suggest it, but there seems to be a poignant irony here: Plato's cave allegory exposes his own ignorance.

Another example of Plato's enthusiasm for Pythagorean ideas, this time from *The Charmides Dialogue*, is of particular interest, because it refers indirectly to a Pythagorean view of healing through the mysterious Zalmoxis, who, as Herodotus told us, is closely connected to Pythagoras, being variously said to have been his slave or his pupil.

Such, Charmides, is the nature of the charm, which I learned from one of the physicians of the Thracian king Zalmoxis, when serving with the army. He was one of those who are said to give immortality. This Thracian told me that in these notions of theirs, which I was just now mentioning, the Greek physicians are quite right as far as they go; but Zalmoxis, he added, our king, who is also a god, says further, that "as you ought not to attempt to cure the eyes without the head, or the head without the body, so neither ought you to attempt to cure the body without the soul; and this," he said, "is the reason why the cure of many diseases is unknown to the physicians of Hellas [Greece], because they are ignorant of the whole, which ought to be studied also; for the part can never be well unless the whole is well." For all good and evil, whether in the body or in human nature, originates, as he declared, in the soul, and overflows from thence, as if from the head into the eyes.[144]

144 Plato: *Charmides, From The Dialogues of Plato, in 5 vols* (Jowett ed.), Oxford, 1892.

It wasn't just healing techniques that Pythagoras taught. He was famed for his psychic abilities and his remarkable empathy with animals. We would call him today an "animal whisperer" for his ability to talk to animals and change their behaviour. He is said to have tamed and petted a marauding bear and persuaded it to stop attacking people and killing living creatures, and he once called out to an eagle, which alighted on the sage's arm and let itself be stroked while he talked to it. The very earliest reference to Pythagoras that has come down to us is a fragment written by his contemporary Xenophanes: He reports that "once when he was passing by a puppy being beaten, he pitied it and said 'stop, don't keep hitting him, since it is the soul of a friend, which I recognized, when I heard it yelping.'" [145] Although Xenophanes is always said to be mocking Pythagoras here, this story is a good example of the kinship with all things that Pythagoras taught. Whether Pythagoras meant that a friend of his had actually been reborn as a dog is not certain, but it is understood that the Orphics and Pythagoreans did believe that humans could be reborn as any kind of animal, depending on what was best suited to the development of their soul.

What Pythagoras certainly seems to have been able to pass on to some of his followers are some of his elemental magic techniques. Porphyry relates the following:

> Verified predictions of earthquakes are handed down, also that he immediately chased a pestilence, suppressed violent winds and hail, calmed storms both on rivers and on seas, for the comfort and safe passage of his friends. As their poems attest, the like was often performed by Empedocles, Epimenides and Abaris, who had learned the art of doing these things from him. Empedocles, indeed, was surnamed Alexanemos, as the chaser of winds; Epimenides, Cathartes, the lustrator. Abaris was called Aethrobates, the walker in air; for he was carried in the air on an arrow of the Hyperborean Apollo, over rivers, seas and inaccessible places. It is believed that this was the method employed

---

145 Xenophanes, Fragment 7.

by Pythagoras when on the same day he discoursed with his friends at
Metapontum and Tauromenium.[146]

Although Porphyry suggests that the common explanation for the widely attested story of Pythagoras appearing in Metapontum in southern Italy and Tauromenium in Sicily on the same day was that he used Apollo's arrow, the orthodox esoteric explanation (to risk an oxymoron) would be *bilocation*, an apparently miraculous phenomenon that has been reported on countless occasions in connection with saints and wonder-workers of all religions all over the world. Aristeas, we may remember, is also credited with this ability, and other famous examples in history include the Christian mystics Seraphim of Sarov, Padre Pio, and St. Joseph of Cupertino, all of whom shared Pythagoras's habit of ascetic living and the minimum of food. In Roman Catholicism, bilocation is one of the recognised signs of sainthood that is noted during the process of canonisation. A good example is the case of St. Alphonsus Maria de Liguori.

On September 22, 1774, Alfonso de Liguori was meditating and fasting while locked in his prison cell at the Palace del Goti in Arezzo, Italy. After emerging from a trance, he told his fellow prisoners that he had been at the bedside of the dying Pope Clement XIV in Rome. Rome was a day's journey away and official word of the Pontiff's passing did not arrive until late the next evening.

Accompanying the news was a list of the clerics who attended to the Pope in his last hours. Included in that list was the same Alfonso de Liguori, who was reported to have been praying at his bedside for several hours before the Pope's passing. Dozens of eyewitnesses all agreed that he had been in Rome, praying and speaking to others, while in fact he was in his locked cell in Arezzo more than one hundred miles away. This instance of bilocation was investigated by the Church during the procedure that led to Liguori's canonisation.

---

146 Porphyry: *Life of Pythagoras*, 29.

When I visited the Himalayan state of Sikkim in the early 1990s, I stayed with the son of the Chogyal's bodyguard[147] at the monastery school he ran in Pemayangtse. He showed me old black and white photographs of Buddhist lamas with heavy iron chains slung over their shoulders. He had known some of them in his youth and explained that they wore these in order to stop them from floating away. They too practised a strictly ascetic way of life. Perhaps when Jesus said that prayer and fasting are the way to the Kingdom of Heaven he was also indicating the method of travel.

The Wind-Walkers

My host in Sikkim also told me that some of the sages shown in his old photographs were adept at weather magic, particularly controlling the winds. He mentioned certain adepts who were known as "wind-walkers," practising the art of *lung-gom-pa*, an esoteric meditational technique that required intensive spiritual training while secluded in a hermit's cave for a minimum of three years. The only Westerner known to have observed a wind-walker in action was the redoubtable Alexandra David-Kneel, the first European woman to make it to Lhasa. She describes what she saw in her book *Magic and Mystery in Tibet*:

> I noticed, far away in front of us, a moving black spot which my field-glasses showed to be a man. I felt astonished. Meetings are not frequent in that region [Chang Thang in northern Tibet]...But as I continued to observe him through the glasses, I noticed that the man proceeded at an unusual gait and, especially, with an extraordinary swiftness...The man did not run. He seemed to lift himself from the ground, proceeding by leaps. It looked as if he had been endowed with the elasticity of a ball and rebounded each time his feet touched the ground.[148]

---

147 The Chogyal was the last monarch of Sikkim, which had been an independent kingdom for centuries before being swallowed up by India in 1975.

148 Alexandra David-Neel, *Magic and Mystery In Tibet*.

Lama Anagorika Govinda wrote about the wind-walkers in his wonderful book *The Way of the White Clouds*.[149] He tells us that the mastery of lung-gom-pa allowed them to cover large distances at great speed for up to forty-eight hours at a time while carrying a phurba (small dagger) in their right hand. This is such a close match to the travelling style of Abaris Skywalker that any further dispute about his racial and geographical origins would seem rather churlish. As for the influence that this ambassador from Hyperborea would continue to exert among Pythagoreans, Kingsley states that at the site of the Pythagorean school of Archytas in Tarentum, the one visited by Plato, archaeologists discovered an ancient painted image: the portrait of a man with distinctly Mongol features.

---

149 Once rare and expensive, it is now easy to find, following a long overdue reprint.

CHAPTER 6

SORCERERS IN PHILOSOPHERS' CLOTHING

It would be a mistake simply to conclude that Pythagoras may have been a bit odd, but that after him, Greek philosophy dispensed with all that mystical nonsense and progressed along ever more methodically logical and rational lines, culminating two hundred years later with the splendidly reasonable colossus that was Aristotle, who would remain a towering authority for one and a half thousand years. Such a mistake, however, has been made by most classical scholars ever since. Our next wizard is a man who is variously cherished to this day by classicists and students of philosophy as the Founder of Logic, the Father of Rationalism, or the Father of Metaphysics. The great nineteenth century classicist John Burnet even dubbed him the Father of Materialism. He is supposed to be the first philosopher to specifically understand that the Earth is a sphere and articulate the fact that it has two poles and a central torrid zone bordered by temperate regions. His more stolid admirers would be scandalized that I should have the temerity to smear dear old Parmenides with the foul taint of magic, the whiff of sorcery. And yet to pay close attention to what he actually wrote (the fragments that have survived on ancient papyrus and the quotes recorded by later writers) is to be amazed that his primary concerns were not picked up on, were misunderstood, or were simply ignored, perhaps even suppressed.

Parmenides, the Playing Mantis

Most of what remains of his writing consists of a single poem, generally known as *On Nature* and usually divided into three parts. It begins with a frantic chariot ride as Parmenides is carried away by wild, but "knowing" mares, that carry him, carry him ever on, led by the maiden "Daughters of the Sun," who had left the "Mansions of Night" to set him on the "legendary road of the daimon that carries the man who knows" [150] and bring him to the towering gates that di-

---

150 The quotations of Parmenides are largely based on translations by the following (referenced in the bibliography): Cornford, Freeman, Gallop, Geldard, and Kingsley, 1999.

vide the "highways of Night and Day," to which stern Justice holds the keys. His maidenly escorts charm Lady Justice into opening the gates through which they then charge, driving the chariot straight on down the road.

Parmenides uses repetitive phrasing and driving rhythms to create a compelling, incantatory effect. Then suddenly there's a change of scene and pace. From galloping, galloping down the road we are suddenly stilled in the presence of a nameless goddess, who welcomes him kindly, reassuring him that his arrival is no evil accident of fate, but that he is required "to learn all things: both the unshaken heart of self-evident Truth and the opinions of mortals, for which there is no reliable evidence at all." She tells him of the "roads of inquiry" that he might follow, advising him to follow the path of what is, rather than is not. She then talks at some length in a riddling and confusing, but ultimately logical fashion about the nature of reality. She warns him off the path that does not exist (because a path that is not cannot exist), as well as the path "that mortals fabricate." This is a dismal, delusional path created by ignorance and wrong-thinking "that keeps turning backwards on itself." The path to trust is the one that "never was nor ever will be, because it is now, all together, one, continuous in itself. For where could you seek its beginning? How and whence could it have grown?" And don't say "From what is not," she warns him, because that, being impossible, is not allowable. Nothing can be created and nothing can be destroyed. Everything is now and forever; "And also: there is no dividing it, because it is all alike"; "Everything is continuous with everything," "without beginning or end," "perfectly complete," "just like a perfect sphere." I was stunned when I first read that last bit, "just like a perfect sphere," because I have come across this nowhere else, except in a vision:

In the midst of nothing, I gazed upon a world, which appeared much as Earth does from the moon, but I knew it was not a planet; it was the whole world, the universe itself; and not just the universe; it was the whole of time and space rolled up in a ball. Everything that ever had been, was, or could ever be was contained within this sphere. Which meant that my life as Guy Ogilvy had already been lived, had always been lived, and was eternally living.

Everything has happened. Everything is done, dusted, and immortal. That thorny old problem of free will versus predestination was solved in an instant. You have complete free will and yet, because everything has already happened, your next step is inevitable, because it always was, is, and was going to be that precise next step. How could it be anything else? Which means that your life is completely real and meaningful and illusory and meaningless at the same time, and also completely known and understood in all its inevitable, eternal, infinite context. There is only being without possibility of non-being; clearly no such thing as death in the sense of my consciousness ceasing to exist, because here I was, beyond all possibility of living and dying; my consciousness was consciousness itself, contingent upon nothing other than itself. "You ponder that!" as the goddess says to Parmenides.

I still treasure that vision as amazingly illuminating and liberating. And Parmenides is the only person whose words have reflected it back to me. The founder of logic; the father of rationality, two and a half thousand years ago, wearing a toga, somewhere in ancient Greece. Who was this guy? Now I needed to know, and what I have discovered certainly thickens the plot. But before I tell his fragmentary story, you should read his fragmentary story, or at least some of it. It's out of this world.

> *The mares that carry me as far as spirit can reach*
> *Fetched and escorted me down the legendary road*
> *Of the daimon, that carries the man who knows,*
> *Ever on through all that is. And on the mares*
> *Carried me, knowing just where to go, carrying, carrying,*
> *Straining the chariot; and maidens led the way.*
> *And the axle at the wheels-hubs shrieked like a pipe*
> *Ablaze from the driving of the two whirling wheels*
> *On either side, as the young women led rapidly on: maidens,*

Daughters of the Sun, who had headed for the light from
The Mansions of Night and pushed back the veils from their faces.
There stand the gates on the roads of Night and Day,
Fixed by a lintel and a threshold of stone.
They stretch up into the heavens, replete with mighty doors
Whose switching keys are closely held by ever-reckoning Justice.
And with soft, beguiling words the maidens cunningly persuaded
Her to hastily push back, for them, the bar that bolts the gates.
The bronze posts with their rivets and pins spun backwards
In their sockets as the gates flew open, creating a gaping chasm.
Straight through and onwards the maidens steered
The chariot and horses, heading them down the road.
And the goddess received me kindly, and took
My right hand in hers, and addressed me with these words:
"Young man, accompanied by immortal charioteers,
Who reaches our abode with the mares that carry you, welcome. For it was
No ill fate that sent you travelling this road—so far away
From the more travelled roads of humans—but Right and Justice.
What's needed now is that you should learn all things: both the unshaken
Heart of self-evident Truth and the opinions of mortals
For which there is no reliable evidence at all.
Nevertheless, this too you will learn—
that things must assuredly be as they seem,
Since seeming runs through all that is.
So come, I will do the talking; it is up to you
To take away my words once you have heard them." [151]

Owing to the high standing granted to Parmenides by Plato (the traditional arbiter of all that is interesting and worthwhile), and subsequently Aristotle (the traditional arbiter of all that is reasonable),

---

151 My version of these lines is based on a wide range of translations (referenced in the bibliography), including Diels and Kranz; Kirk, Raven, and Schofield; Taran; Arnold; and Kingsley, 1999.

innumerable scholars and thinkers have had a go at trying to understand his writings, but for thousands of years this opening part of the poem has been wilfully misinterpreted if not entirely ignored, as if it were the prelude to a musical performance, during which it is perfectly reasonable for the audience to chatter away until the real action begins. But this *is* the real action. The words that our hero is encouraged to take away from his encounter with the unnamed goddess are certainly valuable, they are golden truths indeed, but they can only be really understood beyond a purely intellectual "wordy" level by someone "who knows." Often translated as "a man of knowing," I prefer the former, because it is a term used in many parts of the world where travellers beyond the veil are still recognized and valued. In Mexico and South America, I have met people described as men or women who know and discovered them worthy of the title. "Knows" here is *gnosis*, that knowing that only comes from direct encounters with Truth; that higher power that you may imagine to be outside yourself, but which you only find on the inside.

So Parmenides declares himself to be a "man who knows," a man who travels between worlds on "mares that carry me as far as spirit can reach." Horses symbolise the vehicle that carries the knower; be it drugs, drums, or some other transporting technique. Here they are mares, female like all the other beings in the poem, apart from Parmenides himself. They can only carry him "as far as spirit can reach." The word I translate as "spirit" is *thumos*, which could also be translated as passion, yearning, longing, desire, even anger. It expresses the idea of "spiritedness" that is particularly associated with horses. In *Phaedrus,* Plato uses the allegory of a chariot with two horses, one called Eros, the other Thumos. Eros represents hedonism, the love of pleasure, while Thumos is the spirit that yearns for honour, glory, and recognition. I know both those horses only too well and they tend to pull in different directions. The charioteer represents the soul, which must learn how to control and marshal the two horses so that they head down the road of its choosing. Parmenides, however, does not appear to be holding the reins. It is the "knowing" mares that have "fetched" him and are dictating the direction of travel, following the Daughters of the Sun, who then steer the chariot through the great gates. Parmenides is being taken for a ride, far from the beaten track, and "taken" is the classic word to describe someone who is entranced (my American grandmother used to say "took").

But where exactly is it that Parmenides is taken? The standard interpretation is that he is being transported from a state of benighted ignorance to the sunlit realm of reason as personified by the goddess. It seems, to me, however, that Peter Kinsley has got it right in suggesting that it is the other way around. The Daughters of the Sun have "left the Mansions of Night for the light" where they meet Parmenides's chariot and then bring it *back* through the gates that divide "the highways of Night and Day" into the "gaping chasm."

So they have brought him from the light of *apparent* outside reality to the dark side where everything is inside out. Parmenides has gone through the looking glass, where reality has a very different reflection. The unnamed goddess must therefore be one of the goddesses that are found in the darkness, the gaping chasm. Epimenides met Justice and Truth in the dark cave of Zeus and the goddess mentions both of them, which means our mystery goddess can be none other than she-who-cannot-be-named, the Queen of the Underworld herself: Persephone. Parmenides really is on the other side of the veil. His kindly, welcoming hostess is the Queen of the Dead. Fortunately for him she took his right hand in hers, for if she had taken his left, then, according to tradition, he would not have returned to the land of the living.

So the Father of Logic, the original hero of rationalism claims to have received his primary teaching, the one upon which his reputation is founded (the one that caused the great philosopher of science Karl Popper to remark to Einstein that the idea of "block time" reminded him of Parmenides), following a nightmare ride to hell, where the goddess tells him, effectively, that time does not exist, trapping him like a fly caught in a drop of amber. This seems to be extending poetic licence a bit far, particularly since most scholars who are judging the poem on its artistic merits have criticized it for being "clumsy," "naive," and "repetitious." But even if one was tempted to consider the whole journey and encounter with the goddess as a strange poetic device to introduce some weighty theorizing on the nature of existence, there has emerged during my lifetime fresh evidence in the form of archaeological discoveries that establish once and for all the true nature of Parmenides's teaching.

Parmenides was born around 515 BC in Elea (now Velia), a new city founded in southern Italy by former inhabitants of Phocaea just a generation or so before his birth. Phocaea had been a thriving city on the Ionian coast of Anatolia, not far from Samos. Even more so than the Samians, the Phocaeans had established a reputation throughout the Mediterranean as great seafarers (you may recall my earlier mention of Pytheas the Phocaean, the man who sailed as far as the Arctic Ocean) and consequently had a better idea of what was going on far and wide than any other Mediterranean people. They were also a proudly independent and conservative people, so when the Persian invasions of Cyrus the Great threatened their freedom and culture in the mid-sixth century BC, they opted to abandon their homes and establish themselves far from the reach of the Persians from the East and the potential threat of the Carthaginians in the West. They took everything they could carry with them (including their peacocks and their gods), and embarked on an eight-to-ten-year odyssey in search of a new home, before finally settling on the site of Elea, one hundred kilometres south of Naples, around 535 BC, meaning that Parmenides's parents were probably born during the homeless years.

Aristotle mentions that Parmenides was said to be a disciple of a wandering wordsmith called Xenophanes, and this naturally became the prevailing view that holds sway to this day amongst those who profess to know. Xenophanes is believed to have arrived in Elea not long after the colony was founded. This was the same Xenophanes who recalled the story of Pythagoras and the puppy. He was born within a year or two of "the long-haired Samian" in the Ionian city of Colophon, a neighbour of Ephasus looking across the Caystrian Gulf towards Samos. The gulf that separates the birthplaces of these two sages might appear to stand as a metaphor for the differences in their understanding of life. While Pythagoras was famed for his ethics and close attendance to all the finer points of ritual and observance, Xenophanes is remembered principally for his criticisms of Homer and Hesiod and rejection of the Olympian gods, or rather the torrid soap opera that Homer describes; at least that is what a few tiny remaining fragments of his writings suggest:

> Homer and Hesiod have ascribed to the gods all things that are a shame and a disgrace among mortals, stealings and adulteries and deceivings of one another.
>
> But mortals deem that the gods are begotten as they are, and have clothes like theirs, and voice and form.[152]

Further fragments reveal Xenophanes's belief in one supreme god:

> One god, the greatest among gods and men,
> Neither in form like unto mortals nor in thought.
> He sees all over, thinks all over, and hears all over,
> But without toil he swayeth all things by the thought of his mind.

And another fragment suggests he may have shared Parmenides's belief in fundamental motionlessness:

> And he abideth ever in the selfsame place, moving not at all;
> Nor doth it befit him to go about now hither now thither.

Xenophanes spent most of his life travelling far and wide, but he doesn't seem to have been so single-mindedly committed to the pursuit of ultimate reality; he was not, in short, a sorcerer. It is often suggested that Parmenides may have come into contact with Pythagorean ideas.

---

152 All fragments quoted from John Burnet: *Early Greek Philosophy,* 3rd Edition, 1920.

Given that he was born and raised in southern Italy at a time when Pythagoras was still alive and teaching in Croton and his disciples were already, as we have learned, widespread throughout the region and holding important legislative positions in most of the cities in Magna Graecia, it would seem inconceivable that he should not have. Whether or not he was specifically an initiated Pythagorean we shall probably never know; in fact we know very little of his life. His greatest claim to fame is his starring role in the dialogue of Plato, named after him, in which Plato has him as an old man visit a young Socrates in the company of his pupil Zeno. The dialogue is considered perhaps the most intellectually challenging of all Plato's works and has eluded definitive analysis by all comers for 2,300 years. Some consider it to be a rejection of Parmenides's monism, while others insist that Parmenides triumphs over Plato's attempted pluralism. The most cogent and confident summary of it may be that of the Renaissance mage Marsilio Ficino, which is worth including here, as it also provides a very succinct summary of Plato's oeuvre:

> While Plato sprinkled the seeds of all wisdom throughout all his dialogues, yet he collected the precepts of moral philosophy in the books on the Republic, the whole of science in the Timaeus, and he comprehended the whole of theology in the Parmenides. And whereas in the other works he rises far above all other philosophers, in this one he seems to surpass even himself and to bring forth this work miraculously from the adytum of the divine mind and from the innermost sanctum of philosophy. Whosoever undertakes the reading of this sacred book shall first prepare himself in a sober mind and detached spirit, before he makes bold to tackle the mysteries of this heavenly work. For here Plato discusses his own thoughts most subtly: how "the One itself" is the principle of all things, which is above all things and from which all things are, and in what manner it is outside everything

and in everything, and how everything is from it, through it, and
toward it.[153]

What Plato's *Parmenides* does lack, however, is precisely that "heavenly," magical, or divine factor, which Parmenides's poem captures
in his encounter with the divinity at the gateway between Life and
Death, Night and Day. What Plato takes from Parmenides is the fire
of inspiration, that spark of endless creativity perpetuated through in-
tellectualization, which has allowed us to create the world in our own
image by the magical power of rational thought, without the need
ever to return to the source of that inspiration, the interface with
revelation itself that can only occur when we manage to stop thinking completely. Now we live in a technological world of brightly lit
wonder where we are distracted with endless fascinating toys, while
the titans of greed, ignorance, and envy threaten to tear us apart and
consume us whole. For all his extraordinary learning and brilliant discussion of ideas, the one thing that Plato never seems to have been
taught is the one thing that Parmenides's real teacher is said to have
taught him: stillness.

Diogenes Laërtius, who has already proved to be such a helpful
informant in our investigations, shares this crucial snippet with us:

He [Parmenides] associated also, as Sotion recorded, with the Py-
thagorean Ameinias, son of Diochaitas, a poor but noble man, whom
he preferred to follow. When Ameinias died Parmenides, who came of
a distinguished family and was rich, built a shrine to him. It was by
Ameinias rather than Xenophanes that he was converted to the con-
templative life.[154]

---

153 Marcilio Ficino, commentary on Plato's Parmenides, translated by Raymond
     Klibansky in "Plato's Parmenides in the Middle Ages and the Renaissance: A
     Chapter in the History of Platonic Studies," *Mediaeval and Renaissance Studies*, Vol.
     1, London: Warburg Institute, 1943, pp. 281–335.

154 Kirk, Raven, and Schofield, p. 287.

This information, as translated, is interesting enough in itself. It tells us that Parmenides was taught by a Pythagorean whom he revered so much that he built a heroon ("hero-shrine") for him. But if we delve into the original Greek of Diogenes we discover two remarkable things. The first is that the translators, professors Kirk, Raven, and Schofield, all leading Classical scholars, the former being Regius Professor Emeritus of Greek in the University of Cambridge no less, have failed to render the original text correctly into English. What the learned gentlemen translate as "the contemplative life" is *hesuchia*, a most interesting word used by Euripides in *The Bacchae* to describe the state of quiet calm or stillness achieved by initiates into the Bacchic mysteries. Euripides also esteems what he calls "the life of hesuchia," which may have led the learned professors to their choice of words [155]; but while *hesuchia* can further be translated as silence, harmony, peace, conformity, acceptance, or agreement, it does not imply any form of thinking. It implies voluntary inaction: stillness. A more correct translation, I believe, is: "It was by Ameinias, not Xenophanes, that he was led to stillness."

So Parmenides, the father of logic, remarkably chose to follow, not the philosophizing Xenophanes, but a poor man who initiated him into the art of stillness, and for this precious gift he built a hero-shrine to him. The stories about Aristeas, Hermotimus, and Epimenides indicate that the ability to achieve a catatonic, but waking, state of stillness, to die without dying, is the prerequisite for attaining apparently magical powers, but we find no mention of magical powers being associated with Parmenides. Not even Iamblichus or Plutarch have any wild tales to tell, but science, in the form of archaeology, has unearthed some telling clues; for those recent archaeological discoveries in Velia I mentioned earlier are highly suggestive.

---

155 Alternatively, they may just be modifying the misleading version by Hicks (1925), which is still considered standard: "it was Ameinias and not Xenophanes who led him to adopt the peaceful life of a student." Hicks uses seven words to mistranslate one.

Lords of the Lair

In 1958, archaeologists digging in the ruins of old Elea came across a series of marble inscriptions, the first of which read as follows:

> Oulis son of Euxinus citizen of Velia healer Pholarchos in the 379th year [156]

The next two read:

> Oulis son of Ariston healer Phòlarcos in the 280th year
> Oulis son of Hieronymous healer Phòlarcos in the 446th year

Each of the inscriptions share three words: *oulis, healer,* and *phòlarcos.* Oulis meant a devotee of Apollo—Oùlios, an aspect of Apollo who was venerated in western Anatolia, where the Phocaeans originally came from. Oùlioshad: a double-edged meaning that we can see as typical of Apollo, having already encountered him as the wolf that guards the flocks and the plague bringer whose priests cure plagues. Oùlios means both destroyer and healer. According to the meticulous Peter Kingsley, the word *phòlarcos* appears nowhere else other than on these three inscriptions in Velia and a Latinized version of it, also found in Velia in the 1830s. It appears to be derived from two Greek words: *phōleos* and *archos.* The latter means leader, lord, or master (as in *arch*angel), while *phōleos* means den, as in lion's den or lair, a place where fierce predatory beasts can lurk quietly. So *phòlarcos* is a strange title meaning "Lord of the Lair." Kingsley, bless him, in his tireless sifting of ancient texts for helpful clues, found this example of the use of the word *phōleos* in the context of healing. It relates to a cave near Nysa (birthplace of Dionysus!) in Anatolia, just a few miles southeast of Phocaea, at the entrance to which stood:

> the Plutonium, with a costly sacred precinct and a shrine of Pluto [Hades] and Kore [Persephone], and also the Charonium, a cave that lies above the sacred precinct, by nature wonderful; for they say

---

156 All the marble inscription translations are from Kingsley, 1999.

that those who are diseased and give heed to the cures prescribed by
these gods resort thither and live in the village near the cave among
experienced priests, who on their behalf sleep in the cave and through
dreams prescribe the cures. These are also the men who invoke the heal-
ing power of the gods. And they often bring the sick into the cave and
leave them there, to remain in stillness [hesychia], like animals in their
lair [pholeos], without food for many days. And sometimes the sick
give heed to dreams of their own, but still they use those other men,
as priests, to initiate them into the mysteries and counsel them. To all
others the place is forbidden and deadly.[157]

Caves, stillness, fasting, healing, and lairs. These Lords of the Lair
would lie in the dark on behalf of the sick and achieve a state of such
stillness that they were able to divine the correct cure, in the same way
that the Pythia would divine the oracles at Delphi. Alternatively, these
praying mantises[158] could set people up to be taken, as in Parmenides's
poem, on a journey through darkness to a place where absolute reality can be experienced by those who, having forsaken themselves completely, are able to present themselves in utter stillness. The implication
must be obvious to us now. The inscriptions found at Elea-Velia refer to
a line of initiated healer-priests of Apollo, who presided over incubation
techniques in order to induce states of stillness. And just in case the im-
plications were not obvious enough, Fate arranged for a further inscription to be discovered exactly one month after my birthday in 1960:

Ouliades Iatromantis Apollo

The combination of these three little words go a long way in fur-
thering our understanding of exactly what this all might have to do

---

157   Strabo, *Geography*. (Strabo 64 or 63 BC–c. 24 AD) was a Greek geographer, phi-
       losopher, and historian who lived in Anatolia during the transitional period of the
       Roman Republic into the Roman Empire.

158   *Mántis* is an ancient Greek word meaning "prophet," hence the name of the
       insect.

with Parmenides. *Ouliades* [159] means "clansman" or "son" of Oulios, and in case this isn't explicit enough, the name Apollo is right there too. As for *Iatromantis*, it's a combination of two words. *Mantis* means "prophet" or "diviner," as in such words as *cartomancy* or *necromancy*, which mean divination or prophesying by means of fortune cards or the spirits of the dead. *Iatro* means "doctor" or "healer" as in the English word *iatrochemist*, meaning pharmaceutical chemist. *Iatro* was the word translated as "healer" in the previously mentioned inscriptions, and here we have a Greek word meaning "healer-prophet," which Aeschylus, popularly called the father of tragedy, used in reference to both Apollo and his son Asclepius, and which can also be applied to most of the pre-Socratic sorcerers we have encountered— Pythagoras, Epimenides, Hermotimus, Abaris, and, yes, Parmenides; for surely it had to be obvious now that he was one of a long line of healer-prophets in the Phocaean colony of Elea. And yet there remained some die-hard rationalist scholars doggedly insisting that there was still insufficient evidence to taint the Father of Logic with such superstitious nonsense. And then implacable Fate intervened once more to hammer the last nail in the coffin of good old clever clogs Parmenides the Rationalist. In September 1962 a battered old marble block was found, again in Velia, with a two-thousand-year-old inscription that clearly stated:

Parmenides son of Pyres Ouliades Physikos

Thwack, thwack, thwack, the hammer came down, and what the inscription lacked was just as compelling as what it contained: unlike the three "Oulis" inscriptions, it lacks a date, indicating that Parmenides represents Year Zero. He was the first in a line of Apollonian healer prophets that continued for at least 446 years after his death.

---

159 *Ouliades* crops up as a proper name in the figure of one Ouliades the Samian, who achieved prominence as an administrator and healer in the Samian colony Minoa on the island of Amorgos during the fourth century BC. Apollo was the patron of colonists, while Minoa was the name of the pre-Hellenic Cretan civilization and Amorgos is possibly named after the Cretan Dactyl Morgos, whose priest Epimenides may have been.

Nevertheless there was one slight consolation for the rationalists if they were not too bitter to accept it. The word *physikos* is the root of *physician* and *physicist*. It came to mean "natural philosopher," which was the standard term for scientist (and alchemist!) before the Reverend William Whewell coined both physicist and scientist almost in the same breath:

> As we cannot use physician for a cultivator of physics, I have called him a physicist. We need very much a name to describe a cultivator of science in general. I should incline to call him a Scientist. Thus we might say, that as an Artist is a Musician, Painter, or Poet, a Scientist is a Mathematician, Physicist, or Naturalist.[160]

The good reverend has done us a favour here; despite differentiating an artist as "a Musician, Painter, or Poet" from a scientist as "a Mathematician, Physicist, or Naturalist," he has reminded us that Pythagoras, if not Epimenides and Parmenides as well, was all these things, including, probably, a painter[161]; the original "scientartist." And of course he was even more than that: like Parmenides, he was a true philosopher, a son of Apollo, a prophet, and a priest. I would be inclined therefore to give the great man-god the last word here, but of course he left us no words and anyway, there is one more extraordinary character, another great hero of no-nonsense forward thinking, who was also all these things, and whose story also has to be told in the Apollonian light of what we now know.

---

160 William Whewell, "The Philosophy of the Inductive Sciences," London, 1840.

161 Painting was an integral part of Greek education even in the later Archaic period.

Empedocles Alexanemos, the Chaser of Winds

My friends, who dwell in the great city by tawny Acragas,
Which crowns the citadel, busied with goodly works, all hail!
I go about among you an immortal god, no more a mortal,
Rightly honoured by all, crowned with holy diadems and flowery garlands.
In every flourishing city I visit, I am praised by men and women,
And accompanied by thousands, who thirst for deliverance;
Some ask for prophecies, and some beg
for remedies against all kinds of disease.[162]

The colourful vision of Empedocles that history presents to us, mostly painted by his own words, as quoted above, is of a man processing regally through the streets with his entourage, dressed in flowing purple robes bound with a golden girdle, crowned with a Delphic laurel wreath or golden diadem and shod in bronze sandals, declaring himself a transcended master, an immortal god, while dispensing words of salvation for the soul and remedies for the body to the beseeching crowds that flock around him.

He sounds a bit suspect; so, who was this extraordinary character? Empedocles has been variously presented as the founder of rhetoric, a proto-Darwinian, cosmologist, biologist, physicist, poet, miracle-worker,

---

162 The quotations of Empedocles here and following are largely based on translations by Diels and Kranz; Kirk, Raven, and Schofield; Wright; Martin and Primaves; and Inwood. See bibliography.

prophet, healer, magician, charlatan, and statesman. Amongst the early mystic Sufis of Islam, he was considered a great Gnostic teacher, an illuminated Sheikh and the godfather of alchemy. He was born around 490 BC in the Greek city of Acragas in Sicily and descended from an ancient aristocratic family; his father and grandfather are celebrated for winning the wrestling and the horse race respectively at the 71st Olympiad. Empedocles himself is said to have been an Olympic champion, although probably for poetic rather than athletic prowess, and to have caused a scene by substituting the traditional sacrifice of a bull to Zeus, followed by a banquet, with a model of a bull made from frankincense, myrrh, and sacred spices. This reflected his (Pythagorean) vegetarianism and abhorrence of blood sacrifice.

Despite his social status, Empedocles appears to have been a champion of democracy. His father was said to have been instrumental in overthrowing the tyrant Thrasydaeus and Empedocles himself is said to have upbraided two of his fellow citizens for displaying tyrannical tendencies in their mistreatment of foreigners. He is further credited with single-handedly dissolving the aristocratic oligarchy—called "the Thousand," [163] which replaced the tyrant—through the power of his rhetoric.[164] Indeed his eloquence and powers of persuasion were so esteemed that Aristotle dubbed him the father of rhetoric. He certainly had a way with words and he was the last of the so-called pre-Socratic philosophers to have written entirely in verse. Aristotle dubbed him "Homeric," praising his "diction," use of metaphor, and master of all other poetical devices, noting that he wrote, like Homer, in hexameters. Although his works bear no other relation to the legendary Greek writer, one colourful story of Empedocles tells how he saved a hot-headed young man from murdering his host by leaping up and reciting a verse from Homer that had the extraordinary effect of

---

163 An oligarchy numbering so many seems excessive, but Acragas was very prosperous at the time and said to have numbered more than 800,000 inhabitants, of whom the Thousand would have been made up by the most powerful families.

164 He was then offered sovereignty of the city, which he declined.

completely disarming the young man and saving him from the sin of murder, which would have damned his soul to lifetimes of spiritual exile. As we shall discover, a well-directed burst of Homer became an established magical technique that was still being used nearly a thousand years later, as testified by the so-called Paris Magical Papyrus discovered in southern Egypt, probably Thebes, possibly Akhmim.

Like all the great sages of antiquity, Empedocles is believed to have travelled far and wide on the usual "grand tour" of the known world, meeting other sages and priests, observing, learning, and being initiated into mystery traditions in places like Egypt and Crete. He certainly visited Magna Graecia in southern Italy and absorbed Pythagorean influences, if indeed he had not already grown up with them. He is said to have been a pupil of Parmenides in Elea, and been an heir to the so-called Eleatic School of philosophy. A small fragment of his poetry commemorates a man who is usually believed to be Pythagoras or possibly Parmenides:

> There was a man among them [the Pythagoreans] who was transcendent in knowledge, who possessed the most ample stores of intellectual wealth, and in the most eminent degree assisted in the works of the wise. For when he extended all the powers of his intellect, he easily beheld everything, as far as ten or twenty ages of the human race.[165]

Timaeus, in the ninth book of his Histories, says he was a pupil of Pythagoras (or rather his followers), but that he was convicted of stealing his discourses, and therefore, like Plato, excluded from taking part in the discussions of the school. This sounds rather dubious and I think it's more likely that this story was invented much later and probably springs from a concern amongst certain Pythagoreans that Empedocles had revealed too much in his writings. Diogenes Laërtius nevertheless tells the same story, giving Neanthes as his source, saying that:

---

165 As quoted by Iamblichus, *Life of Pythagoras*, Ch. 15.

Till the time of Philolaus and Empedocles, the Pythagoreans used to admit all persons indiscriminately into their school ; but when Empedocles made their doctrines public by means of his poems, then they made a law to admit no Epic poet. And they say that the same thing happened to Plato; for that he too was excluded from the school. But who was the teacher of the Pythagorean school that Empedocles was a pupil of, they do not say; for, as for the letter of Jelanges, in which he is stated to have been a pupil of Hippasus and Brontinus, that is not worthy of belief. But Theophrastus says that he was an imitator and a rival of Parmenides, in his poems, for that he too had delivered his opinions on natural philosophy in epic verse. Hermippus, however, says that he was an imitator, not of Parmenides, but of Xenophanes with whom he lived; and that he imitated his epic style, and that it was at a later period that he fell in with the Pythagoreans. But Alcidamas, in his Natural Philosophy, says, that Zeno and Empedocles were pupils of Parmenides, about the same time; and that they subsequently seceded from him ; and that Zeno adopted a philosophical system peculiar to himself; but that Empedocles became a pupil of Anaxagoras and Pythagoras, and that he imitated the pompous demeanour, and way of life, and gestures of the one, and the system of Natural Philosophy of the other.[166]

Upon his return to Sicily, Empedocles established a reputation as a miracle-working iatromantis in a similar vein to Epimenides and Pythagoras. He was accorded the epithet *Alexanemos*—the Chaser of Winds—as a result of being able to control storms. One specific story recalls how he was able to "catch" a particularly destructive wind in bags made of donkey hides. He also became known as a purifier and on one occasion averted an epidemic by causing two rivers to flow together. As a healer, he induced amazement for being able to keep a certain woman alive for a week or a month, despite the fact that

---

166 Diogenes, *Lives*, Empedocles II.

she was not breathing and had no discernible pulse. These remarkable abilities are attested in Empedocles's own words to his pupil Pausanias in the concluding lines that survive from *On Nature*, where he promises to teach him how to perform these very things:

> *And you shall master every drug that ever*
> *Was made defense against sickness and old age—*
> *For you alone all this I will fulfil—*
> *And you shall calm the power of tireless winds,*
> *That burst on earth and lay waste the cornfields;*
> *And if you wish, you will whip up the winds*
> *And watch them take their vengeance, wild and shrill,*
> *Before you tame them. You shall change*
> *Black rain to drought, at seasons good for men,*
> *And turn the long drought of summer into*
> *Torrents, nourishing the mountain trees,*
> *As down they stream from ether. And you shall*
> *Call back from Hades the life-force of perished men.*[167]

For reasonable admirers of Empedocles down the ages, such promises are something of an embarrassment. He displays such an extraordinary breadth of imagination and even scientifically approved understanding of nature and the cosmos in the preceding lines of the poem; why must he go and ruin it all by making such preposterous claims? At best they put it down to poetic license or the forgivable eccentricities of this splendid and important early philosopher. Usually they just ignore it, but, in truth, weather magic is one of the easiest powers of nature to tap into, if not to master. I have had some extraordinary meteorological interactions myself. The following is no less remarkable for the fact that it involved no (conscious) intent on my part whatsoever. Riddle me this:

---

167 This is basically Leonard's 1907 translation of Empedocles (see bibliography), somewhat modernized and modified by me.

Thunderbolts and Lightning

I was camping with some friends at Worthy Farm near Glastonbury on the first Thursday after the summer solstice in 1994. It had been hot and sunny all day, but gradually became increasingly hazy as we lazed in the grass around mid-afternoon. One of us, me I think, asked: "How hazy does it have to be before we can say that it is actually cloudy?" Someone answered that clouds tend to have discernible definition or movement, if not shapes. Lying back, I gazed up into the deep haze and at first could see no definition at all. Gradually I started to discern a certain stirring directly above me, like a chaotic seething that began to congeal the haze into the vague shape of a face that became increasingly defined. I giggled as the cloud visage started to pull ever more grotesque faces and mentioned the phenomenon to my companions, who strained to see what I was referring to. "Oh-oh, now it's getting angry," I laughed as the face started to turn furiously. I suddenly felt afraid. Behind the roiling cloud shapes there seemed to be a real, awesomely powerful personality and it appeared to be furious, terrifyingly furious. Just as the sky demon brought to my mind the thunder gods Zeus and Thor, I saw an arm being drawn back with murderous intent and knew what was about to happen. Panicking, I leapt to my feet, shouting "Run!" and started sprinting for my tent. No more than a second or two later there was a clap of thunder directly overhead and a simultaneous bolt of lightning that struck the ground maybe one hundred yards away. Fat, heavy drops of rain immediately began to fall, but I had reached my tent before getting wet. My friends appeared a few minutes later in dribs and drabs, soaked to the skin and totally astonished by my performance. Some were convinced I had caused the storm inadvertently; one suspected, despite my protestations, that I had done it deliberately. We all agreed, however, that it was a very rum thing indeed.

I have had various unusual meteorological encounters before and since that day, and even convinced myself on occasions that I have been able to affect the course of winds and the shapes of clouds, but nothing as dramatic as my meeting with the mighty thunder god. Who was he—Thor, Zeus, or simply an unconscious, but highly responsive anthropomorphisation of an unfolding meteorological phenomenon? I leave it to you, gentle reader, to decide. One of Zeus's epithets is Cloud Gatherer, which will do for me. As a result of such experiences, I don't have much difficulty keeping an open mind with regard to the weather magic attributed to Empedocles and other ancient Greek sorcerers. As for calling back the shades of the dead, well, my experiences go some way to supporting those notions too, but there's no need to go there just yet.

Truth be told, there are many strange things way beyond the ken of reductive rationalism, and the likes of all the ancient sages we have met here in these pages seem to have been up to their eyeballs in them. And yet it is not for their amazing abilities to master these anomalies that they are remembered, but for their ability to make seeming rational sense out of the extraordinary situation we humans find ourselves in.

Despite his linguistic gifts, the meaning of some of Empedocles's surviving words remains hotly disputed nearly two and a half thousand years after he wrote them. The inevitable rationalising tendencies of subsequent scholars and philosophers have desiccated his poetry of its magic, requiring students of the esoteric tradition to revivify them as best they can. The likes of Burkert and, above all, Kingsley have breathed new life into the surviving fragments and allowed their words to once again work their ancient magic. Fate too has played its part: in 1992 fifty-two fragments of papyrus scroll purchased in Egypt in 1904, which had languished (like the Lion Man) unrecognised for decades, were discovered to be inscribed with some of Empedocles's writings. The papyrus roll, known today as the Strasbourg Papyrus, appeared to have been part of a wreath, possibly a funerary wreath from a necropolis in ancient Panopolis, present day Akhmim in southern Egypt. It contains about seventy-four lines of

Empedocles's writing, which just happens to overlap perfectly with the fragment long considered the most important of his surviving words, "Fragment 17." "Further adding to this good fortune," the scholar Simon Trépanier notes, "a stichometric mark on the last line of 'ensemble a' indicates that the line was the 300th verse of that particular book. This allows us to estimate that fr. 17, which Simplicius quotes as from the first book of the Peri Phuseos [*On Nature*], must have begun at about line 233 of that same book. Thus, not only is fr. 17 now the longest extant passage of Presocratic philosophical poetry, it is also one of the best attested." [168]

Father of the Four Elements

The identification, transcription, and translation of the Strasbourg Papyrus fragments have not just added a few lines to the surviving Empedocles corpus; they caused such an academic sensation that Empedocles became very much the centre of attention again, just as he would have liked. This attention has, of course, highlighted recent scholarship on the extraordinary old mage, which in turn has drawn more people, scholars and seekers alike, to the exciting and controversial work of Peter Kingsley. Kingsley has combined rigorous scholarly investigation with profound insight and imagination to create by far the most complete and satisfying, if still tantalisingly mysterious, picture of Empedocles. Perhaps the most interesting aspect of his approach is that Kingsley considers himself, first and foremost, a mystic rather than a scholar. For him, Empedocles and Parmenides are living teachers with whom he has a mystical relationship on a plane that is very far removed from the pedantic intellectual confines of academia. This, of course, makes his work even harder for a lot of classical scholars to accept, despite the recognition it has earned from such towering authorities as Walter Burkert. The best his opponents can do is to engage in (usually) unsubstantiated nit-picking. A good exam-

168 Trépanier, 2004.

ple of this concerns Empedocles's theory of the four elements. As acknowledged by Aristotle, Empedocles was the first to suggest that the fundamental building blocks of the universe are the four classical elements of Fire, Water, Earth, and Air,[169] which he refers to as "roots." These elements, as Plato was the first to call them, are central to the understanding of such traditional esoteric disciplines as alchemy, astrology, Hermetic magic, and Kabbalah, as well as Wicca, (neo-)Druidism, neopaganism, and Western interpretations of many aboriginal traditions, such as Native American shamanism. Where would we be without them?

Even if we knew absolutely nothing else about him, this contribution would in itself be enough to ensure Empedocles's immortality in the annals of Western esotericism. But for Empedocles, these four creative principles aren't just material building blocks vivified (as they later came to be) by their corresponding elemental spirits (such as salamanders and sylphs); they are, *a priori*, immortal divinities in their own right. And it is in the attribution of the "roots" to their presiding deities that Empedocles set a neat little riddle to trip up the uninitiated and have them still bickering two and a half thousand years later. Empedocles initially introduces them to us as deities first and foremost:

> *Hear first the four roots of all things:*
> *Dazzling Zeus, life-bearing Hera, Aidoneus,*
> *and Nestis who moistens the springs*
> *of mortals with her tears.*[170]

Aidoneus is an occasional name for Hades, while *Nestis* presents the first riddle, being either an invention of Empedocles or a local Sicilian name for She Who Must Not Be Named, the dread Queen of the Dead, Persephone. The root of the name relates to fasting,

---

169 The classical elements are always capitalised to distinguish them from the mundane substances of the same name—H_2O, soil, etc.

170 Empedocles, Fragment 6, Leonard.

which was one of the techniques used by Pythagoreans for shamanic descents into the underworld and also an activity directly related to Persephone who, like mortals on earth at the end of winter, would fast during the last days of her annual underworld confinement before her release from Hades heralded the advent of spring.

Empedocles's text clearly reveals Persephone/Nestis as the elemental goddess of Water, but in the rest of the surviving fragments he refers to the elemental divinities as Fire, Water, Earth, and "Aither," and does not specifically link them to their respective deities. Such apparent vagueness might seem unhelpful, if not deliberately obscure, but we should bear in mind the fact that Empedocles was accused, possibly erroneously, of revealing too much Pythagorean lore. Anyone familiar with alchemical texts of any period, be they of Greek, Egyptian, Jewish, Christian, or Islamic origin, will not be surprised by such light-handed evasiveness, which renders things opaque while appearing to reveal, but in fact even a little alchemical understanding makes matters quite clear; not that you would know it from the scholarly debates that continue to this day.

For the sake of brevity I will spare you the endless wranglings and try to put them in some sort of nutshell. It will be worth your while to understand the main bones of contention though, because they will reveal the unfolding of a secret tradition that surfaces clearly for the first time with Empedocles and reappears in some very interesting places over the ensuing centuries, to establish itself a thousand years later as abiding alchemical lore: suffice to say that there is one school of thought that insists that Zeus is Fire, Hera Air, and Hades Earth. From the point of view of the relative volatility of the elements, it makes superficial sense that celestial Zeus should be Fire, the lightest of the elements, while the heaviest of the elements, Earth, should be accorded to Hades in his underground fastness. Support for this viewpoint is drawn from the fact that Hera and "air" are both spelt as *aer* in Greek. The fact is, however, that Empedocles always refers to elemental Aither, and where he occasionally uses the word *aer*, he is referring to mist, a mixture of Water and Air.

Another school of thought agrees that lightning-wielding Zeus should be equated with Fire, but insists that when Empedocles refers to "life-bearing Hera" he is clearly associating her with Earth, because the Earth goddess in all cultures is Mother Earth, the womb from which all terrestrial life is delivered.

The only school of thought that makes complete *alchemical* sense, however, recognises that the elemental deities represent two couples. Hera is the wife of Zeus, and despite their numerous infidelities, mostly his, she is *always* the wife of Zeus. Their marriage may be a lot more "open" than Hera would like, but it is essentially monogamous, as is that of Persephone and Hades, the King and Queen of the Underworld. Hades raped Zeus's daughter Persephone and abducted her by force into his inner domain, causing her mother, the harvest goddess Demeter, such distress that the crops failed and famine ensued. Pressed by Hera to intervene on behalf of mankind, Hades was forced into letting her go, but through trickery contrived to ensure that she would have to spend the winter months as his queen.

From an alchemical perspective it doesn't simply make sense, but is imperative, that the attribution of the four elemental roots corresponds to these conjugal pairings, and in alchemy Fire is always paired with Water and Earth with Air, as indicated by their symbols: Fire = N; Water = P; Air =M ; Earth = O. These simple icons represent complex and profound understandings regarding the nature and origin of the cosmos, which Empedocles may have elaborated on in the 1,500-odd lines that are missing from *On Nature*. The union of Fire and Water symbolises the *Chemical Wedding* in alchemy, which in turn is symbolised by the Philosophers' Stone (more often, but incorrectly, spelled Philosopher's Stone, with the apostrophe in the wrong place), the culmination of the Magnum Opus, which equates with the achievement of divine immortality that Empedocles claims to have achieved. So, as the husband of the Water element Nestis/Persephone, Aidoneus/

Hades equates with Fire, leaving the sky god Zeus lord of Air (which is in accordance with the Derveni Papyrus), and his wife Hera, the goddess of Earth.

The objections to the equating of Hades with Fire are superficially obvious. How can the most volatile and, in a sense, primary element, which surely represents the principle of light, possibly correspond to the dark and murky Lord of the Underworld? The explanations can be found on many levels, the most immediate, if unexpected, of which is geographical. Empedocles's homeland was Sicily, an island subject to intense volcanic activity, then as now, with Etna and Stromboli still dangerously active. A single-line fragment of Empedocles directly alludes to this activity:

Many fires burn between the surface of the earth.[171]

Empedocles is in fact inescapably associated with volcanoes, for a pernicious legend sprung up shortly after his lifetime that he had died by throwing himself into the fiery mouth of Etna. His detractors liked to think that he did it to prove his immortality, but died, proving himself a charlatan. Diogenes states that he threw himself into the volcano so that his body would vanish and convince the people that he was indeed the immortal god he claimed to be, but that the volcano spat out one of his indigestible bronze sandals, thus exposing his deceit. Ironically, Empedocles recently achieved earthly immortality when a massive underwater volcano off the coast of Sicily was named after him in 2006, emphatically giving the old trickster the last laugh in a way that would no doubt have delighted him.

It can be argued that volcanic associations indelibly mark the Greek worldview. Around 1600 BC the volcanic island of Santorini, which was settled by the Minoan culture of Crete, was almost sunk by a cataclysmic eruption that generated such powerful tsunamis that the Minoans' 1,500-year maritime domination of the Eastern Medi-

---

171 Empedocles. Fragment 52, Inwood.

terranean collapsed. The Greek settlers that established Acragas, including Empedocles's forbears, came from Minoan Crete and the Minoan colonies of Rhodes, bringing apocalyptic volcanic folklore with them. It is easy to imagine a cosmogony in which the fiery centre of the planet erupts to produce not just life on earth, but the sky, the stars, and even the sun itself. In his poem Empedocles describes how primordial Aither first established the outer bounds of the cosmos, which was then glazed by the eruption of Fire (*"And fire sprang upward with a rending speed"*) to form the dazzling inner surface of the sphere, making it top heavy and causing it to tilt, establishing the celestial pole and making the Fire ball up into the sun, which then proceeded to orbit the interior, establishing a centrifugal force that keeps everything in suspended balance.

The primordial inner Fire generates the outer cosmic fire through its interaction with the other root elements, and for alchemists, the discovery or encounter with the secret inner fire or "black sun" is decisive on the path to the transcendent, transmuting Stone, which itself represents immortal godhood. The inner Fire is the spark of the divine in all "mixtures," i.e. created things, being mixtures of the elements. The idea of the fire in the darkness is not, of course, Empedocles's invention. We remember Parmenides being taken by the Daughters of the Sun to meet the nameless goddess in the realm of night and the encounters of Pythagoras and Epimenides with Apollo shining in the darkness of their own cave-like stillness. The darkness of Hades is where the sun resides when not about its daily rounds, and it is in the darkness that the true philosopher can encounter the true light of reality face to face without being blinded, but rather illuminated.

Empedocles makes no direct mention of Apollo, but ancient authorities refer to him having written a long-since lost *Hymn to Apollo*, while the Alexandrian philosopher Ammonius states that Empedocles's Fragment 134 (to which we can add Fr. 133) from *On Nature* describes the non-anthropomorphic nature of Apollo as God per se:

He is not equipped with a human head on a body;

Two branches do not spring from his back;

He has no feet, no swift knees, no shaggy genitals,

But he is mind alone, holy and inexpressible,

Darting through the whole cosmos with swift thoughts.[172]

The adjectives *swift* and *darting* are epithets of Apollo and the Neo-Platonists insist that the Pythagoreans identified Apollo as the Monad, the indivisible, singular God,[173] while Menander Rhetor tells us that the hymns to Apollo of Empedocles and Parmenides are discussions on "the nature of the sun." So if Apollo is in fact the inner sun of blackest night, why does Empedocles tell us that this secret Fire is in fact Hades? Welcome to magical paradox! The single greatest obstacle to understanding magical and alchemical texts, as already mentioned, is their tendency to present us with riddles and paradoxes. It would be a mistake, however, to assume that this is simply to mislead and put off those unsuited to their understanding. The fact is that we are dealing with domains that are both parallel and opposed to each other, such as the realms of Life and Death, the Outer and the Inner; we must understand that they are the inverse of each other, mirror images that reverse polarities, each turning the other inside out.

When reading esoteric texts written by genuine masters, one must always be ready to recognize that what is really being said may be the opposite of what appears to be said. No wonder Aristotle, initially respectful of Empedocles, would later describe his supposed attempts to combine poetry with philosophy as "laughable" and ac-

---

172 Empedocles, Fragment 134, Stamatellos.

173 Empedocles is credited to this day—even in current Classical dictionaries—with the famous quote that states: "God is a circle whose centre is everywhere and circumference nowhere." No such fragment of his survives, however, and Brian Parshall has tracked back the earliest such reference to the thirteenth century encyclopaedist Vincent de Beauvais. I like to think that Empedocles may have said it though, just as I like to think that primordial humans may have framed such a frameless and timeless idea thousands of years earlier.

cuse him of trickery and pretentiousness. Aristotle did not have or, perhaps, chose not to develop, a capacity for magical insight; he had no intention of catching himself out and sneaking around the back of his own pedantic, rationalising ego. Which, of course, helped him to establish his own enduring reputation as the supreme no-nonsense Captain Clever-Clogs for more than two thousand years, but ensured that he would never achieve true revelation in that still dark place on the other side of reason. For on the other side of reason the many becomes the One and the one becomes the Many, which is too much for mere mortals to understand. Empedocles is, of course, perfectly aware of this as he tells Pausanias of the limitations of mundane experience:

> Narrow hints of knowing are scattered through their limbs,
> But countless mean surprises blunt their careful thoughts.
> They see so little of life in their lifetimes,
> And then they are gone, off like a puff of smoke.
> Each believe only what they happen to experience,
> While bumping haphazardly first this way then that,
> Idly declaring that they get the whole picture.
> Living thus they will never see nor hear,
> Nor understand these teachings.
> But you, since you have turned aside here, you will learn.
> Mortal metis can achieve no more.[174]

Those of us, who like Pausanias have "turned aside here," by moving out of the knockabout torrent of mundane life to pay attention to his words, have a chance of learning what Empedocles has to teach. And the casually glossed equation of Hades and the Maiden with the primordial root elements of Fire and Water should warn us that he plans to lead us, should we choose to follow his words, to an encounter with the awesome Other on the hidden side of being.

---

174 Empedocles, Fragment 2, My translation, largely based on translations by Diels and Kranz; Kirk, Raven, and Schofield; Wright; Martin and Primaves; and Inwood.

In the last line quoted above I have left a word untranslated. The word is *metis*, which means cunning, craftiness, or resourcefulness and is often used by Homer to describe the famous cunning of Odysseus as exemplified in the famous story of the Trojan Horse in the *Iliad* and his tricking of the Cyclops in the *Odyssey*. This line of Empedocles has, inevitably, been endlessly misunderstood by everyone, no matter how clever, whose intelligence is limited to the mortal sphere. What Empedocles is telling us here is that in order to *really* understand the true nature of existence we need a teacher who has been through the looking glass; who has not only realised his immortality, but has achieved godlike powers of understanding. Mere mortal powers of understanding, no matter how resourceful, are inevitably unequal to the task. So Empedocles proceeds to lay out the situation we are all in by spelling it out for us and, of course, he kicks off with a riddle that almost no-one understands:

> *A double tale I'll tell. At one time one thing grew to be just one*
> *from many, at another many grew from one to be apart.*
> *Double the birth of mortal things, and double their demise.*
> *Union of all begets as well as kills the first;*
> *the second nurtures them but shatters as they grow apart.*
> *And never do they cease from change continual,*
> *at one time all uniting into one from Love,*
> *while at another each is torn apart by hate-filled Strife.*[175]

Double, double, toil and trouble! No one, as far as I know, has ever suggested that the famous words spoken by Shakespeare's immortal witches, as they stir their fateful cauldron, might be directly inspired by Empedocles, but his words here sum up the tragic helplessness of individual existence, against which the dastardly mortal *metis* of Macbeth is doomed from the start.

---

175 Fragment 17, lines 233–240 of Strasbourg Papyrus. (Translated by Richard Janko in: Empedocles, "On Nature" I 233-364: A New Reconstruction of "P. Strasb. Gr." Inv. 1665-6, Zeitschrift für Papyrologie und Epigraphik, Bd. 150 (2004), pp. 1–26.)

Empedocles has turned everything inside out. Instead of diversity emerging from a singularity, which in the fifth century BC, as always, would have been the usual order of things, he tells us that *"it grew to be one alone from many"* before growing apart to becoming many from one. Our fate is then described as a double coming into existence and a double dying in a ceaseless round of contraction and expansion governed by the dynamic principles of love on the one hand and strife on the other. Help! Are we just being stirred endlessly backwards and forwards, in and out, like the fell ingredients in a witches' cauldron? And if this dynamic is ceaseless, why are our livings and dyings only double and not infinite? This can only be understood from an Orphic and Pythagorean perspective in which mortal existence signifies a temporary "dying" of immortal reality, while physical death returns us temporarily to immortality before the whole process repeats again ad infinitum. The perpetual motion machine predicated upon love and strife appears to be inescapable, forever joining and separating the material ingredients of the universe. What's worse, as he confirms elsewhere, is that love seems to be responsible for contracting us into mortal existence,[176] while strife liberates us. Everything seems to be inside out. But Empedocles is not simply being perverse, and he is not the first to have his reservations about the goddess of love. In revealing to Parmenides some of the secrets of creation, the Queen of the Underworld, his teacher's teacher, says:

> In the middle of these is the goddess who governs all things.
> For she rules over hateful birth and union of all things,
> Sending the female to unite with male and in opposite fashion,
> Male to female.[177]

"Hateful birth and union!" Empedocles names his principle of love as Aphrodite, the Greek goddess of love, called Venus by the Romans.

---

176 "A soft, immortal stream of blameless Love kept running in, and straightway those things became mortal which had been immortal," Empedocles, fr. 36.

177 Parmenides. Fragment B12, McKirahan.

In Empedocles's scheme she presides over a scenario where everything is reduced from its elemental constituent parts into one cloying, undifferentiated mass. The divine roots of life lose their individual identities and only gradually, through the separating action of strife, do the manifested features and creatures of the world emerge. Empedocles describes a grotesque hit-and-miss evolution of creatures:

> Many creatures with faces and breasts
> looking in different directions were born;
> Some, offspring of oxen with faces of men, while others, again,
> Arose as offspring of men with the heads of oxen, and creatures
> In whom the nature of women and men was mingled, furnished with
> sterile parts.[178]

Here he mixes the mythic idea of man-beasts, such as the Minotaur of his ancestral Crete, with what might be considered a proto-Darwinism. The more harmoniously membered things prevail and a Golden Age ensues where:

> All things were tame and gentle to man, both beasts and birds,
> And friendly feelings were kindled everywhere.[179]

This Golden Age, devoid of Strife, was, of course, ruled over by Love alone:

> Nor had they any Ares for a god nor Cydimus,
> nor King Zeus nor Kronos nor Poseidon,
> but Cypris the Queen ...[180]

---

178 Empedocles. Fragment 61, Burnet.

179 Empedocles. Fragment 130, Burnet.

180 Cypris is another name for Aphrodite, after the island of Cyprus, where she traditionally emerged from the foam of the sea. Cyprus also gives its name to copper, being the main source of the metal that, alloyed with tin, gave birth to the Bronze Age. In alchemy, copper is governed by the planet Venus, the Roman equivalent of Aphrodite.

Her did they propitiate with holy gifts,
With painted figures and perfumes of cunning fragrancy,
With offerings of pure myrrh and sweet-smelling frankincense,
Casting on the ground libations of brown honey.
And the altar did not reek with pure bull's blood,
But this was held in the greatest abomination among men,
To eat the goodly limbs after tearing out the life.[181]

There is no doubting that Empedocles reveres this idyllic period, especially as a zealous Pythagorean vegetarian, who believed that humans could be born as animals. In a passage describing a later period, such as his own, under the increasing rule of Strife he bewails:

And the father lifts up his own son in a changed form and slays him
with a prayer.
  Infatuated fool! And they run up to the sacrificers, begging mercy,
  While he, deaf to their cries, slaughters them in his halls and gets
ready the evil feast.
  In like manner does the son seize his father, and children their mother,
  Tear out their life and eat the kindred flesh.[182]

From Empedocles's point of view, this Golden Age is nevertheless (if we are to read between some of his other lines) tainted by the fact that everything is held under Aphrodite's controlling spell. Indeed, if Aphrodite had her way there would be no individuality at all, since it is only the influence of Strife[183] that allows any differentiation of species. Golden Age humanity, blameless though it is, is transfixed by the illusory glamour cast by Aphrodite, completely unaware of its immortality and truly divine nature, the implication being that there is not much difference between man and beast. Any mortal existence is for Empedocles a curse:

---

181 Empedocles. Fragment 134, Burnet.

182 Empedocles. Fragment 137, Burnet.

183 Strife is personified as Ares (Mars, god of war).

From what honour, from what a height of bliss have I fallen
To go about among mortals here on earth.[184]

His original sin would seem to have been an inevitable blood crime: the eating of flesh.

There is an oracle of Necessity, an ancient ordinance of the gods, eternal and sealed fast by broad oaths, that whenever one of the dae-mons, whose portion is length of days, has sinfully polluted his hands with blood, or followed strife and forsworn himself, he must wander thrice ten thousand seasons from the abodes of the blessed, being born throughout the time in all manners of mortal forms, changing one toilsome path of life for another. For the mighty Air drives him into the Sea, and the Sea spews him forth on the dry Earth; Earth tosses him into the beams of the blazing Sun, and he flings him back to the eddies of Air. One takes him from the other, and all reject him. One of these I now am, an exile and a wanderer from the gods, for that I put my trust in insensate Strife.[185]

Mortal existence, as all the followers of Orpheus and Pythagoras would agree, is a curse. And yet there seems to be a way out of the maze; but in order to glean the answer from his words we have to tend them carefully like seeds, as he tells us in a fragment that only came to light in 1842 with the discovery of a manuscript preserved in the monastery of Mount Athos in Greece:

For if, supported on thy steadfast mind, thou wilt contemplate these things with good intent and faultless care, then shalt thou have all these things in abundance throughout thy life, and thou shalt gain many others from them. For these things grow of themselves into thy heart, where is each man's true nature.[186]

---

184 Empedocles. Fragment 119, Burnet.

185 Empedocles. Fragment 115, Burnet.

186 Empedocles. Fragment 110, Burnet.

He then goes on to warn us that if we allow ourselves to be distracted by "the ten thousand empty treasures that blunt the minds of men" then these living words of wisdom, our chance of freedom, may leave us entirely to seek a better home; for all things, he assures us, "have their share of knowing and intent."

To take you through the whole of Empedocles's poem line for line would be to try your mortal patience. You would need to "turn aside" and give the matter your fullest attention. You would also need to be in the hands of a sure guide, someone with a profound knowledge of the meaning and context of Empedocles's original words, for double is the teaching required to guide us twenty-first century mortals through the maze. We need a teacher to teach us what the teacher means, and that teacher who taught me what his own teacher gleaned from the teachings imparted by the divine teacher of his teacher took the best part of a thousand pages to break down my presumptions and teach me right. I can only hope that my brief distillation will inspire you to turn aside in turn.

Reassured though we may be that we need do nothing more than carefully plant Empedocles's wise words inside that central organ of intelligence within our breast,[187] he makes it clear that we must tend to them attentively in order that they take root and grow in their own time. In order to assist that process, he openly conceals one more teaching, which is nothing less than a magical technique to bring us face to face with the truth. Scholars who value Empedocles most for his contribution to the development of rational thought and the emergence of a reasonable natural philosophy from the murky grip of mythology, even while considering it part of the "first bungling attempts" to understand the true nature of things,[188] like to point out that he differs quite reasonably from Parmenides in describing a

---

187 The word Empedocles uses is *prapides*, an area approximating to the diaphragm, which the ancient Greeks believed to be a centre of cognition. It is the point where spirit becomes breath.

188 Millerd 1–2, 79–81, and similarly Guthrie, 229–230.

universe in a state of constant flux, as opposed to the absolute motionless that Parmenides described and that his pupil Zeno went on
to prove in his famous paradoxes. In Fragment 17 he points out that,
doomed though humans are to be ever caught in the ceaseless flux of
Love and Strife,

> *In that they never cease continuously changing,*
> *In that respect they are forever, motionless in the cycle.*[189]

And here we have another splendid magical paradox, because
it is the very factor that seems to trap us inescapably that offers us
our one means of escape. The universe appears to be at a balancing
point between the forces of contraction and expansion, humanity is
fully formed and while the forces of Strife might be considered to be
in the ascendant, if you were living in the countryside and ignoring
the media you could be forgiven for imagining that everything is just
as it should be. If you could afford to relax and get into the natural
rhythms of the day; if your diet allowed your body to be at ease; if,
in other words you were living a good, healthy, reverent, community-
conscious Pythagorean lifestyle, and were meditating on Empedocles's words and paying attention to everything at the same time, just
as he suggests:

> *Consider with all thy powers in what way each thing is clear. Hold not*
> *thy sight in greater credit as compared with thy hearing, nor value thy*
> *resounding ear above the clear instructions of thy tongue; and do not*
> *withhold thy confidence in any of thy other bodily parts by which there*
> *is an opening for understanding, but consider everything in the way it*
> *is clear.*[190]

What Empedocles is trying to teach us here is an uncommon understanding of common sense. I'm going to take the liberty of spelling out more clearly what I believe he is alluding to here. Trapped

---

189   Empedocles. Fragment 66, Trépanier.

190   Empedocles. Fragment 4, Burnet.

though we appear to be in a universe that is endlessly changing and therefore fundamentally illusory, if you take advantage of the fact that we are essentially motionless within the flux; if you get quiet enough and still enough and give your undivided attention to every single sensation in your body, until it has nothing more to tell you that you need to hear; and if you then allow yourself to become conscious of using all your senses equally at the same time a funny thing can happen: a sixth sense, that all the others in common, emerges that can give access to what we might otherwise call extra-sensory perception, an occult power of awareness; a state in which the true nature of reality becomes apparent in a way that our wake-a-day humdrum experience completely fails to match. This gives access to enormous awareness and insight, which can be of a very practical nature and much valued by your community when you return armed with apparently godlike powers. If everything goes particularly well. I'm still practising.

There are various other hints amongst Empedocles's fragments that can also be useful. In reference to his myriad incarnations he mentions having been a boy, a girl, a bush, bird, and fish in the sea, but he singles out as the choice incarnation in an animal form that of "the tawny lion that has its lair in the mountains." The carnivorous lion might seem a strange preference for the meat-deploring Empedocles, but perhaps Empedocles considers the king of the beasts as the perfect balance of Love and Strife, with its equal capacity for cruelty and affection. To bring a certain leonine quality to one's practice in achieving presence can be most helpful in becoming Lord of one's own lair. Perhaps that is what the Lion Man really represents; primordial, supra-sensory consciousness; complete mastery of the eternal moment. We are truly free, wholly healed when we realise that absolutely nothing is the matter after all.

The ability to achieve zero-state consciousness is the opposite of a dead end, as the fruits of its most famous ancient practitioners bear out only too well. The likes of Pythagoras, Epimenides, Parmenides, and Empedocles were intensely practical people whose achievements brought great advantages to their communities. They advanced our understanding of medicine, engineering, mechanics, mathematics, and the humanities in general, playing a decisive role in shaping Western philosophy. History has contrived to give us the impression that their philosophical achievements were subsumed by the superior intellectual understandings of Plato and Aristotle, but this can now be seen as a very "Athenocentric" view, which belies the fact that their specific teachings and techniques (independent of subsequent Athenian rationalisations [191]), particularly in the fields of holistic healing and what is now fashionably referred to as "consciousness-hacking," continued to be disseminated and developed far and wide for thousands of years.

Before we leave Empedocles, there are a few loose ends that need to be addressed. At some stage, he left his ancestral home of Acragas, probably due to renewed enmity from members of the oligarchy of the Thousand that he was instrumental in deposing—an act for which he continues to be revered as a champion of Italian democracy in the same breath as Garibaldi and Santini. He is said to have resumed his earlier travels, but no more is heard of him for certain, and the time, manner, and place of his death remains a mystery. Accounts of his death range from the grotesque to the mundane to the miraculous. A grotesque one has him hanging himself, while a mundane one has him drowning on account of being weakened by old age. As for the miraculous, Diogenes relates several versions of his death, including one in which he quotes Heraclides as relating that:

[Empedocles] celebrated a sacrifice in the field of Pisianax, and that some of his friends were invited, among whom was Pausanias. And

---

191   The great Persian polymath, al-Razi (known as Rhazes in the West), who made enduring contributions to various fields, particularly medicine, was scathingly critical of Aristotle's corruption of the Presocratic philosophical tradition, and he wasn't the only one.

then, after the banquet, they lay down, some going a little way off, and some lying under the trees close by in the field, and some wherever they happened to choose. But Empedocles himself remained in the place where he had been sitting. But when day broke, and they arose, he alone was not found. And when he was sought for, and the servants were examined and said that they did not know, one of them said, that at midnight he had heard a loud voice calling Empedocles; and that then he himself rose up and saw a great light from heaven, but nothing else. And as they were all amazed at what had taken place, Pausanias descended and sent some people to look for him; but afterwards he was commanded not to busy himself about the matter, as he was informed that what had happened was deserving of thankfulness, and that they behoved to sacrifice to Empedocles as to one who had become a God.[192]

This story is, of course, amazing, but one particular detail catches my attention. After hearing the witness's account of Empedocles's apparent "translation" into heaven, his pupil Pausanias, apparently unconvinced, sends people out to look for him. Later, however, "*he was commanded not to busy himself about the matter, as he was informed that what had happened was deserving of thankfulness.*" Who or what "commanded" him to call off the search and "informed" him that his master had indeed ascended as a god and should therefore be sacrificed to? We can only guess; suffice to say that Pausanias had an experience that, like Doubting Thomas, convinced him of Empedocles's divinity.

Another story related by Diogenes is that Empedocles fell from a chariot and broke his thigh, whereupon he fell ill and died aged seventy-seven. This story rings a bell, recalling Pythagoras's golden thigh and the idea that it marks his successful shamanic descents into the underworld. A broken thigh is a shamanic injury, a mark of initiation for those able to survive it, which in the ancient world would have been very few indeed. The femur is the largest bone in the human body

---

192 Diogenes, *Lives*, Empedocles XI.

and has always been imbued with certain magical properties. The crossed bones in the piratical skull-and-crossbones motif are thigh bones and what piracy offers is death or gold.

The most famous story of Empedocles's death, however, rings more specifically magical bells—bronze ones. This is the story that Empedocles threw himself into the crater of Mount Etna, which subsequently spat out his bronze sandal. The idea of a shaman who specializes in descents into the Underworld throwing himself into the very volcano which local folklore holds to be the entrance to Hades has a certain symbolic ring to it, but it is the bronze sandal that holds the most magical clue. The story appears to be the oldest of all the death legends associated with Empedocles and may even have been circulated by his followers, albeit in a different original form, now lost.

The discovery of the famous Paris Magical Papyrus ("PGM IV" [193]) which I mentioned at the beginning of this chapter with regard to Homeric quotations still being used to spellbind people intent on violence) provided an extraordinary and eclectic wealth of magical ingredients, charms, curses, deities and epithets. Probably dating from the second century AD, it includes a terrific curse aimed at an unfortunate individual named as "NN," or rather an appeal to a certain divinity to assist in a curse. Known as *Document to the Waning Moon*, it addresses itself to a goddess, whose first epithet is "Ruler of Tartarus." Tartarus is the utmost pit of Hades, the lowest reach of the Underworld, and since the operator further refers to the goddess as "Maid" and "Kore" it would appear that the goddess in question is, shush, you-know-who, the wife of Hades. But there are specific references to a key, black dog, and, above all to a bronze sandal, which

---

193   PGM stands for *Papyri Graecae Magicae*, Latin for Greek Magical Papyri. This is a collection of papyri addressing the use of magic from Graeco-Roman Egypt, Volume IV of which consists of the Paris Magical Papyrus. It is to be hoped that more such papyri will be discovered and added to the body of PGM texts. The Strasbourg Papyrus previously mentioned is not part of the PGM collection, as its subject matter is not specifically magical.

make it clear that the goddess in question is actually Hecate,[194] one of only two goddesses referred to by their true name in all of Empedocles's surviving fragments.[195] The first reference in PGM IV is:

For I have hidden this magic symbol
Of yours, your sandal, and possess your key.[196]

The second is decisive:

Then, too, I'll speak the sign to you:
Bronze sandal of her who rules Tartarus,
Her fillet, Key, wand, iron wheel, black dog,
Her thrice-locked door, her burning hearth, her shadow,
Depth, fire, the governess of Tartarus.[197]

The idea of Hecate's secret sign and symbol being a bronze sandal is clearly ancient, and is mentioned by Porphyry: "Hecate...goddess of the brazen sandals." As a metempsychotic Pythagorean, a pupil of Parmenides and a Sicilian, Empedocles's relationship with the underworld is bound to have been profound and complex, but Hecate is something of a surprise. She has always been an enigmatic goddess of mysterious origin and function. Although she appears in the Homeric Hymn to Demeter, she is not a central Olympian deity and her origins, like those of Dionysus, may lie outside the Greek world. Like Dionysus she may have entered via Thrace, where her cult was particularly strong, but one of the many epithets used for her in PGM

---

194 Hecate berates the witches in *Macbeth* for not consulting her before assisting Macbeth's evil plans and commands them to meet her "at the pit of Acheron," the principal river in Tartarus according to Virgil.

195 Fragment 142 refers to "the house of dire Hecate."

196 PGM IV, 2291–2292. Betz.

197 PGM IV, 2334–2338. The full text makes impressive reading and I was prepared to transcribe it from my copy and pay a copyright fee to add it as an appendix in this book, but it's quite expensive and I have since found that if you search for it on the internet it is easy enough to find reproduced, with permission, on various websites.

IV is "Persian" and her most important and enduring sanctuary was in Anatolia. In terms of attributes, she is a shape-shifter most closely associated with the Moon, magic, margins, and secret entrances. The *Document to the Waning Moon* reveals her in a bewildering array of guises, many of which stray intriguingly onto the territory of two other gods we have become familiar with. Like Apollo she is a "swift," "far-famed," "wolf-formed," "shooter of arrows," while, as Kore the Maid, she is an underworld ruler, dread goddess of the dead. Tartarus is the terrifying realm where the souls of the dead are judged and punished, an abyssal dungeon of torment and eternal hellfire. It is Hell as we in the West have grown up to imagine it. It gives its name to an extraordinarily complex substance collected from the inside of old wine barrels. Alchemists still use it as a *Grenzsubstanz*, a borderline substance that connects the plant and mineral kingdoms. It contains the Secret of the Salt and can be turned into hundreds of different things. It is the Salt of the Earth that melts into a volatile dark tar wherein the cunning may find the Secret Fire, the element of Aidoneus, King of the Underworld whose name is almost an anagram of that other chthonic god, the god of wine, Dionysus.[198] Riddle me that![199]

These clues to the significance of Empedocles's bronze sandal should not lead us to suspect that he was a practitioner of the kind of low black magic referenced in the *Document to the Waning Moon*. His dazzling pupil and successor Gorgias the Sophist is famously said to

---

198 Helena Blavatsky in her monumental *Isis Unveiled (Subtitled "A Master-Key to the Mysteries of Ancient and Modern Science and Theology,"* 1877) quotes the *Codex Nazaraeus* of the splendidly heretical Mandaeans (1, 47): "Thou shalt not worship the sun, who is named Adonai, whose name is also Kadush and El-El" and also [it declares elsewhere] Lord Bacchus." Adonai is a Hebrew appellation of Yahweh, which also sounds uncomfortably like Aidoneus.

199 It is rich in tartrate compounds such as cream of tartar, a bright white salt used as a leaven for baking.

have seen Empedocles performing magic with his own eyes,[200] but just what kind of magic is left unsaid. The word used in this reference is a verbal form of *goēteía*, meaning sorcery or wizardry, which in its Latinized form, *goëtia*, came to refer to a specific type of magic involving the conjuration of demons, as exemplified by the famous seventeenth-century grimoire *The Lesser Key of Solomon*. The bronze sandal clearly associates Empedocles with Hecate, the only goddess he mentions by her true name apart from Hera,[201] but as for the exact nature of his relationship with her, that is likely to forever remain a mystery. As we will discover, Empedocles was to leave an enduring legacy in esoteric tradition, but one that was associated specifically with alchemy.

---

200 Diogenes attributes this intriguing detail to Satyrus, a so-called Peripatetic philosopher of the third century BC, who wrote many biographies of famous people, all of which were thought lost until a few fragments of a life of Euripedes were discovered on a papyrus scroll in Egypt around 1912. Diogenes, *Life of Empedocles, IV.*

201 He refers to Aphrodite as *Cypris.*

SECTION 3

THE WESTERN
ALCHEMICAL
TRADITION

CHAPTER 7

GRAECO-EGYPTIAN AND
ISLAMIC ALCHEMY

It is not surprising that even well-educated people tend be a little vague about what exactly alchemy is. It has always been a mysterious, even obscure art. Its origins are shrouded in mystery and steeped in myths and legends. Even the derivation of the word *alchemy* itself is uncertain, but worth considering. There are three main possibilities, each of which sheds light on the purpose and origins of the art. The first is from *Khem*, the ancient name of Egypt, with the Arabic prefix "al." The second derives from the Greek word *chemeia*, meaning the art of casting metal, while the third is derived from *chumeia*, another Greek word, meaning the art of extracting juice or medicinal properties from plants. The first explanation has been the most widely held, but there is disagreement as to what *Khem* really means. It is usually thought to mean "black"; Egypt therefore being "the Black Land"— an allusion to the black alluvial silt that for millennia was borne down the Nile and annually flooded the flat lands of Upper Egypt before the building of the Aswan dam. Some scholars maintain that *Khem* is actually derived from a root meaning "wise." Alchemy would therefore be the "Art from the Land of the Wise" or "the Wise Art."

Whatever its origins, alchemy is a word that is familiar to most of us, and yet it remains one of the most mysterious and least understood of all the esoteric wisdom traditions. Most people associate it with a medieval obsession for turning base metal into gold, or with a vague notion of magical transformation. We will find that these views are not baseless, but they are incomplete.

Definitions

Until recently, science historians have tended to consider alchemy as a forerunner of modern chemistry and alchemists the deluded practitioners of an illusory pseudo-science, who nevertheless managed to establish some useful scientific facts in the course of their misguided experiments. But what of all the prelates, princes, saints, popes, queens, and even emperors that have practised this art? To say nothing of such eminent scientists as Isaac Newton, Robert Boyle, and Jan Baptista van Helmont.

In the late nineteenth century it became fashionable amongst esotericists to consider alchemy a mystical symbolic system for self-realization. The elaborate symbolic language and reference to laboratory operations were considered to be a blind, disguising the true purpose of the art. C. G. Jung developed this theory in enormous detail in the twentieth century from the point of view of psychology. As we have already seen from the writings of Zosimus, however, the earliest known alchemists combined material operations with the highest spiritual aspirations.

The Philosophers' Stone

The great bone of contention about the plausibility of alchemy is a mysterious substance called the Philosophers' Stone. Methods for confecting this "stone which is not a stone" provide the avowed basis of the great majority of alchemical texts. This "stone of the wise" is claimed to transmute "base metal" into the purest gold. Dream on, say rational sceptics, and who can blame them? Low energy transmutation defies scientific belief (although the discoveries of Louis Kervran suggest otherwise, as we shall discuss later). It is much easier to accept the idea that the true object of such a transmutation is the alchemist himself; that the Philosophers' Stone actually represents perfect spiritual enlightenment. The attainment of enlightenment is equated with sainthood, the highest calling of all religions. The transcendent lives of some of the saints testify to the attainability of such a goal. Miracles appear to occur in the presence of saints. Could such miracles include transmutation?

Harry Potter fans with good memories will recall that the Philosophers' Stone confected by the alchemist Nicolas Flamel became a matter of perilous importance because it could not only transmute base metals into gold, but also confer immortality on humans. The Elixir of Eternal Life plays a significant role in historical alchemical lore, but in a material sense, it is gold that is both the beginning and end of alchemy; indeed, it could be argued that human civilisation itself begins with the pursuit of gold. There are only three metals that are to be found lying on the earth in their elemental form: native copper, native gold, and meteoric iron. The latter is not native, which is to say not of this earth, because it has fallen as meteoric fragments from the heavens. It is not easy to spot, because it tends to be a dark rust brown. It has a metallic ring to it, however, and is impressively weighty and indestructible, which gave it considerable totemic value to primordial humans, despite the fact that it was completely unworkable. Native copper is almost never found on the earth's surface, but native gold, though of course rare, can be found in nuggets alongside rivers and streams. Being the only metal that never oxidises, gold always glints like the sun, catching the eye and dazzling the imagination. Satisfyingly weighty and yet wonderfully malleable, gold has been prized by humans for as long as we have invested value in things purely for their beauty, which is to say an extremely long time. The Aurignacians who made the Lion Man over 40,000 years ago appear to have worn jewellery and decorated their clothing. It may even be that one of the things that defines our humanity is a capacity to perceive and value beauty.

Entering the Goddess

So we followed the lovely shiny metal upstream. Shepherds noted that when they set fleeces in gold-bearing streams to slip the wool they became heavy with tiny flecks of gold—hence the golden fleece that Jason and the Argonauts sought. We learned to sift the gold from sand and eventually prized open the fissures whence the lode-bearing springs issued forth. This would not have been done lightly. What strikes me most about primordial cultures is the sense of awe, wonder, and respect they have for all aspects of nature. Water springs were always honoured as sacred, producing as they do the single most vital substance needed for life, apart from invisible air. The earth is, of course, the life-bearing body of the Great Mother, so to feel our way into her secret cracks and fissures in order to pry free her magical gold would inevitably assume enormous significance and place an unenviable responsibility upon those who dared to do it. All the appropriate deities and spirits would have to be propitiated with prayers and offerings and, probably, some form of sacrifice. The ones who assumed the authority to take responsibility for these operations would become the holders of powerful arcane knowledge as the earth yielded up her most intimate secrets to these daring individuals who were to become smith-shamans.

Following the seams of gold into the earth, we encountered native copper and other metals that glinted in the rock and could be freed by fire. Quicksilver mercury was astonishing not only for its fluidity, but also for the fact that it could absorb all the other metals into itself. But it was the hardness of smelted copper that created a huge breakthrough. This was the first substance that was hard enough and pliable enough to replace stone for tools that required sharpness as well as heft; and not just tools, such as ploughshares, axes, and sickles, but also weapons. From copper we forged the first swords, and in no time we learned to alloy the copper with tin to make bronze, which was harder and could keep a sharper edge for longer. Once we had entered the Bronze Age, the pace of technological progress picked up rapidly, creating, arguably, more problems than it solved. By the time we had mastered the art of fire to the point where we could smelt iron—the one metal that mercury could not absorb—the cat was truly out of the bag and things would never be the same again.

Despite the usefulness of the other metals, they could not challenge the hold that gold held over us. The smith-shamans, discovering that copper and silver naturally alloyed themselves with gold, deduced that they were really just unperfected gold and that all metals were gradually ripening in the earth's belly towards attaining the perfection of gold. The birth of alchemy begins with the idea that the smith-shaman is acting as a magical midwife who has aborted the unripe child from the earth's womb and is incubating it and manipulating it within the artificial womb of her furnace in order to bring the sacred foetus to its full maturity in the smallest fraction of the time it would take nature to achieve. As you can imagine, such sensitive, not to say sacrilegious, acts would require the utmost contrition, humility, and purity of intent in order to avoid damnation for such hubris. Moreover, the subtlety and sensitivity required to approach Nature in this way, and the intimacy between subject and object that opened up led the sincerest practitioners to identify with their patient/victim with all the sympathy, indeed empathy, of a true lover or parent, which is why the process was as transformative for the actor as that which was being acted upon. Indeed, if all proceeds to the heart of the matter, a point is reached where the roles reverse and the object acts upon the subject and in that moment both are transfigured. Such moments are, of course, infinitely rarer and more precious than gold itself. In the brief history of alchemy that follows, we will meet some of those who are said to have achieved the extraordinary trick of *chrysopoeia*, the art of making gold. Along the way we will come across some remarkable testimonies and a few unfortunates who fell victim to the traps and pitfalls of this most tricky of the occult arts, starting where we left off, with the link between alchemy and Empedocles.

The Assembly of the Philosophers

I first encountered ideas directly associated with Empedocles when I read an extremely influential alchemical text of the twelfth century called the *Turba Philosophorum* (The Assembly of the Philosophers[202]), in which a gathering of nine Greek philosophers (all Presocratic and including Empedocles) met to discuss alchemical philosophy, presided over by Pythagoras. The Turba is a partial Latin version of an original Arabic text called *Mushaf al-jama'a* (Tome of the Gathering), the authorship of which was finally established as recently as the 1950s as belonging to an alchemical author called Uthman Ibn Suwaid, who lived in Akhmim, Egypt around 900 AD. Akhmim is where the most recently discovered fragment of Empedocles was found and it appears to have had a very long association both with alchemy and Presocratic philosophy, as the extraordinary depth of familiarity and understanding of early Greek philosophy, in all its exoteric and esoteric aspects, in the *Mushaf al-jama'a* reveals, despite the fact that it is at the same time very much rooted in Islam.

In the Turba, Empedocles likens the arrangement of the elements in the cosmos to an egg, with Fire, as the Sun, in the centre, and the "point of the Sun" as the chick. This example echoes both Pythago-

---

202 Although the Presocratic philosophers are not considered alchemists as such, the word *philosopher* is what alchemists called themselves—hence "the Philosophers' Stone."

rean and Orphic ideas, and the positing of the element of Fire as central tallies with our earlier understanding of "Aidoneus" being the Fire god. Various works surfaced in Islam attributed to Empedocles, now known under the umbrella of "Pseudo-Empedocles." These exercised a wide influence in Sufi circles and even left their mark on the great Andalusian saint Ibn Arabi (1165–1240), the *Shaikh Al-Akhbar* ("greatest master").[203] A text attributed to the enormously influential Muslim alchemist Jābir ibn Ḥayyān (c. 721–c. 815) refers to the alchemical practices of the *ta'ifat anbadaqlis*, the "followers of Empedocles."

The great Islamic martyr and mystic al-Suhrawardi, founder of the Ishraqi line of Sufism and often referred to as *Shaikh al- 'Ishraq* "Master of Illumination," wrote in the twelfth century of a primordial wisdom tradition, an "pre-eternal leaven" (*al-hamirah al-azaliyyah*) which had divided into a western and an eastern branch at an unspecified time in the distant past. The western branch came to be exemplified by such rare masters as Pythagoras and Empedocles. He describes how it survived the rationalising predations of Aristotelianism and was preserved in Egypt, whence it was reunited with the eastern branch in Persia. He specifies the line of transmission: "The Pythagorean leaven fell to the brother from Akhmim and passed from him to the traveller from Tustar and his companions." [204] The brother from Akhmim was Dhul Nun al-Misri, venerated to this day as one of the first great Sufi saints of Islam and sometimes called "the head of the Sufis." His pupil, "the traveller from Tustar" was Sahl al-Tustari, via whom the esoteric Pythagorean tradition entered into various subsequent Sufi lineages and spread throughout Islam.

Akhmim was where the Strasbourg Papyrus with its important fragments of Empedocles was found and it was there that Dhul Nun lived just a generation or so before the author of the *Turba*, Ibn Suwaid, who

203 Cf. the recent biography of Ibn Arabi, *Quest for the Red Sulphur* by Claude Addas, edited and translated by Peter Kingsley.

204 Al-Suhrawardi, *Kitab al-Masari' wal-mutarahat (ed. H. Corbin, Opera Metaphsica et Mystica, Vol I, Istanbul, 1945, p. 502f.).*

he may even have taught. Another of Ibn Suwaid's alchemical texts was the first of many subsequent Sufi books to be called *Book of the Red Sulphur* (Kitab al-kibrit al-ahmar).

Zosimos of Panopolis

Evidence of a much earlier and presumably continuous line of alchemy related to Pythagorean currents in Akhmim is provided by the famous Zosimus of Panopolis (the earlier Greek name of Akhmim) who flourished there around 300 AD, some five hundred years before Dhul Nun.

Zosimus was the author of the earliest known specifically alchemical texts, in which he describes the art as "the composition of waters, movement, growth, embodying and disembodying, drawing the spirits from bodies and bonding the spirits within bodies."[205] He writes specifically about metallic transmutations of copper and lead into silver and gold, while at the same time always emphasizing that the art mirrors an internal process of purification and liberation:

> *The symbol of chemistry is drawn from the creation by its adepts, who cleanse and save the divine soul bound in the elements, and who free the divine spirit from its mixture with the flesh.*

205 This and the following quotations of Zosimos are from *The Visions of Zosimus*, translated by F. Sherwood Taylor: Ambix 1,1, May 1937.

This Pythagorean aspect of his work shows that the spiritual factor was always central in the most sincere alchemical traditions and exonerates the Sufis from any accusation of adapting alchemy to purely spiritual concerns where it had once been purely material. There is no basis for either misunderstanding. Zosimus was a Gnostic mystic, with clear Hermetic and Judaic influences, as well as an alchemist, and completely free from the "corrupting influence" of Aristotelian rationalism. The relationship of Pythagorean and Empedoclean ideas to Gnosticism and Hermeticism will be explored in another book. For now, suffice to say that Zosimus refers frequently to the *krater* (mixing bowl), which recalls a Sicilian Orphic/Pythagorean poem of that name, from around the time of Empedocles, that inspired a mythic topography of huge underground rivers and fires in Plato's *Phaedo*, in which Socrates discusses death and the immortality of the soul. More specifically, Zosimus, in one of his surviving works, speaks of the sun in a way that is particularly reminiscent of Empedocles:

> As the sun is, so to speak, a flower of the fire and (simultaneously) the heavenly sun, the right eye of the world, so copper when it blooms—that is when it takes the colour of gold, through purification—becomes a terrestrial sun, which is king of the earth, as the sun is king of heaven.

Zosimus's surviving work is, alas, very fragmentary. There are fifteen known manuscripts scattered around various libraries, but recent studies suggest that there remains a rich vein of Arabic tradition to be explored, further supporting the understanding of how much European alchemy owes to both Greek and Arab sources.

How Empedocles's teachings reached so far down the Nile is not difficult to understand. There had long been a close connection between Sicily and Egypt dating back to the earliest times of Greek colonisation in the eighth century BC; at the famous sanctuary of the Gaggara at Selinus, on the southwestern coast of Sicily, various Egyptian magical objects were found, including some that suggest links with Orphic cults. When Alexander the Great conquered Egypt in the fourth century BC, he founded the city that still bears his name, Alexandria, where many Sicilian Greeks were to move, particularly during the third century BC when the island was seized by the Romans. Many moved directly to cities farther up the Nile, such as Panopolis and Thebes, where there were long-established Greek communities, and there, as in Alexandria, the religious and magical currents of the Greeks and Egyptians blended to create a richly syncretic stew, as exemplified by the Greek Magical Papyri. The writings of the third century BC Greek magus Bolos of Mendes in the Nile delta show the overlapping of Pythagorean, magical, and alchemical ideas, which were to become ever more potent with the commingling of early Christian, Jewish, Hermetic, and Gnostic currents, all of which were to influence each other profoundly. Hermeticism was to emerge as the most influential carrier of magical and alchemical ideas, helmed by a daimon referred to in the Document to the Waning Moon as "Hermes, the Elder, chief of all magicians." The "elder Hermes" is a syncretic fusion of the Olympian Greek god Hermes, the one who gave Apollo the lyre he had invented and protected Dionysus from Hera. He will be a central character in the next volume of the Great Wizards, but for now we will follow the development of alchemy in Islam.

Jābir ibn Ḥayyān and the Rise of Islamic Alchemy

The Quran encourages the faithful to seek knowledge and within decades of the Prophet's death the most important works on philos-

ophy, mathematics, medicine, astronomy, indeed all areas of learning, were being identified and translated, primarily from Greek into
Arabic. Islam soon showed itself to be devoted to culture and learning, with enlightened rulers such as the Caliph of Baghdad Harun al-
Rashid (764–809) patronising scholars and establishing academies all
over what had become a great empire stretching from the Pyrenees to
the Indus.

Morienus was a Byzantine Greek monk, a disciple of the Alexandrian alchemist Stephanos. Legend has it that he, in turn, was the
teacher of a certain King Calid, who was, in fact, an Ummayad prince
called Khālid bin Yazīd (died 704), who forfeited his chance of becoming Caliph in order to study alchemy.

Interest in alchemy was right at the forefront of Islam's cultural revolution. Indeed, the very first books to be translated into Arabic were
Greek and Coptic works on alchemy from Egypt, especially Alexandria.
These were translated by Greek scholars in Damascus for Prince Khālid
bin Yazīd around 690. Khalid was in line to become caliph, the most
powerful man in Islam, but he chose instead to devote his life to learning, including the study of alchemy. Legend has it that, despite surrounding himself with self-professed alchemists, he made little progress
in the Art until hearing of a true adept called Morienus, who was then
in Jerusalem. Morienus was a Byzantine Greek monk, who had learned
the Art from the Alexandrian alchemist Stephanos. When Morienus
performed a successful transmutation for him Khālid promptly had all
his court alchemists executed as charlatans. Several alchemical texts attributed to Khalid have survived, including *The Paradise of Wisdom*.

Probably Islam's greatest alchemist was the Sufi Abū Mūsā Jābir
ibn Ḥayyān (c.721–c.815). Jābir was famed for his medicinal elixirs
produced as court alchemist to Harun al-Rashid. The famous caliph's
court in Baghdad represented the epitome of Arabian culture and romance. This is the Baghdad of the Arabian Nights—Aladdin, genies,
magic, mystery, and intrigue. Ancient folklore and old magic combined with Hermeticism and Islamic mysticism to produce a potent

new alchemy. Jābir derived further inspiration from China. Amongst the precious goods carried along the Silk Route were some of the treasures of Chinese alchemy, including the magic square of the Ming Tang, the Temple of Light, known as the Lo Shu.[206]

The Magic Square

The magic square consists of the numbers one to nine, with the number five in the centre, arranged in such a way that each row, column, and diagonal adds up to a magic constant of fifteen. The gnomon (which you may recall Pythagoras's teacher Anaximander was the first to use in Europe) consists of the L-shape formed by the upper row and right-hand column of numbers. The word gnomon has the same Greek root as gnosis and means "the knower" or "that which knows." From the numbers in the gnomon the other four numbers and their positions in the magic square can easily be calculated. Jābir invested the four numbers "known" by the gnomon with great significance, equating them with the qualities of the Empedoclean Elements (1 Fire hot; 3 Earth cold; 5 Water wet; 8 Air dry). These four elemental numbers are seen as the foundation stone of Creation. These, together with the number seventeen, being the sum of these numbers in the magic square, and twenty-eight, being the sum of the numbers in the gnomon, are the six key magic numbers for manipulating the Elements employed by Jābir in his Theory of Balance, one of Jābir's most important contributions to the Art. Jābir also adopted the Chinese concept of Mercury being the soul of metals and introduced the Sulphur-Mercury theory which we will explore later. Suffice to say for now that they represent principles rather than the elements of the same name. One reason for using them as ciphers is that the two elements combine to produce mercury sulphide or cinnabar, which is

---

206 The Lo Shu is still used in the elegant divinatory system know as the *I Ching*, which is still very much in use today.

used as the pigment vermillion, a bright red colour traditionally associated in China with immortality and the Philosophers' Stone.

Jābir's work became the foundation stone for Western alchemy some four centuries later. Known in the West as Geber, Jābir wrote many works on alchemy, although most of those attributed to him were written by disciples and admirers as much as seven hundred years after his death. It is in one of Jābir's own works that we find the first reference to the Emerald Tablet. His name entered the vernacular in the form of "gibberish"—an indication of just how complex and riddling his writing can appear. After his death, his laboratory was found to contain a solid gold mortar weighing two pounds.

Other Muslim alchemists whose work was of enduring influence include al-Razi and Ibn Sina, known in the West as Rhazes and Avicenna respectively. Rhazes (c.860–925) was a merchant's son from Ray in Persia, who gave up a life as a musician to devote himself to philosophy and medicine. He studied in Baghdad and returned a man of science, critical of religious superstition and fanaticism. His writings are less mystical than Jābir and reveal a powerful intellect. He added salt as a third principle to Jābir's mercury-sulphur theory. Rhazes remained an authority at European universities into the seventeenth century. He wrote some twenty books on alchemy and classified a great number of substances, medicines, apparatus, and processes. He famously declared "Who knows not chemistry does not deserve the name of philosopher."

Avicenna (980–1037), another Persian, was born in the old Silk Route city of Bokhara. He was a prodigious intellect and, having outlearned his tutors at an early age, he devoted himself to the private study of medicine. By the age of seventeen he was physician to a prince and went on to lead an enormously colourful and productive life. His massive "Canon of Medicine" earned him the title "Prince of Physicians" and made him an oracular authority until well into the Renaissance. His greatest alchemical work is the "Book of the Remedy," in which he concurs with Jābir and Rhazes on the generation of metals, but expresses scepticism about transmutation. For all his brilliance Avicenna lacked a certain magical understanding. Like Rhazes he was more a scholar than a seer.

CHAPTER 8

CHRYSOPOEIA IN
CHRISTENDOM

Arabian culture and knowledge began to be transmitted to Europe after Islamic Moors invaded Spain under Ṭāriq ibn Ziyād in 711, and built three great universities there at Toledo, Cordoba, and Seville.

Gnostic and Neo-Platonic works were brought to France in the ninth century, where they were translated from the Arabic by Johannes Scotus Erigena, a Scottish mystic from Ireland. Subsequently, Christian mysticism re-emerged as the Mystery of the Holy Grail. However, despite the practice of alchemy among the ancient Greeks, alchemy was generally unknown in Europe prior to the Moorish invasions. After Toledo was retaken from the Moors in 1105, Archbishop

Raymond founded the College of Translators there for the purpose of translating Arabic works for Europeans. The earliest known translation of Arabian alchemy into Latin was Englishman Robert of Chester's translation of the *Book of the Composition of Alchemy* by Morienus in 1144. Robert was also the first to translate the Quran and the Arabian form of mathematics known as "algebra." His most influential work was the translation of the "Emerald Tablet" from Jābir's writing. Increasingly, scholars such as Gerard of Cremona, in Lombardy, Adelard of Bath, Roger of Hereford, and Maimonides the Jew revealed the vast Arabic knowledge to Europeans. As a result, a wave of alchemical studies was generated throughout Europe.

Some of the greatest minds of the time took up the study of alchemy. These included the German Bishop Albertus Magnus, born in Swabia in 1193, and his famous student, St. Thomas Aquinas; the Franciscan Friar Roger Bacon, born in Somerset in 1214; and Arnold of Villanova, physician to kings and popes, born in Valencia in 1235. The idea of the Philosophers' Stone also laid a powerful hold on the less lofty aspects of the medieval mind, attracting the greedy, gullible, and dishonest, who were only interested in material gold. Such "puffers" [207] led the Art into disrepute, but this materialist emphasis served to protect alchemy from being branded heretical by the Church. Even so, the production of alchemical gold from powder that had fallen into unworthy hands, or, more commonly, cleverly faked gold, reached such levels that Pope John XXII issued a decree prohibiting the practice of alchemy in 1317.

The extent to which "puffing" had become a common practice in England by the late fourteenth century can be gauged from "The

---

207 The term is a double slur, meaning, on the one hand, endless (futile) blowing upon the flames in alchemical operations and, on the other, the puffed-up conceit of those professing knowledge of the Art.

Canon's Yeoman's Tale" in Chaucer's *Canterbury Tales*, the most famous literature of the period. Chaucer's familiarity with the language of alchemy and laboratory operations, which he brilliantly and satirically evokes, suggests an assumed familiarity on the part of his readers, while also indicating that he himself had wasted time and money pursuing the Stone.

In spite of royal and papal bans and the fraud and failures associated with gold-making, alchemists continued to study and publish throughout Europe, and a significant number of alchemists were members of the clergy, including abbots, bishops, and cardinals. Alchemy came to be known as the Royal Art, for many kings and princes were taken up with it, and either had their own alchemical laboratories or paid for those of the many alchemists they hired. It was not uncommon for alchemists to be extremely learned men, many of them physicians, who traveled widely in search of alchemical knowledge at a time when such travel was dangerous.

What drove these people was a belief in the sacred, transformative value of the Art and also the tantalising rumours of genuine transmutations. Some of the latter were supported by reliable witnesses, including goldsmiths and churchmen. Indeed, were it not for the prejudice against transmutation, some well substantiated accounts would be accepted as historical fact. Such examples include those associated with the names Seton, Sendivogius, Helvetius, James Price, Lascaris, and Van Helmont, which we will examine in due course. As a taster, the case of Van Helmont is worth relating here as it is a typical and reliable example, which even hardened sceptics find hard to dismiss out of hand.

The Testimony of Van Helmont

Jan Baptista van Helmont (1577–1644) was a pioneering Flemish chemist, physiologist, and physician, who identified carbon dioxide and is considered the father of pneumatic chemistry. He was a follower of Paracelsus and shared his mystical view of nature. He was sympathetic to alchemical ideas, but had expressed himself sceptical of transmutation. One day he was visited unexpectedly by a stranger who engaged with him in conversation about the Philosophers' Stone as if it were a matter of fact. Van Helmont challenged his assumptions, whereupon the stranger produced a container full of a powder, of which he gave him a tiny amount. The stranger told him how to use the powder and then made to leave. When van Helmont expressed surprise that he did not wish to observe the outcome of the operation, the stranger replied that the outcome was assured. Van Helmont asked him why he had sought him out in this way. "To convince an illustrious scientist whose work does honour to his country," replied the stranger, and left. Van Helmont followed the stranger's instructions to the letter and successfully performed a transmutation.

Later he wrote: "For truly, I have divers times seen it [the Philosophers' Stone], and handled it with my hands: It was the colour of powdered Saffron yet weighty, and shining like powdered Glass. There was once given unto me one fourth part of one Grain: But I call a

Grain the six hundredth part of one Ounce: This quarter of one Grain therefore, being rolled up in Paper, I projected upon eight Ounces of Quicksilver made hot in a crucible; and presently all the Quicksilver, with a certain degree of noise, ceased its flux, and being congealed, settled like unto a yellow lump: but after pouring it out ... there were found eight Ounces, and a little less than eleven Grains of the purest Gold: Therefore one only Grain of that Powder, had transchanged 19186 Parts of Quicksilver, equal to itself, into the best Gold." [208]

Such accounts of strangers performing transmutations in front of reliable witnesses or providing specimens of "projecting powder" to be proven in their absence persisted throughout the seventeenth and eighteenth centuries, and several coins and medals made from alchemical gold are preserved in museums and private collections in Europe. Even more remarkable than the testimony of van Helmont, perhaps, is the remarkably similar account given by Johann Friedrich Schweitzer, physician to the Prince of Orange-Nassau, later William III of England. Even confirmed skeptics like the noted historian of alchemy E. J. Holmyard have found themselves unable to dismiss the account of such a reliable witness out of hand. His testimony can be found in the appendices.

The Fulcanelli Phenomenon

In the 1920's an unusual book appeared in Paris called *The Mystery of the Cathedrals*, written under the alchemical pseudonym of Fulcanelli. This book elaborated with great authority on the idea that the Gothic cathedrals of Europe were nothing less than alchemical texts written in stone, containing within their architecture all the symbols of the Great Work. As the distinguished scholar Walter Lang wrote in the introduction to the English edition of *The Mystery of the Cathedrals*, "It has long been believed that the Gothic cathedrals were secret textbooks of some hidden knowledge; that behind the gargoyles and the

---

208 Van Helmont, p. 807.

glyphs, the rose windows and the flying buttresses, a mighty secret lay, all but openly displayed. This is no longer a theory."

Fulcanelli suggests that esoteric Hermetic philosophy was the impulse behind the astonishingly sudden flourishing of Gothic architecture in medieval Europe. Not only did Gothic architecture display extraordinary technical advances on the preceding Romanesque style, but it was executed on such a vast scale. Between 1170 and 1270 some eighty cathedrals and five hundred churches of near-cathedral size were started in France alone. This same impulse inspired the legends of the Holy Grail, written during the same period. This was the time of the troubadours and the courtly love poets who heralded the Age of Chivalry and the institution of mystical knightly orders like the Order of the Garter.

Where did this impulse come from? Probably from the Holy Land. The First Crusade and the establishment of the Christian Kingdom of Jerusalem at the beginning of the twelfth century had brought Europeans into direct contact with Islam. The Knights Templar, founded to protect the pilgrimage routes through the Holy Land, have always been linked with secret knowledge and it is probable that some of their rank were initiated into Sufism. This mystical, not to say magical, current of Islam had embraced a profound understanding of Hermeticism, Neo-Platonism, and alchemy since at least the time of Jābir. Sacred geometry, erotic religious symbolism, and quasi-shamanic techniques for manipulating consciousness were also part of the Sufi mix, and some of these elements started to enter Europe in the twelfth century.

Fulcanelli also elaborated at length on the phonetic cabala, a system of puns and wordplay used by adepts both to conceal and reveal esoteric meaning. This form of cant or argot (hence "l'art Gothique"—Gothic art), also known as the "language of the birds" is a crucial key to deciphering alchemical treatises and symbolism and reading nature's signs.

Fulcanelli remains one of the most enigmatic and mysterious occult figures of the twentieth century. He rediscovered the long-lost alchemical process which produced the famous blue and red stained glass of such cathedrals as Chartres and is said to have performed a transmutation before reliable witnesses before disappearing in the 1930s. In *The Morning of the Magicians*[209] Jacques Bergier describes an unexpected visit from a stranger he believed to be Fulcanelli in 1937. At the time he was engaged in nuclear research with the noted scientist Andre Helbronner. He asked his visitor to explain the nature of his work, to which the stranger replied that he could hardly be expected to summarize in four minutes four thousand years of philosophy in a language for which such concepts were not intended. He was nevertheless prepared to say the following:

> *Relativity demonstrates the extent to which the observer today intervenes in all these phenomena. The secret of alchemy is this: there is a way of manipulating a force-field, which acts upon the observer and puts him in a privileged position in relation to the universe, from which he has access to the realities which are normally concealed from us by time and space, matter and energy. This is what we call the Great Work.*

When Bergier asked about the Philosophers' Stone and gold the stranger replied:

> *Those are only applications of it. The vital thing is not the transmutation of metals, but that of the experimenter himself. It is an ancient secret that a few people rediscover each century.*

Bergier was impressed by the stranger's knowledge of nuclear energy, which surpassed his own and proved highly prescient. He was warned of the appalling dangers involved in nuclear fission. After the

---

209 An international bestseller, first published in France as *Le Matin des Magiciens* in 1960, then in Britain as *The Dawn of Magic* in 1963, and subsequently in the USA as *The Morning of the Magicians* in 1964.

war, Bergier, who had worked in intelligence, was debriefed by the forerunner of the CIA. His testimony pursuaded the authorities to try and track Fulcanelli down. They never found him. The only person who claims to have seen Fulcanelli since Bergier is his former pupil Eugene Canseliet. Summoned by his master to a castle in the mountains of Spain in 1952, Canseliet described his master as appearing twenty years younger than he had twenty years earlier.

The Comte de Saint-Germain and the Elixir of Life

An ingredient of the perennial lure and romance of alchemy, second only to the Philosophers' Stone, is the Elixir of Life. Stories of immortal adepts abound in both Eastern and Western alchemical traditions, as we have already seen, but there is one particular figure who made a most extraordinary impact upon his (extended) time.

The Comte de Saint-Germain is one of the most enigmatic figures in the history of alchemy. His ancestry has never been definitely established, but he claimed to be a son of Francis II Rákóczi, the Prince of Transylvania, and there is sufficient circumstantial evidence to suggest that may have been true. Whatever the circumstances of his background, the impression he made was so dramatic that his appearances at the highest levels of European society between 1710 and 1822 are a matter of extensive and detailed historical record, from which a fascinating picture emerges. He always appeared to be aged around forty-five to fifty years old; of pleasant, but unremarkable appearance;

habitually dressed simply, but elegantly in black, adorned with large diamonds. He never touched meat or wine, and if he did eat, it was alone. He was a great linguist, speaking at least eleven languages fluently, including Arabic, Sanskrit, and Chinese; an accomplished musician, composer, and artist; possessed a remarkable memory; and was universally admired for his charm, erudition, and consideration. Frederick the Great, whose confidence he enjoyed, described him as "the man who does not die," while the great French philosopher Voltaire, the sharpest intellect of his time, said of him (without, it seems, his usual sarcasm): "He is the greatest philosopher I know, a man who never dies, never seems to age, and who knows everything." The great adventurer Jacques Casanova mentions him several times in his famous autobiography, which has proved a surprisingly reliable document. Casanova considered Saint-Germain to be an adventurer and imposter (much like himself), but could not help admiring him, as the following quote demonstrates:

It may safely be said that as a conversationalist he was unequalled.

St. Germain gave himself out for a marvel and always aimed at exciting amazement, which he often succeeded in doing. He was scholar, linguist, musician, and chemist, good-looking, and a perfect ladies' man.

This extraordinary man, intended by nature to be the king of impostors and quacks, would say in an easy, assured manner that he was three hundred years old, that he knew the secret of the Universal Medicine, that he possessed a mastery over nature, that he could melt diamonds, professing himself capable of forming, out of ten or twelve small diamonds, one large one of the finest water without any loss of weight. All this, he said, was a mere trifle to him. Notwithstanding his boastings, his bare-faced lies, and his manifold eccentricities, I cannot say I thought him offensive. In spite of my knowledge of what he was and in spite of my own feelings, I thought him an astonishing man as he was always astonishing me.[210]

Saint-Germain travelled extensively, mediating in important affairs of state, mingling gracefully at royal courts from Portugal to Russia and performing such wonders as removing flaws from precious stones. His true agenda can only be guessed at, but his most assiduous biographer, Isabel Cooper-Oakley, writes that "the most interesting and important work done by M. de Saint-Germain, lies buried in the secret archives of many princely and noble families."[211] There are many documented proofs that he was a Freemason and Rosicrucian—he is recorded as having attended two major Freemasonic and Rosicrucian conferences in 1785—the year following his supposed death in Germany. He was generally considered an adept alchemist— he often spoke extensively on the subject—in possession of the Stone, but given his extraordinary vigour and longevity, it is with the Elixir that he is most closely associated. Madame de Pompadour, the mistress of Louis XV, said that Saint-Germain gave a lady of the court an elixir which had preserved her beauty for more than twenty-four years beyond the norm. The Viennese writer Franz Gräffer records a meeting between a "stranger" assumed to be Saint-Germain and Franz Mesmer (the hypnotist, after whom the verb "to mesmerise" was coined) around 1789 where "their conversation centred round the theory of obtaining the elements of the elixir of life by the employment of magnetism in a series of permutations."[212]

Saint-Germain's appearances became much less frequent after the 1820's, but he is considered an immortal Adept or Hidden Master by many occult and esoteric New Age and Rosicrucian organisations to

---

210 Casanova de Seingalt, chapter 3.

211 Cooper-Oakley, p. 2.

212 Gräffer, Franz: *Kleine Wiener Memoiren*, vol. 1, 1845–6, quoted in Cooper-Oakley, p. 156.

this day.[213] If anyone ever perfected or received the Elixir, it was he. But what actually is the Elixir of Life? According to esoteric tradition, it is an alchemically prepared substance that can extend human life by up to a thousand years. The adept who manages to make it will anyway achieve complete enlightenment, and therefore conscious immortality, in the process. It is called the White Stone and is also capable of transmuting metals into silver. It can be elaborated one stage further into the Red Stone, the Philosophers' Stone, the "red powder of projection." The elixir is thus a very highly evolved substance, which has powerfully energising effects. According to remarkably similar accounts from India, China, and Europe, the effects of taking the elixir are rather alarming. If more than a tiny amount of the elixir is taken, the recipient is likely to die a swift and violent death. If the right dose is taken the recipient can expect the purging from the body of all toxins together with the sudden loss of hair, teeth, and nails. These grow back within a few weeks, healthier and stronger than before. Muscular tone is reestablished, affording a youthful appearance. There is no further need to eat and all natural elimination is performed through the sweat glands. Consciousness is greatly expanded, leading to profound spiritual insight. This, coupled with a very greatly extended lifespan, provides someone thus reborn with an extraordinary opportunity to achieve divine union without the need of further lifetimes. In the Indian and Chinese traditions, the preparation of life-extending medicines while working towards the Stone has always been more important than the manufacture of gold.

As for Saint-Germain, he has further been immortalized in many fictional works over the centuries, while his purported immortality and Transylvanian origins have inevitably afforded him hero status amongst vampire enthusiasts, whose numbers are legion.

---

213 Including the Theosophical Society, whose leaders, Mme Blavatsky and Annie Besant, both claim to have met him on different occasions.

Paracelsus the Great: The Devil's Doctor

The Renaissance physician Theophrastus Philippus Aurelius Bombastus von Hohenheim, known to history simply as Paracelsus, was one of the most remarkable men of his or any other age. Like Pythagoras, Empedocles, and Apollonius, he spent years wandering the world in the pursuit of knowledge. He revolutionized medicine and made great contributions to the understanding of alchemy. He is considered the father of both chemical medicine and modern surgery, and the forefather of homeopathy. This legendary figure, described by the great nineteenth century mage Eliphas Lévi as "marvellous Paracelsus, always drunk and always lucid, like the heroes of Rabelais," [214] remains, nevertheless, an enigmatic, contradictory figure who divides opinion to this day.

Born in Switzerland in 1493, Paracelsus received his early education from his physician father. His mother committed suicide when he was young, whereupon he moved with his father to a mining district in Carinthia (now part of Austria), where he attended the local school and shared his father's interest in alchemy. At the age of sixteen he attended university before spending some time with Johannes Trithemius, abbot of Sponheim, one of the greatest mages of the sixteenth

214 Lévi, p. 11.

century.[215] Whatever he learnt from Trithemius was to help forge an undying faith in alchemy and the conscious forces of nature. He then worked at the mines of a wealthy alchemist in the Tyrol. There he learned the physical properties of ores and metals, studied extraction and purification, and noted the curative effects of mineral waters. He observed the accidents and diseases that befell the miners and decided to become a physician.

In the sixteenth century, medicine was still subject to such classical authorities as Aristotle, Galen, and Hippocrates, which is to say it had not advanced for nearly one and a half millennia. Physicians tended to live in ivory towers of scholasticism, studying the texts of the ancients, most of which were over a thousand years old, and concerning themselves entirely with theory. They seldom dealt with patients and had little or no practical experience. They couldn't disinfect a wound, let alone sew it up. If informed of a patient's symptoms, they would simply prescribe a remedy to be supplied by the apothecary. This suited physician and apothecary, but seldom the patient. This was not the kind of physician that Paracelsus wished to become.

Upon receiving his doctorate from the University of Ferrara, Paracelsus hit the road for seven years, travelling all over Europe and beyond, often by foot. Rejecting university libraries, he chose instead to "read in Nature's book." He learned all he could of medical folklore and plant-cunning from gypsies and midwives, and much else besides from all the people he engaged with in places as diverse as England, Spain, Italy, Scandinavia, Portugal, Poland, Turkey, and Russia. He learned surgery on the battlefront, for whenever his wanderings led him into a warzone he simply joined the first army he encountered

---

215 Trithemius wrote perhaps the first book devoted to cryptography (*Polygraphia*) and can therefore be considered a grandfather of Bitcoin.

as a surgeon and healer. He even served at times on opposing sides, which is typical of the man.[216]

Legend tells us that in one war he was captured by the Tartars and taken to the Khan in India. How long he stayed there and how much he learned is a mystery, but he introduced several concepts known in India, which were hitherto unknown in Europe, such as the seven principles of man,[217] the qualities of the astral body, and elemental spirits. He is said to have accompanied the Khan's son to Constantinople, where he met the equally itinerant adept Solomon Trismosin, author of the extraordinarily beautiful and enigmatic alchemical emblem book *Splendor Solis*, who is said to have given him a portion of transmuting powder. Legend has it that Paracelsus kept the powder in the jeweled pommel of his sword.

Paracelsus eventually returned to Switzerland where he was received with great honour, being made town physician of Basel in 1527. His legendary cures established his reputation, but he soon outraged his peers by mocking and insulting them and lecturing in German rather than time-honoured Latin. When he went as far as burning books in public, the faculty tried, unsuccessfully, to stop him from lecturing. He made further enemies amongst the apothecaries, who he accused of exploiting the sick.

Things reached a critical point when a rich prelate refused to pay Paracelsus the huge sum he had promised him for a cure. Paracelsus

---

216 He never supported causes, seeking knowledge of medicine alone. Born a Roman Catholic just two years after Martin Luther, he never renounced his Catholicism, but, unlike with so many other matters, he never took great issue with Protestantism.

217 This concept is addressed by Mme Blavatsky in *The Key to Theosophy (pp. 90–93)*. She defines the principles as: Atma—Spirit or Self—one with The Absolute as Its Radiation; Buddhi—Spiritual Soul—vehicle of pure universal spirit; Manas—consisting of Higher Manas, the spiritual, inner, or higher Ego; and Lower Manas, the ordinary mind; Kamarupa—the "desire body," seat of animal desires and passions; Prana—the vital principle; Linga Sharira—the double, or astral body; and Sthula Sharira—the physical body.

sued him. When the court awarded him just a fraction of his fee, he published a scathing attack on their integrity. This was a punishable offence. In peril of imprisonment, Paracelsus took the advice of his remaining friends and slipped out of the city, never to return.

He never achieved such a prominent position again and returned to a life of wandering. Over the remaining years of his life he wrote, or dictated, a great body of work. Only his two books on surgery were published during his lifetime (1536), but they were widely acclaimed and remained an authority for many years. By this time Paracelsus had reestablished his reputation, and in 1540 he was invited to settle in Salzburg. But just when it seemed he might find some rest, he died, probably murdered by his enemies.

Paracelsus was intolerant of hypocrisy and pompousness. He was no respecter of academic position and it was this that made him so many enemies. When accused of being an unlearned vagabond and challenged to name his authorities, he retaliated: "Whence have I all my secrets? From what writers and authors? Ask rather how the beasts have learned their arts. If Nature can instruct irrational animals, can it not much more men?"[218]

Paracelsus understood that just as animals instinctively recognise the virtues of things like plants, humans too can redevelop an instinctive rapport with Nature, which can then transmit its secrets. We can know the true nature of things, not by reading about them or even thinking about them, but by *being with* them. He perceived Nature as a conscious, mystical, living force able to engage directly with people whose hearts and souls are open. This appreciation is true alchemy—the ability to identify with something on the most intimate level, allowing both to be all that they are.

Paracelsus developed the *Doctrine of Signatures*, which describes how Nature reveals itself through its signs. The shape or colour of

---

218 Ferguson, "Paracelsus," *Encyclopædia Britannica: A Dictionary of Arts, Sciences, and General Literature, Volume 18*, Philadelphia: J. M. Stoddart Co., 1885, p. 238.

a plant, for example, can indicate its medicinal use. For those able to read it, Nature was an open book. Paracelsus tells us how: through prayer, faith, and imagination. Prayer is "a strong desire and aspiration for that which is good. We must seek and knock and thereby ask the Omnipotent Power within ourselves, and remind it of its promises and keep it awake, and if we do this in the proper form and with a pure and sincere heart, we shall receive that for which we ask, and find that which we seek, and the doors of the Eternal that have been closed before us will be opened, and what was hidden before our sight will come to light."

Faith, he tells us is not mere belief, but an "unwavering confidence" based upon *knowing,* "a faith that may move mountains and throw them into the ocean, and to which everything is possible."

"Faith is a luminous star that leads the honest seeker into the mysteries of Nature. You must seek your point of gravity in God, and put your trust in an honest, divine, sincere, pure and strong faith and cling to it with your whole heart, soul, sense and thought - full of love and confidence. If you possess such a faith, God (Wisdom) will not withhold His truth from you, but He will reveal His works to you credibly, visibly, and consolingly." [219]

As for imagination, Paracelsus equates it with meditation, a cognitive awareness that receives the messages and translates the revelations that prayer and faith allow us to receive. As the mystic Jacob Boehme declared and as the psychologist C. G. Jung was later to discover, alchemy is a language which speaks to the active imagination when opened in man.

Although a pious Christian, Paracelsus's concept of the Absolute is not the divine intellect of a paternal God; it is the *Mysterium Magnum* (Great Mystery), the source from which all things issue and to which all things return, like the Brahma of Hinduism and the Dao of Chinese mysticism. Native American mysticism shares this concept and also has in common with Paracelsus an all-embracing definition

---

219 All Paracelsus quotes taken from Hartmann.

of medicine as the language of nature, through which meaning is transmitted to us.

Paracelsus's greatest contribution to alchemy is the emphasis he put on its medicinal, transformative value, bringing Western alchemy in line with the Chinese and Indian systems. He developed a series of alchemical processes for making medicines, which he called "spagyrics"[220] that are still being used all over the world. In Germany there are several commercial laboratories that produce spagyric remedies that are sold in pharmacies throughout the country.

Spagyrics provide the neophyte with the simplest access to practical alchemy both from a practical and theoretical perspective. One of Paracelsus's most useful innovations was to emphasise the importance of a third principle in addition to Sulphur and Mercury. The latter correlate to Spirit and Soul, to which Paracelsus not so much added as emphasized the principle of Salt, which correlates to the body. From an alchemical perspective, nothing can manifest in this dimension without these *Tria Prima*. Without a soul we would be zombies; without a spirit we would be comatose; and without a body we would not be here.

In alchemy the work begins with the identification of each principle, which must then be isolated and purified. The vegetable kingdom exemplifies the principles very clearly and allows us easy access. Sulphur/Soul is the principle that represents the essence of a thing, that which distinguishes it from all other manifestations. In the plant kingdom, this essence is to be found, fittingly, in the essential oils, which allow us to identify a plant even in the dark through the primary sense of smell. Mercury/Spirit represents vitality or life-force and, again fittingly, this principle manifests as alcoholic spirit. Whereas Soul is essential and identifying, Spirit is universal, being the same throughout each kingdom. All plants will produce alcohol in the right conditions and once alcohol is distilled beyond 96 percent it becomes undifferentiated, which

---

220 From the Greek words *spao and ageiro*, which mean draw out, extract, and put together, recombine.

is to say that you can no longer tell which plant it came from. The Salt/ Body principle is to be found in the "secret salts," the water-soluble salts that can be extracted from the incinerated ashes of the plant.

Here is an example of a Paracelsan process which he called a *Magistery*.

Take a plant with a high proportion of essential oil, such as rosemary. Steam distil it and reserve the distilled essential oil (Soul). Ferment the remaining plant matter and distil off the resulting alcohol (Spirit). Evaporate the remaining plant soup and incinerate the resulting solids. Grind the ashes and leach out the water-soluble salts with hot, distilled water. Filter, evaporate, and calcine (roast to whiteness) the remaining salts. Dissolve in distilled water and repeat until pure white. The three purified principles are then recombined as a *Magistery*, which is a highly resonant and effective preparation, more highly attuned to the original "idea"[221] of the plant than any other preparation that does not isolate, purify and recombine the Tria Prima.

One of Paracelsus's most infamous contributions to magical and alchemical lore is the concept of the *homunculus*, a miniature human being that he claimed to be able to generate in the alembic, a sealed glass vessel, from human sperm:

> *Human beings may come into existence without natural parents. That is to say, such beings may grow without being developed, and born by a female organism; by the art of an experienced spagyricus. The generatio homunculi has until now been kept very secret, and so little was publicly known about it that the old philosophers have doubted its possibility. But I know that such things may be accomplished by spagyric art assisted by natural processes. If the sperma, enclosed in a hermetically sealed glass, is buried in horse manure for about forty days, and properly "magnetized," it may begin to live and to move. After such a time it bears the form and resemblance of a human being, but it will be*

---

221   In accordance with Plato's concept of "forms," which are the divine "ideas" of things that precede manifestation. Nothing that has not been dreamed up in the divine *nous* can possibly come to be.

transparent and without a corpus. If it is now artificially fed with the arcanum sanguinis hominis[222] *until it is about forty weeks old, and if allowed to remain during that time in the horse manure in a continually equal temperature, it will grow into a human child, with all its members developed like any other child, such as may have been born by a woman, only it will be much smaller. We call such a being a homunculus, and it may be raised and educated like any other child, until it grows older and obtains reason and intellect, and is able to take care of itself. This is one of the greatest secrets, and it ought to remain a secret until the days approach when all secrets will be known.*[223]

As Paracelsus suggests, the idea is not his own, but he is the first person known to have used the word homunculus. C. G. Jung opined that some of the visions of Zosimos allude to the idea of the homunculus, citing passages in which a man appeared to Zosimos who attacked him with a sword before undergoing terrible torments reminiscent of a classic "shaman's death" scenario, eventually changing into "the opposite of himself, into a mutilated anthroparion, and he tore his flesh with his own teeth, and sank into himself."[224] He describes other "men," such as "the Brazen Man" and "the Leaden Man" who go through similar grotesque ordeals, but it seems to me that these characters are symbolic anthropomorphic representations of materials undergoing alchemical transformation in the laboratory. The artificial creation of life, such as Paracelsus' homunculus," a concept known as takwin in Arabic, was one pursued by certain Islamic alchemists, including Jābir some seven hundred years earlier, while in Prague some hundred and fifty years after Paracelsus, Rabbi Loew is said to have created his famous Golem using kabbalistic arts. Another century later Goethe returns to the theme in Faust:

---

222 "Arcanum sanguinis hominis" means "secret potion made from human blood" in Latin. An Italian alchemist who was the chief lab practitioner for a well-known German spagyrics company produced such an Arcanum from his own blood, which was made available to the public on order through pharmacies.

223 Paracelsus: *De Natura Rerum, Vol I.*, quoted in Hartmann, p. 174.

224 Jung, p. 60.

And brains, with thoughts to celebrate,
A Thinker in the future will create.[225]

Around the same time, Mary Shelley, inspired by a visit to the castle of the pioneering German alchemist Conrad Dippel, wrote the most famous story ever written about the artificial creation of life in the laboratory: *Frankenstein*. Faust and Frankenstein ended badly, both paying for their hubris with their lives, and, at least in the case of Faust, with their souls. Although Paracelsus's homunculus recipe will strike most of my readers as grotesque and ethically dubious at best, it is important to bear in mind just how pious and principled Paracelsus was. Unlike the tragic Dr. Frankenstein such operations, regardless of their efficacy, would only be undertaken by Paracelsus with the utmost humility. In order to achieve the desired result, he would attempt to connect the *archaeus* of the matter in the vessel with his own *archaeus*. For Paracelsus, the archaeus is a spiritual entity that resides in all living things and is responsible for all processes governing growth and health. Most people who use the term these days tend to consider it more like an aura or subtle body that manifests as a luminous energy field. Be that as it may, such concepts as homunculi and the archaeus were to prove beyond the pale for the brave new rational physicians of the eighteenth century. This is no doubt why Samuel Hahnemann, the inventor of homeopathy, was careful to conceal his indebtedness to Paracelsus who, two hundred and fifty years earlier, had declared that "everything is medicine, everything is poison, only the dosage decides."

---

225 Goethe: *Faust, Part Two, Act 2.*

CHAPTER 9

THE STRANGER OF ONE
NIGHT'S ACQUAINTANCE

On Saturday May 25, 1782, a distinguished group of gentlemen found themselves gathered at Stoke, near Guildford, England, in the splendidly equipped laboratory of the celebrated young chemist James Price. They were there to witness an experiment that, they had been assured, would convince them of the reality of alchemical transmutation. The fifteen witnesses included Lords Palmerston (father of the future prime minister), Onslow, and King; Sir Robert Barker; Sir Philip H. Clarke; the reverends O. Manning and B. Anderson; a Dr. Spence; and Mr. William Mann Godschall. Four of them had witnessed previous, seemingly successful experiments and the whole company had, only shortly before, witnessed the apparent transmutation of a quantity of mercury into silver. Now their host proposed to turn mercury into gold.

The atmosphere in the laboratory was calm, but electric. Everyone there was fully aware of the enormity of the occasion. Should the experiment be successful, then they would all be witness to an event of seminal importance, such as would likely be recounted to schoolchildren for generations to come. Several of the company were Fellows of the Royal Society, the world's most prestigious scientific institution. Their testimony would be crucial in deciding success from failure; fact from fraud. Mr. Price, himself a Fellow of the Royal Society, asked them all to pay the closest attention to every part of the process—an injunction he repeated throughout the experiment—and invited Lords Palmerston and King to stand closest to the action. The room was therefore humming with the keenest attention as Price commenced proceedings by passing around a pestle and mortar for all to inspect.

He then invited two of the company to first select a small amount of charcoal and borax from large quantities which he had available; then place them in the mortar and grind them to a powder. Lord Palmerston was then asked to select a crucible from a quantity arranged on a shelf. His Lordship duly obliged, choosing a small round porcelain crucible, which he was asked to examine closely and pass around the company for further inspection. All appeared satisfied, as before, and the crucible was finally passed to Price, who placed it on a table in front of them and tipped into it the ground charcoal and borax. Pressing the powder down with the pestle, he announced that this was to act as a flux. He then asked the Rev. Anderson to produce some mercury and declare its provenance. The reverend brought out from his coat a small bottle containing, he said, half an ounce of pure quicksilver derived from cinnabar, which he had himself procured from an established dealer.

Thanking him, Price asked him to show it to the gentleman on his left, whom he then asked to pour the mercury into the depression that he had made in the flux.

Price now produced from his waistcoat pocket a small wooden box. This, he declared, contained the red powder of projection, also known as the Red Lion or the Philosophers' Stone. Requesting that they not touch it he held the box open for all to see. It was several minutes before all present had had the opportunity to peer closely at the powder and try to gauge its qualities. At first glance it had a dull, waxy appearance, but as it drew the eye in, it appeared more translucent and even to glitter subtly as if it were a mass of incredibly tiny cut gems. Its colour changed too on closer inspection from a citrine yellow to an ever-deeper blood red. A modern astronomer may have been reminded of a red dwarf star.

When all had finally stood back reluctantly, Price closed the lid and allowed them all to hold the wooden box. As they passed it gingerly around, many openly expressed their amazement at how heavy it was—considerably heavier than if it had contained lead or even gold. Retrieving the box at last, Price took a scalpel and weighed out a bare half grain of the powder, equivalent in size to a mustard seed, on a pair of very fine scales. Handing Lord Palmerston the scalpel, he invited him to scrape up the weighed out powder and place it on top of the mercury in the crucible. The crucible was then covered with a lid (selected as before from among many others and inspected by all) and placed in a furnace surrounded by red-hot charcoal. After a few minutes, the crucible began to glow red, whereupon the lid was removed and the mercury observed to be quite unagitated, neither boiling nor smoking even when it became red-hot. At that point the lid was replaced and the heat raised to white-hot and held there for thirty minutes. The crucible was then lifted out with tongs and allowed to cool. As it did so, it broke in half and a globule of yellow metal was found at the bottom which, as Lord Palmerston then demonstrated, exactly fitted the concavity in the vitrified flux like the yolk of a hard-boiled egg. It was found to weigh about ten grains. Lord Palmerston then passed the globule around for the company's inspection together with other fragments of yellow metal that were diffused through the scoriae attached to the sides of the crucible. The yellow metal had both the appearance and the pliability of gold. Price asked Mr. Godschall to collect up all the yellow metal and give it to Lord Palmerston, who had undertaken to have it submitted to expert examination. The Assay-Master (who had been recommended to Mr. Godschall by the clerk of the Goldsmiths' Company) duly reported the metal to be perfectly pure gold. A goldsmith in Oxford called Mr. Lock later confirmed the gold as purer than "gold of the English standard."

News of Mr. Price's astonishing experiments soon spread and they were widely reported in the press, causing a great sensation. In all Price had performed nine different experiments, some of which were repeated several times, between the sixth and twenty-eighth of May. In eight of these Price appeared to have been successful, transmuting mercury into gold using the red powder and silver using a white powder. All of the witnesses appear to have been convinced by what they had seen (they all agreed to sign Price's account) and Price was widely hailed as a genius. Lord Onslow, a Lord of the Royal Bedchamber and former Treasurer of the Household, presented some of the alchemical gold to King George III who, in Price's words "was pleased to express His approbation." On July 2, Oxford University conferred on him the degree of MD on account of his "knowledge, ingenuity and skill in experiments,"[226] while Price responded to public interest by publishing a very detailed account of the experiments.[227] This was well received by the popular journals and was summarized at length in the *London Chronicle*. It ran to two editions, which quickly sold out. It was also translated into German and became a *cause célèbre* on the Continent.

The majority of the lay public seemed ready to accept what Price and, indeed, his witnesses attested. And who could doubt him? He had, after all, the approbation of both Oxford University and the King. Many hailed his success as a great boon for the nation. As Chambers notes: "The more sanguine and less scientific of the community saw in this work the approach of an era of prosperity for England such as the world had never previously witnessed."[228]

There were others, however, who remained far from convinced. Some suggested that he was a clever trickster, others that he had fooled himself. But his fiercest critics were to be found among his colleagues in the Royal Society, in particular Richard Kirwan, who had headed Price's list of sponsors for election to the RS the previous year. It seems to have been Kirwan who first drew the matter to the attention of the Royal Society's president, the autocratic Sir Joseph Banks. In a letter to Dr. Charles Blagden, MD (a close friend whom he was to appoint as secretary of the Royal Society two years later), dated July 14, 1782, Banks writes:

> We have been entertained by Mr. Price, formerly Higginbotham, fixing mercury into gold and silver at his pleasure. He exhibited several times at Guildford to the neighbourhood and made all the spectators write their names in a book recording the mode of experiment.

226 Sir William Ramsay, *The Life and Letters of Joseph Black*, London, 1918, p. 63.

227 An account of some experiments on mercury, silver, and gold, made at Guildford in May 1782 in the laboratory of James Price MD FRS to which is prefaced an abridgement of Boyle's account of a degradation of gold. Oxford, 1782

228 *Chambers' Book of Days*, 1, 602–4, London, 1863. http://www.thebookofdays.com /months/may/6.htm.

Kirwan, who at first thought he was in jest, went in search of him but found he had left Guildford a few days before he arrived. A letter however passed from which we are informed that Mr. P is now printing at Oxford a small impression of a detail of the mode of his experiments and their success, authenticated by the names of those who saw him. Kirwan and indeed all the Chymists are angry at such an apparent charlatanerie.[229]

On July 19 Blagden replied:

Before I left town Mr. Price had begun to exhibit his alchemical operations. I was the first that mentioned them to Mr. Kirwan who then fancied that Price meant nothing more than to make the country people stare, but since the matter is become too serious. Either his reputation as a chemist must be raised to the highest pitch or he must be contented to occupy a seat in the noted paradise of the lunar regions.[230]

The chemists of the Royal Society were furious with Price for a number of reasons. For a start, some felt slighted that they had not been invited to witness the experiments themselves. As Price's sponsor, Kirwan, in particular, felt that he should have been privy to the whole business. To hear about it second-hand from Blagden, who wasn't even a chemist, must have been galling. The fact that he had been excluded also made him suspicious about Price's motives. Above all the chemists were angry because they were largely agreed that transmutation was impossible and that alchemy was therefore nonsense. This orthodoxy was all the more fiercely defended for being of quite recent foundation.

Belief in alchemy, which had pertained in all the great civilizations for thousands of years, had been eroded by the surging tides of the Age of Reason and the Scientific Revolution. In the seventeenth

---

229 Blagdon-Banks correspondence in the Royal Society Library (Hereinafter referred to as Bla. B.R.S.), p. 8.

230 Bla. B.R.S. p. 9.

century, chemistry, as distinct from alchemy, could be defined as "a kinde of praestigious, covetous, cheating magick."[231] By Price's day, the tables had turned. Chemistry had superseded alchemy and begun to catch up with mathematics and physics as a highly promising branch of natural science, whose foremost practitioners were held in high esteem within scientific circles, if not yet in society as a whole. These modern chemists were radical, rational, and revolutionary in both spirit and approach. To give an idea of just how far chemistry had come as a respected science in its own right, one need only check out its entry in the very first edition of the *Encyclopaedia Britannica*, a triumph of the Scottish Enlightenment, which was published in 1768, fourteen years before Price's bombshell. Chemistry is accorded no fewer than 114 pages (somewhere in the region of 140,000 words), while alchemy is contemptuously dismissed in just thirty-eight words, thus:

> *That branch of chemistry that had for its principle objects the transmutation of metals into gold; the panacea, or universal remedy; an alkahest, or universal menstruum; an universal ferment; and many other things equally ridiculous. See CHEMISTRY, Introduction.*[232]

Alchemy is very much in the past tense. As far as the new chemists were concerned, the traditional theory of the four elements had been exploded by that "Skeptical Chemist" Robert Boyle, a founder of the Royal Society (RS), more than a hundred years before. Science was moving towards the atomic theories of John Dalton and Antoine Lavoisier, whose "Elementary Treatise of Chemistry" described thirty-three of the elements we know today and appeared to prove transmutation impossible. Although this work was still seven years away from publication, while Dalton wouldn't propose his atomic theory until 1803 (the official end of the age of alchemy), the reaction of the Royal Society chemists shows that by 1782 alchemy had become, to them

---

231 *The Oxford English Dictionary*, 1989.

232 Online version: https://babel.hathitrust.org/cgi/pt?id=mdp.49015002322619;view=1up;seq=9.

at least, an embarrassing anachronism whose taint they wished to remove from their brave new science. (A good example of this was the ongoing publication of a "Complete Works" of Sir Isaac Newton, the great hero of the Scientific Revolution and former president of the RS, compiled by Bishop Samuel Horsley and William Mann Godschall, one of Price's witnesses, that contrived to exclude any evidence of Newton's alchemical interests, despite the fact that his alchemical papers were easily the most voluminous. It would be another two centuries before Newton came to be recognised as an alchemist, and I believe it safe to assume that the embarrassment of the Dr. Price affair encouraged Godschall to seek to protect Newton from the taint of alchemy. According to Banks, Kirwan became "violent, almost determined to propose his (Price's) expulsion from the R.S."[233] Kirwan, the modern chemist, was convinced that his former protégé must be guilty of a "prestigious, covetous, cheating magic," precisely the thing that the new chemists wanted to distance themselves from.

Blagden, however, appears to have reserved judgment regarding Price's claims. He was infuriated rather by Price's apparent refusal to reveal the composition of the powders he had used and scandalised by Oxford University's haste in conferring further honours upon him. As he wrote to Banks:

> *Was ever any country more completely disgraced than ours has been by the conduct of our University? For, granting that Price has made the discovery held out in his book, should it not have been said to him that the man who having hit upon an improvement in science, keeps it from the world deserves rather to be excluded from the Society of learned men than to be adorned with extraordinary academical honours? … Why were casual people called in as witnesses when the author was acquainted with the most eminent chemists?*[234]

---

233 Bla. B.R.S., p. 9.

234 The Dawson Turner Copies of Banks' correspondence, Volume II (Hereinafter referred to as D.T.C. II.), p. 169, British Library.

What happened next we can glean only from a few surviving letters. One of these, sent to a Professor Lichtenberg in Germany and dated 30 September, 1783, was published in the *Goettingisches Magazin der Wissenschaften und Litteratur* in 1783.[235] The source, unfortunately unnamed, claims to be a friend of a friend of Price. He informs us that Price spent from November 1782 until the end of January 1783 in London trying to come to terms with Banks and the RS chemists. We can imagine that the main bone of contention was Price's apparent refusal to reveal the process for making the powders. A note in Banks's hand written on the back of a letter received by him from William Godschall provides us with Price's excuse for his secrecy:

> *The invention of extracting gold from mercury is Price's own, but that of extracting silver from it was communicated to him by another person who has laid him under an injunction not to publish it. As the former was deduced from the latter by analogy he considers himself bound to conceal that also. So he said, but would allow nothing but the former words to be wrote down as his declaration.* [236]

Price's declaration has disappeared and there is no record that the matter was ever formally addressed in the Minutes of Council of the Royal Society. Nevertheless, it would seem from his words that Banks confronted Price face to face over the matter on at least one occasion (probably in London in November/December 1782), for Godschall alludes to a proposed meeting in his letter:

> *Agreeable to my allegiance I ought to tell you I saw Dr. Price and told him one of two things was expected, either to repeat the experiment at a foreign laboratory or disclose the composition of the powder. He said he would wait on you previous to the next meeting and learn, ex Cathedra, all that was required of him.*[237]

---

235 *Goettingisches Magazin der Wissenschaften und Litteratur, 3, 886–9.*

236 D.T.C. II, p. 232.

237 D.T.C. II, p. 232.

What Banks required of him, failing the actual recipe for the powders, was that he should repeat the experiments in front of experts approved by the Society. Price demurred, saying that his supply of the powders had run out and that they were too expensive, time-consuming, and poisoning to merit producing another batch. Dashing the hopes of the empire builders, he declared that his process could never be a source of profit as the expense involved exceeded the value of any resulting gold.[238] (A keen student of alchemy would note here that Price had failed to master the process of "multiplication," by which the potency and quantity of the powder can be continually increased). When Banks insisted, Price retorted that his experiments had been conducted under the most transparent conditions in front of men of honourable and esteemed reputation, including members of the RS. What purpose would further demonstrations serve? What would Banks's "experts" be able to spot or deduce that the others had missed? Price had already pointed out in the preface to his published account that "as the spectators of a fact must always be less numerous than those who hear it related, so the majority must at last believe, if they believe at all, on the credit of attestation."

Price, it seems, was no longer interested in shouldering the burden of proof. Such was the pressure brought to bear on him, however, that he at last relented and consented to make up another quantity of his powders and repeat the experiments before official delegates of the RS. According to Professor Lichtenberg's informant, Price immediately contacted "chymists" in Germany in an attempt to track down information on "Hermetic processes," including work by well-known contemporaries, such as Andreas Marggraf and Karl Wenzel.

Whether he discovered what he was looking for is not clear, but he left London at the end of January for his home in Surrey promising to have everything ready for his next demonstration in six weeks'

238 Cameron, H. C., *The Notes and Records of the Royal Society of London,* Vol. 8, p. 112. London, 1951.

time. Our informant tells us that his friend invited Price to stay at his house for a while, but he demurred, saying that he would be engaged in very important business for six weeks. During this period, the people around him noticed that he often appeared angry and upset. He expressed his amazement that the public were not content to accept the truth of his discovery based on the testament of the witnesses of his first experiments. In March, with the six weeks well past and having presumably given the matter up, he made a large quantity of laurel water (a lethal poison distilled from laurel), which he redistilled many times down to a small quantity and gave to the maid to look after. Then he wrote his will, beginning: "Since I will probably soon be in a better place..." (despite being known as an atheist) and bequeathed various things to people who were much older than him. Thereafter he lived quietly for a few months, "though still expressing his amazement at the incredulity of the world."

Accounts vary regarding the next twist in the tale. According to the standard account reported by Chambers, Price "reappeared in London and formally invited as many members of the Royal Society as could make it convenient to attend, to meet him in his laboratory at Guildford on the 3rd of August. Although, scarcely a year previous, the first men in England were contending for the honour of witnessing the great chemist's marvellous experiments, such was the change in public estimation caused by his equivocal conduct, that, on the appointed day, three members only of the Royal Society arrived at the laboratory, in acceptance of his invitation. Price received them with cordiality, though he seemed to feel acutely the want of confidence implied by their being so few. Stepping to one side for a moment, he hastily swallowed the contents of a flask of laurel-water. The visitors seeing a sudden change in his appearance, though then ignorant of the cause, called for medical assistance; but in a few moments the unfortunate man was dead." [239]

---

239 *Chambers' Book of Days,* 1, 602–4, London, 1863.

Professor Lichtenberg's informant gives a significantly different, but similarly tragic, account. He tells us that Price had invited "people" to visit him on a particular day in early August. On that same day he breakfasted and lunched as usual. He received no visitors. At teatime he asked the maid to bring him the laurel water and a glass. He then came downstairs with the empty and cleaned bottle and glass and went back up. The maid followed him and saw him fall. She called for help, but the doctor found him dead on his bed.[240]

The most reliable account of the time and manner of Price's death would seem to be contained in a letter sent by Godschall to Banks dated August 1, 1783:

> *Tho I don't love relating disastrous events I think you ought to be informed of the fate of poor Dr. Price. Dr. Spence our provincial Hippocrates was sent for to him last night. He found him in agonies, but got down some Ipecacuanha Wine as it was suspected he had taken Laurel Water. It however had no effect and he expired soon after: he had lately talked with the doctor about the effects of that water and was known to have distilled some. What a melancholy end of a man of five and twenty, but I attribute his fate to hereditary disease for his father died insane.*[241]

In a later letter to Banks Godschall elaborates on Price's possible insanity:

> *The poor man had many weeks before given many instances of his insanity, he had beaten a servant so badly much as to make him fear he had killed him and in a fit of despair attempted to take some Laurel Water when the maid snatched the phial out of his hand, another time he ran suddenly out of his room down the garden across a field to the brink of a chalk pit, ran back again without the least reason.*

---

240 Goettingisches Magazin der Wissenschaften und Litteratur, *3, 886-9.*

241 Bla. B.R.S. p. 9.

He was often low spirited, disoriented and in short so unfortunately
constituted as not likely to be happy himself or to make others so. [242]

Price's suicide was a shocking end to what had been a very rum business. "Many and various were the speculations hazarded on this strange affair," notes Chambers. Some imagined like Godschall that Price was insane, others that he had been hounded to death by jealous contemporaries, while many will have shared Chambers's view that it was "most probable that Price had in the first instance deceived himself, and then, by a natural sequence, attempted either wilfully or in ignorance to deceive others, and, subsequently discovering his error, had not the moral courage to confess openly and boldly that he had been mistaken."

Genius, scapegoat, charlatan, or lunatic? A man could possibly be all of these things, but which of these was Price? Despite his immediate fame and subsequent notoriety, James Price proves to be an elusive subject. Biographical material on him is disappointingly scanty and that which is easily found is often contradictory. His date of birth, which is usually given as 1752, is recorded as "1757/8" in the new Oxford Dictionary of National Biography. Godschall's assertion that Price was "a man of five and twenty" when he died informs or supports the latter date. In which case Price was only fourteen or fifteen when he entered Oxford in 1772, nineteen or twenty when he graduated with an MA, and only twenty-three or twenty-four when elected fellow of the RS in May 1781, making him one of the youngest fellows ever elected. The man was a prodigy. Richard Kirwan, some twenty-five years older than Price and one of the most respected chemists in the land, had himself only been elected fellow the previous year.

On top of his professional prestige, Price seems to have had an attractive personality and to have counted artists, politicians, and high-ranking courtiers amongst his friends, as well as eminent scientists. He was a man of good family and high social standing, whose portrait still hangs in the National Portrait Gallery. Shortly after his

---

242 Bla. B.R.S. p. 10.

election, Price had changed his name from Higginbotham to Price in order to qualify for a substantial legacy left him by a relative. Never poor, Price was now a man of considerable wealth. The first thing he did was to take a country house near Guildford in Surrey and furnish it with a well-equipped laboratory. These details do not paint the portrait of a man likely to resort to deception in order to establish for himself a reputation. The late eighteenth century was a time of great scientific discovery. A man with the qualities and means of Price had only to tinker around with things in his lab to be sure to come up with some interesting discoveries that would sustain his reputation. Moreover, Price was known to be an atheist. He did not even share the religious faith of the vast majority of his peers, far less the notable piety expressed by alchemical authors. There was nothing fey or even traditionalist about him. On the contrary, he seems to have been infused with the pioneering spirit of the age. Had Price expressed any interest in alchemy or even professed an open mind about the possibility of transmutation to the likes of Richard Kirwan he would have been viewed askance and would never have been sponsored for election to the Royal Society.

Nevertheless, upon taking up his new residence he apparently announced to friends that he planned to conduct some experiments using old alchemical texts, and within just a few months it appeared that he had succeeded where so many had failed. For centuries the legendary quest for the secret of turning base metals into gold had consumed the lives of countless philosophers, saints, chancers, puffers, princes, and popes in Europe, China, India, and the lands of Islam. And yet Price seemed to have succeeded in confecting this rarest of all substances: the fabled Philosophers' Stone. Or, at least, so it seemed to those of his contemporaries who either scorned or were not up to speed with the latest scientific theories. Prevailing scientific prejudice insists now, more so than then, that transmutation is impossible and since Price could not have been mistaken in his claims, he must therefore have been lying, in which case the public experiments were a series of elaborate and impressive conjuring acts. Having successfully fooled several distinguished companies that included five fellows of the RS (and no fewer than seven persons of sufficient importance to warrant inclusion in the latest *Dictionary of National Biography*), why should Price have been so wary of repeating the deception? Why should he be prepared to commit suicide rather than attempt it again? The RS chemists' complaint that they were insufficiently represented at the demonstrations is a red herring. Would an apparent performance of the Indian rope trick be any more believable if witnessed by a bunch of physicists? There is no suggestion that Price could have been using chemical tricks to dupe his audiences, producing substances that merely looked like gold or silver. The yellow metal produced in the experiment described above was professionally assayed and since we must, in all fairness, accept the evidence of the assayers, we must also accept that either gold and silver appeared legitimately in the crucibles or else they did not. There appears to have been no room for such old tricks as using a hollow stirring rod filled with powdered gold.[243] The only possibility for trickery would seem to be a highly dextrous sleight of hand. Are the RS chemists likely to have had greater powers of observation than any of the other witnesses?

There is no reason to believe so. It might be objected that the possibility of deception could at least have been reduced if Price had given up some of his powders for analysis. Although analytical techniques remained comparatively limited in those days, resistance to analysis would nevertheless have sustained the powders' mystery. His claim to have used up all the powder is unfortunate, but not necessarily implausible. What is most unsatisfactory is that, having finally agreed to produce another batch of the powders, he failed to do so. What's more, he appears to have sought help from German sources. None being apparently forthcoming, he distils a deadly poison and writes a will in the professed belief that death is near. In the last weeks of his life he exhibits some very odd behaviour and is considered by Godschall to have succumbed to hereditary madness. Finally, having allegedly invited the RS to attend a demonstration to take place in

---

243 As infamously employed by Thurneisser in the late sixteenth century.

early August, he commits suicide on the last day of July. The verdict appears inescapable: James Price, charlatan and lunatic.

That would appear to be that. Those familiar with alchemical history and sympathetic to its philosophy and traditions, however, may yet nurture nagging doubts about the matter. A clue to an alternative theory is contained in the first edition of Price's "Account" (Banks's copy of which is preserved in the British Library), in which Price provides a summary of a very rare paper written by the chemist's hero Robert Boyle, titled "A Degradation of Gold," which describes an experiment demonstrating an apparent reverse transmutation. Boyle claims that this was achieved using a tiny amount of a red powder presented him by a foreigner. Those acquainted with transmutation histories will immediately spot one of their most significant and enduring motifs: the anonymous adept providing the eminent scientist with a fragment of the Philosophers' Stone.

As we have already seen, several well documented transmutation stories, such as that of Van Helmont, begin with the unexpected appearance of a stranger in possession of the powder of projection. One of the most famous is that recorded by the distinguished seventeenth-century physician Johann Schweitzer, known as Helvetius (1630–1709), who became physician to the Prince of Orange. The noted science historian (and sceptic) E. J. Holmyard writes of Helvetius that as "a man of culture, education, and discernment, he can scarcely be suspected of having lied, or of wilfully misreporting the remarkable events he describes. In most accounts of 'transmutations' it is not difficult to perceive where trickery could have entered, but in the case of Helvetius no one has yet discovered the loophole." [244]

Helvetius recounts that a stranger, who he refers to as Elias the Artist, came to his house in The Hague in December 1666 and engaged him in discussion, suggesting that he had come in order to convince him of the reality of the Philosophers' Stone. He himself had

---

244 Holmyard, p. 259.

been instructed in the alchemical arts by an anonymous master and shown how to confect the stone. The stranger produced some lumps of the fabled substance and allowed Helvetius to handle them, but could not be constrained to perform a transmutation. He promised, however, to return, and three weeks later he reappeared. This time he gave the physician a tiny crumb of the mysterious matter, saying that it could transmute a little more than half an ounce of lead. He promised to return the next day and perform a transmutation, but Helvetius never saw him again. Perplexed and disconsolate, he was inclined to believe that the stranger had been an impostor after all, but his wife persuaded him to attempt a transmutation with the crumb he had been given, which he performed according to the method he had gleaned from Elias. They were astonished when the addition of the powder to half an ounce of molten lead instantly transmuted it into gold. Rumour of the wonder circulated quickly and many illustrious citizens came to visit and hear tell of the miracle, including the Assay-Master of the province, who persuaded Helvetius to allow him to put the alchemical gold to various tests. These tests, which Helvetius describes in useful detail, resulted in the further transmutation of two scruples of silver into gold.[245]

Between 1602 and 1604, a mysterious wandering adept performed a series of transmutations in Holland, Italy, Germany, and Switzerland, some of which were well-documented. He became known as the Cosmopolite and was believed to be English or Scottish. He often used the name Alexander Seton, although Seton, being an anagram of "stone," is most likely pseudonymous. His grand tour came to an end when he was imprisoned and brutally tortured by Prince Christian of Saxony, who wished to prize from him the secret of the Stone. He was nearly dead by the time he was daringly rescued by an aspiring Moravian alchemist called Michał Sędziwój (better known as Michael

---

245 John Frederick Helvetius: *The Golden Calf, Which the World Adores, and Desires ...*, London, 1670. http://www.levity.com/alchemy/helvet.html.

Sendivogius), to whom he bequeathed his remaining supply of powder before dying shortly afterwards (although he was apparently sighted in Basel two years later).

Sendivogius performed several transmutations, including one commemorated in a famous painting before the Holy Roman Emperor Rudolph II at his Hermetic court in Prague. He was never able to confect the Stone himself, but went on to make several important scientific discoveries leading to the identification of oxygen.[246]

But what of these mysterious adepts? Elias Artista, also known to Rosicrucians as Helie Artiste, is a legendary messianic figure who Paracelsus prophesied would transform the world through alchemy. Helvetius, being a Paracelsian, probably gave his stranger that name himself in ignorance of his true identity.[247] The true identity of the Cosmopolite also seems destined to remain a mystery, but one episode in his European tour of 1603 will bring us back to the story of Dr. Price.

In the summer of 1603 a stranger turned up at the house of a Strasbourg goldsmith called Gustenhover and asked permission to use his workshop. The goldsmith agreed and left him to it. Before departing a while later, the stranger presented Gustenhover with a small amount of red powder and showed him how to use it to make gold. Gustenhover couldn't resist performing a transmutation in front of his friends and neighbours, foolishly allowing everyone to think that he had discovered the secret himself. The news of this wonder ran riot throughout Strasbourg, resulting in a visit from the city council, who demanded a demonstration. Gustenhover not only acquiesced, he invited the delegation to perform the miracle themselves. News soon reached the fascinated ears of Emperor Rudolph who immediately summoned the goldsmith to court. Gustenhover had by this

---

246 Cf. Zbigniew Szydło: *Water which does not wet hands. The alchemy of Michael Sendivogius.* London-Warsaw, 1994.

247 Paracelsus's prophecy was based on astrological patterns due to unfold in 1603.

time squandered all his powder and, when threatened with imprisonment if he did not make more, broke down and admitted that he had not confected the powder himself nor had he any idea how to do so. His protestations availed him nothing and he was locked up in Rudolph's White Tower until the end of his miserable days.

When pressed by Banks to reveal the means of composition of his powders, Price claimed that he could not do so because he had been given the recipe for the white powder in the strictest confidence by an unnamed person. The red powder he said had been made from the white powder. According to alchemical convention this would figure. The white powder, also known as the White Lion and the Elixir, transmutes base metals into silver. By further careful processes, including sustained heating in the sealed alembic, the Elixir becomes the Stone, the red powder that transmutes base metals into gold. Who was it who had given Price the precious recipe? And if he had been able to make it once, why could he not make it again? When he had initially refused to even try, Price had objected that the process, as well as being expensive and laborious, was "injurious to the health." From the detailed descriptions that Price gives of his experiments, it is clear that he is more than likely to have suffered from mercury poisoning. The vapour given off by heated mercury is extremely toxic and all too readily absorbed into the blood stream. Constant exposure over a period of months would have made him very vulnerable to chronic poisoning. According to the US Environmental Protection Agency, "People with chronic mercury poisoning often have wide swings of mood, becoming irritable, frightened, depressed or excited very quickly for no apparent reason. Such people may become extremely upset at any criticism, lose all self-confidence, and become apathetic. Hallucinations, memory loss and inability to concentrate can occur." [248]

---

248 http://publichealth.uic.edu/sites/default/files//public/documents/great-lakes /other/HARTS_library/mercury.txt.

These symptoms could hardly more closely mirror Price's behaviour as described by Godschall. The memory loss and inability to concentrate could possibly account for Price's failure to reproduce the powders, but it would be more in keeping with alchemical tradition if, like Boyle, Helvetius, Gustenhover, and Van Helmont, Price had in fact been given a quantity of the white powder by a person who subsequently disappeared from his life, probably a stranger, who showed or told him how to convert it into the red powder, but not how to make it from scratch. Price, perhaps out of vanity, made the same mistake as Gustenhover and claimed to have confected the powders himself. Like Gustenhover he paid severely for his imposture.

Despair and mercury-madness conspired to drive him to suicide. Had he been honest with his colleagues he would probably have fared no worse than Van Helmont or Helvetius. If he had performed his transmutations in full transparency in open collaboration with peers such as Kirwan, Joseph Priestley, and even Lavoisier across the channel, not only would his reputation have survived unscathed, but the evolving atomic theories might have been less triumphantly delivered. The modern chemists may have done better to hearken to those words of Robert Boyle, the founder of their science, with which Price had prefaced his "Account":

> We may among other things learn from it this lesson, that we ought not to be so forward as many men otherwise of great parts are wont to be, in prescribing narrow limits to the power of Nature and Art, and in condemning and deriding all those that pretend to, or believe, uncommon things in Chymistry, as either Cheats or Credulous.[249]

---

249 Robert Boyle: *Of a Degradation of Gold made by an anti-elixir: a strange chymical narrative*. London, 1678.

ALCHEMY TODAY

The Psychology of Alchemy

Following the tragedy of James Price, the study of alchemy was confined to occultists and historians of science. In the early 1920s, however, the pioneering psychologist and former student and colleague of Sigmund Freud, Carl Gustav Jung started studying alchemy when he realised that many of its key symbols were surfacing in the dreams of his patients. His own nervous breakdown a few years earlier had already made him aware of a mythic realm of what he called archetypes—powerful images arising from the "universal unconscious" shared by all humans. His studies and lectures on alchemical symbolism were collated in his book *Psychology and Alchemy*. Richly illustrated with a great number of previously unpublished alchemical images, it was published in 1944 and has remained in print ever since. Its influence was considerable and almost single-handedly presented alchemy as a subject worthy of profound investigation.

Jung established that the body of alchemical works presents an astonishing consistency and complexity of ideas and images—in spite of its apparently riddling and often contradictory language. This, he contends can be no accident: "A symbolism as rich as that of alchemy invariably owes its existence to some adequate cause, never to mere whim or play of fancy." The alchemists, he realised, were neither deluding, nor simply amusing, themselves. They were on to something of enormous significance.

Jung's study of alchemy inspired his concept of "individuation"—man's liberation from his own psychic labyrinth, the resolution of the personal psycho-drama. His work with Freud on sexual psychology gave him insights into the erotic aspect of alchemy with its emphasis on the union of opposites—the *Chemical Wedding*. While many alchemists and mystics reproach Jung for confining alchemy to purely psychological models, it is fair to say that he recognized that alchemy is concerned not just with the resolution or redemption of man alone, but also of nature itself. His main interest lay in how the psyche responds to the riddle of existence rather than the nature and purpose of Creation. Jung's subject is the psychology of man, not life. The alchemist's subject is life itself and his relationship with it; the intense and intimate study and experience of which reveals the alchemist and life to be the same thing, the All in One.

In this respect, Jung's view of alchemy is limited to a psychological viewpoint, although Manfred Junius told me that he heard on good authority that in the latter years of his life Jung set up a laboratory for practical work.

Jung's other major books on alchemy are *Alchemical Studies* and the monumental *Mysterium Coniunctionis*, which explores the nature of opposites, particularly the polarity of male and female as represented in alchemy by Sun and Moon and the Red King and White Queen. He also elucidates the understanding that the world is a reflection of the inner psyche, that in a very real sense each individual is responsible for their experience of the outside world. This is the key to understanding the true significance of man as microcosm—As Above, So Below; As Within, So Without.

Of particular interest to me is Jung's therioanthropic experience of becoming a lion-headed deity, which he recounts in his confessional *Liber Novum*, also known as the Red Book, which was published after his death. Jung identifies this lion-headed entity with Mithras / Aion, the personification of eternal life, the ancient Greek prototype of which is Phanes, the "first-born" deity of the Orphic mystery religion, described in the Derveni Papyrus as "the first-born king, the neverend one; and upon him all the immortals grew, blessed gods and goddesses and rivers and lovely springs and everything else that had then been born; and he himself became the sole one."

Phanes is generally depicted emerging from an egg-shaped opening, which is bordered in several instances with the signs of the zodiac. Like Mithras / Aion, Phanes is depicted with wings and encircled by a serpent. Two Mithraic reliefs (one discovered at Hadrian's Wall) show Mithras emerging from a zodiacal egg, while a Greek inscription found in Rome includes a dedication "To Zeus Helios Mithras Phanes, by the priest and Father Venustus together with the attendants of the god." In Orphism Phanes is also equated with the dying and reborn Dionysus. Aion is also identified with Dionysus by various Neoplatonic writers, while both Phanes and Aion are associated with the dualistic concept of the Demiurge. In this experience Jung would seem to have found himself at the very heart of a primordial mystery tradition that stretches back through the Orphic mysteries at least as far as the Lion Man 44,000 years ago.

The Redeeming of Alchemy

Over the course of the twentieth century, alchemy experienced a revival that would have been unimaginable during the nineteenth century. The 1968 edition of the *Encyclopaedia Britannica*, which I grew up with, accorded alchemy some three thousand words; up from the thirty-eight-word put-down from the first edition exactly two hundred years earlier. There can be no doubt that Jung has played the major role in this renaissance, but there have been other significant contributors in different fields.

During the 1920s to 1940s, Dr. Lili Kolisko, a colleague of the philosopher and mystic Rudolf Steiner, undertook a series of experiments to validate his theories regarding subtle forces at work in plants and soil. She then used a form of chromatography called capillary dynamolisis, which validated the alchemist's ancient association of the seven classical planets with their corresponding metals—sun/gold, moon/silver, etc.[250] These experiments were successfully repeated by others, including the English hermeticist Nick Kollerstrom.

In 1962 the French scientist Louis Kervran, then director of conferences at the University of Paris, published a book called *Biological Transmutations*, which described a series of experiments showing that low energy transmutation of certain elements is a biological reality in both plants and animals, including humans. Physicists were, of course, highly sceptical, but Kervran's work was subsequently confirmed by Japanese, French, and Swiss scientists. In the '90s Oliver Costa de Beauregard, professor of theoretical physics at the Institut de Physique Théorique Henri Poincaré (Faculty of Sciences, Paris), evolved a theory that places these discoveries within the framework of modern physics.

Concurrent with scientific validations of alchemical theories, there has been a resurgence of practical medicinal alchemy, based in particular on the teachings of Paracelsus. The most significant figure behind this fresh impetus has been the Austrian alchemist Albert Riedel, known as Frater Albertus. He attended a series of alchemy lessons provided by AMORC, the California-based Rosicrucian society. In 1960 he published *The Alchemist's Handbook,* providing straightforward instructions for the product of Paracelsian plant elixirs, made with modern laboratory apparatus. He founded the *Paracelsus Re-*

---

250 If you dip a length of blotting paper into a bottle of ink, the paper will draw the ink up and gradually separate out into different shades or colours according to the particle sizes and specific gravity of the ingredients. This is basic chromatography. I whiled away many a dull moment in this way at the Dragon School.

search Society in Salt Lake City, teaching alchemy to students at a very low cost and producing a quarterly magazine from 1960 to 1972. He gave lectures and seminars throughout the USA and in various other countries, including Europe and Australia. He made contact with other practising alchemists and gave hundreds of people their first real introduction to alchemy, including many of the best contemporary teachers. He emphasised the spiritual and medicinal virtues of alchemy.

Following Frater Albertus's death in 1984, former students of his, looking for another teacher, contacted Jean Dubuis, a French alchemist and nuclear scientist, who ran an organization called *Les Philosophes de la Nature* providing courses in herbal and mineral alchemy as well as Kabbalah. Jean Dubuis donated his lessons to the American students who had them translated into English and formed The Philosophers of Nature, publishing a quarterly magazine and holding annual seminars. The group is currently less active, but still provides courses and seminar videos.

One of the most widely respected alchemists of recent years was Professor Manfred Junius, who was born in Germany in 1929. He spent thirty-five years in India practising ayurvedic medicine, which led to his initiation into Brahminic alchemy, which emphasises medicinal work. Upon his return to Europe in the 1970s he studied Western alchemy with the Italian Augusto Pancaldi, who soon encouraged him to attempt the *Circulatum Minus*, a notoriously difficult plant work, which had not been perfected since the pseudonymous Baron Urbigerus published his treatise on the subject in 1690. Unconvinced of his readiness, Junius was nevertheless persuaded and achieved success after about six months of work, producing a clear, colourless liquid with certain remarkable qualities that defy scientific explanation. In a matter of minutes it separates out the soluble properties of fresh plant matter *without* dissolving them into itself, this despite the fact that it consists predominantly of plant alcohol. Such a peculiar solvent is unknown to modern chemistry. It can be used over and over again with any variety of plants without being affected in any way. It remains an extremely difficult work, but with Junius's help a further six individuals have since achieved the same success.

Junius's book *The Practical Handbook of Plant Alchemy*[251] is a modern classic that is recommended to anyone who wishes to explore laboratory alchemy. There is no better place to start. With the help and encouragement of the South Australian Department of Trade and Industry Professor Junius established a commercial laboratory, Australerba, producing spagyric medicines, herb honeys, and tonics. It is still in operation and exports its products around the world.

In Germany, where alchemy survived more continuously than elsewhere, there is an alchemy association with about 120 members, a good number of whom hold practical workshops on a fairly regular basis. There are several commercial laboratories that have been selling spagyric remedies for as long as eighty years, including Phönix Laboratorium GmbH near Stuttgart and SOLUNA Heilmittel GmbH in Donauwörth. SOLUNA has continued the work of an important German alchemist and poet called Alexander von Bernus, who was first encouraged to establish a laboratory by Rudolf Steiner. Von Bernus's book *Alchemie und Heilkunst* is an inspired work that I hope to finish translating one day.

---

251 Third edition published under the new title of *Spagyrics* by Healing Arts Press, Rochester, Vermont, 2007.

APPENDICES

Appendix 1

Extract from Plato's Critias, Benjamin Jowett translation, 1860s.

O Solon, Solon, you Hellenes (Greeks) are but children, and there is never an old man who is a Hellene. Solon, hearing this, said, "What do you mean?" "I mean to say," he replied, "that in mind you (Greeks) are all young; there is no old opinion handed down among you by ancient tradition, nor any science which is hoary with age. And I will tell you the reason of this: there have been, and there will be again, many destructions of mankind arising out of many causes. There is a story which even you have preserved, that once upon a time Phaethon, the son of Helios, having yoked the steeds in his father's chariot, because he was not able to drive them in the path of his father, burnt up all that was upon the earth, and was himself destroyed by a thunderbolt. Now, this has the form of a myth, but really signifies a declination of the bodies moving around the earth and in the heavens, and a great conflagration of things upon the earth recurring at long intervals of time: when this happens, those who live upon the mountains and in dry and lofty places are more liable to destruction than those who dwell by rivers or on the sea-shore; and from this calamity the Nile, who is our never-failing saviour, saves and delivers us. When, on the other hand, the gods purge the earth with

259

a deluge of water, among you herdsmen and shepherds on the mountains are the survivors, whereas those of you who live in cities are carried by the rivers into the sea; but in this country neither at that time nor at any other does the water come from above on the fields, having always a tendency to come up from below, for which reason the things preserved here are said to be the oldest. The fact is, that wherever the extremity of winter frost or of summer sun does not prevent, the human race is always increasing at times, and at other times diminishing in numbers. And whatever happened either in your country or in ours, or in any other region of which we are informed—if any action which is noble or great, or in any other way remarkable has taken place, all that has been written down of old, and is preserved in our temples; whereas you and other nations are just being provided with letters and the other things which States require; and then, at the usual period, the stream from heaven descends like a pestilence, and leaves only those of you who are destitute of letters and education; and thus you have to begin all over again as children, and know nothing of what happened in ancient times, either among us or among yourselves. As for those genealogies of yours which you have recounted to us, Solon, they are no better than the tales of children; for, in the first place, you remember one deluge only, whereas there were many of them; and, in the next place, you do not know that there dwelt in your land the fairest and noblest race of men which ever lived, of whom you and your whole city are but a seed or remnant. And this was unknown to you, because for many generations the survivors of that destruction died and made no sign."

Appendix 2
Porphyry: The Life of Pythagoras
Translated by Kenneth Sylvan Guthrie, 1920.

1. Many think that Pythagoras was the son of Mnesarchus, but they differ as to the latter's race; some thinking him a Samian, while Neanthes, in the fifth book of his Fables states he was a Syrian, from the city of Tyre. As a famine had arisen in Samos, Mnesarchus went thither to trade, and was naturalized there. There also was born his son Pythagoras, who

early manifested studiousness, but was later taken to Tyre, and there entrusted to the Chaldeans, whose doctrines he imbibed. Thence he returned to Ionia, where he first studied under the Syrian Pherecydes, then also under Hermodamas the Creophylian who at that time was an old man residing in Samos.

2. Neanthes says that others hold that his father was a Tyrrhenian, of those who inhabit Lemnos, and that while on a trading trip to Samos was there naturalized. On sailing to Italy, Mnesarchus took the youth Pythagoras with him. Just at this time this country was greatly flourishing. Neanthes adds that Pythagoras had two older brothers, Eunostus and Tyrrhenus. But Apollonius, in his book about Pythagoras, affirms that his mother was Pythais, a descendant, of Ancaeus, the founder of Samos. Apollonius adds that he was said to be the off-spring of Apollo and Pythais, on the authority of Mnesarchus; and a Samian poet sings:

"Pythais, of all Samians the most fair;
Jove-loved Pythagoras to Phoebus bare!"

This poet says that Pythagoras studied not only under Pherecydes and Hermodamas, but also under Anaximander.

3. The Samian Duris, in the second book of his "Hours," writes that his son was named Arimnestus, that he was the teacher of Democritus, and that on returning from banishment, he suspended a brazen tablet in the temple of Hera, a tablet two feet square, bearing this inscription:

"Me, Arimnestus, who much learning traced,
Pythagoras's beloved son here placed."

This tablet was removed by Simus, a musician, who claimed the canon graven thereon, and published it as his own. Seven arts were engraved, but when Simus took away one, the others were destroyed.

4. It is said that by Theano, a Cretan, the daughter of Pythonax, he had a son, Thelauges and a daughter, Myia; to whom some add Arignota, whose Pythagorean writings are still extant. Timaeus relates that Pythagoras's daughter, while a maiden, took precedence among the maidens in Crotona, and when a wife, among married men. The Crotonians made her house a temple of Demeter, and the neighbouring street they called a museum.

5. Lycus, in the fourth book of his *Histories,* noting different opinions about his country, says, "Unless you happen to know the country and the city which Pythagoras was a citizen, will remain a mere matter of conjecture. Some say he was a Samian, others, a Phliasian, others a Metapontine.

6. As to his knowledge, it is said that he learned the mathematical sciences from the Egyptians, Chaldeans and Phoenicians; for of old the Egyptians excelled, in geometry, the Phoenicians in numbers and proportions, and the Chaldeans of astronomical theorems, divine rites, and worship of the Gods; other secrets concerning the course of life he received and learned from the Magi.

7. These accomplishments are the more generally known, but the rest are less celebrated. Moreover Eudoxus, in the second book of his *Description of the Earth,* writes that Pythagoras used the greatest purity, and was shocked at all bloodshed and killing; that he not only abstained from animal food, but never in any way approached butchers or hunters. Antiphon, in his book on illustrious Virtuous Men praises his perseverance while he was in Egypt, saying, "Pythagoras, desiring to become acquainted with the institutions of Egyptian priests, and diligently endeavoring to participate therein, requested the Tyrant Polycrates to write to Amasis, the King of Egypt, his friend and former host, to procure him initiation. Coming to Amasis, he was given letters to the priests; of Heliopolis, who sent him on to those of Memphis, on the pretense that they were the more ancient. On the same pretense, he was sent on from Memphis to Diospolis.

8. From fear of the King the latter priests dared not make excuses; but thinking that he would desist from his purpose as result of great difficulties, enjoined on him very hard precepts, entirely different from the institutions of the Greeks. These he performed so readily that he won their admiration, and they permitted him to sacrifice to the Gods, and to acquaint himself with all their sciences, a favor theretofore never granted to a foreigner.

9. Returning to Ionia, he opened in his own country, a school, which is even now called Pythagoras's Semicircles, in which the Samians meet to deliberate about matters of common interest. Outside the city he made a cave adapted to the study of his philosophy, in which he abode day and night, discoursing with a few of his associates. He was now forty years old, says Aristoxenus. Seeing that Polycrates's government was becoming so violent that soon a free man would become a victim of his tyranny, he journeyed towards Italy.

10. Diogenes, in his treatise about the *Incredible Things Beyond Thule,* has treated Pythagoras's affairs so carefully, that I think his account should not be omitted. He says that the Tyrrhenian Mnesarchus was of the race of the inhabitants of Lemnos, Imbros and Scyros and that he departed thence to visit many cities and various lands. During his journeys he found an infant lying under a large, tall poplar tree. On approaching, he observed it lay on its back, looking steadily without winking at the sun. In its mouth was a little slender reed, like a pipe; through which the child was being nourished by the dew-drops that distilled from the tree. This great wonder prevailed upon him to take the child, believing it to be of a divine origin. The child was fostered by a native of that country, named Androcles, who later on adopted him, and entrusted to him the management of affairs. On becoming wealthy, Mnesarchus educated the boy, naming him Astrasus, and rearing him with his own three sons, Eunestus, Tyrrhenus, and Pythagoras; which boy, as I have said, Androcles adopted.

11. He sent the boy to a lute-player, a wrestler and a painter. Later he sent him to Anaximander at Miletus, to learn geometry and astronomy. Then Pythagoras visited the Egyptians, the Arabians, the Chaldeans and the Hebrews, from whom he acquired experteery in the interpretation of dreams, and he was the first to use frankincense in the worship of divinities.

12. In Egypt he lived with the priests, and learned the language and wisdom of the Egyptians, and three kinds of letters, the epistolic, the hieroglyphic, and symbolic, whereof one imitates the common way of speaking, while the others express the sense by allegory and parable. In Arabia he conferred with the King. In Babylon he associated with the other Chaldeans, especially attaching himself to Zabratus, by whom he was purified from the pollutions of this past life, and taught the things which a virtuous man ought to be free. Likewise he heard lectures about Nature, and the principles of wholes. It was from his stay among these foreigners that Pythagoras acquired the greater part of his wisdom.

13. Astraeus was by Mnesarchus entrusted to Pythagoras, who received him, and after studying his physiognomy and the emotions of his body, instructed him. First he accurately investigated the science about the nature of man, discerning the disposition of everyone he met. None

was allowed to become his friend or associate without being examined in facial expression and disposition.

14. Pythagoras had another youthful disciple from Thrace. Zamolxis was he named because he was born wrapped in a bear's skin, in Thracian called Zalmus. Pythagoras loved him, and instructed him in sublime speculations concerning sacred rites, and the nature of the Gods. Some say this youth was named Thales, and that the barbarians worshipped him as Hercules.

15. Dionysiphanes says that he was a servant of Pythagoras, who fell into the hands of thieves and by them was branded. Then when Pythagoras was persecuted and banished, (he followed him) binding up his forehead on account of the scars. Others say that, the name Zamolxis signifies a stranger or foreigner. Pherecydes, in Delos fell sick; and Pythagoras attended him until he died, and performed his funeral rites. Pythagoras then, longing to be with Hermodamas the Creophylian, returned to Samos. After enjoying his society, Pythagoras trained the Samian athlete Eurymenes, who though he was of small stature, conquered at Olympia through his surpassing knowledge of Pythagoras' wisdom. While according to ancient custom the other athletes fed on cheese and figs, Eurymenes, by the advice of Pythagoras, fed daily on flesh, which endued his body with great strength. Pythagoras imbued him with his wisdom, exhorting him to go into the struggle, not for the sake of victory, but the exercise; that he should gain by the training, avoiding the envy resulting from victory. For the victors, are not always pure, though decked with leafy crowns.

16. Later, when the Samians were oppressed with the tyranny of Polycrates, Pythagoras saw that life in such a state was unsuitable for a philosopher, and so planned to travel to Italy. At Delphi he inscribed an elegy on the tomb of Apollo, declaring that Apollo was the son of Silenus, but was slain by Pytho, and buried in the place called Triops, so named from the local mourning for Apollo by the three daughters of Triopas.

17. Going to Crete, Pythagoras besought initiation from the priests of Morgos, one of the Idaean Dactyli, by whom he was purified with the meteoritic thunder-stone. In the morning he lay stretched upon his face by the seaside; at night, he lay beside a river, crowned with a black lamb's woollen wreath. Descending into the Idaean cave, wrapped in

black wool, he stayed there twenty-seven days, according to custom; he sacrificed to Zeus, and saw the throne which there is yearly made for him. On Zeus's tomb, Pythagoras inscribed an epigram, "Pythagoras to Zeus," which begins: "Zeus deceased here lies, whom men call Jove."

18. When he reached Italy he stopped at Crotona. His presence was that of a free man, tall, graceful in speech and gesture, and in all things else. Dicaearchus relates that the arrival of this great traveller, endowed with all the advantages of nature, and prosperously guided by fortune, produced on the Crotonians so great an impression, that he won the esteem of the elder magistrates, by his many and excellent discourses. They ordered him to exhort the young men, and then to the boys who flocked out of the school to hear him; and lastly to the women, who came together on purpose.

19. Through this he achieved great reputation, he drew great audiences from the city, not only of men, but also of women, among whom was an especially illustrious person named Theano. He also drew audiences from among the neighbouring barbarians, among whom were magnates and kings. What he told his audiences cannot be said with certainty, for he enjoined silence upon his hearers. But the following is a matter of general information. He taught that the soul was immortal and that after death it transmigrated into other animated bodies. After certain specified periods, the same events occur again; that nothing was entirely new; that all animated beings were kin, and should be considered as belonging to one great family. Pythagoras was the first one to introduce these teachings into Greece.

20. His speech was so persuasive that, according to Nicomachus, in one address made on first landing in Italy, he made more than two thousand adherents. Out of desire to live with him, these built a large auditorium, to which both women and boys were admitted. (Foreign visitors were so many that) they built whole cities, settling that whole region of Italy now known as Magna Grecia. His ordinances and laws were by them received as divine precepts, and without them would do nothing. Indeed, they ranked him among the divinities. They held all property in common. They ranked him among the divinities, and whenever they communicated to each other some choice bit of his philosophy, from

which physical truths could always be deduced, they would swear by the *Tetractys*, adjuring Pythagoras as a divine witness, in the words.

"I call to witness him who to our souls expressed the Tetractys, eternal Nature's fountain-spring."

21. During his travels in Italy and Sicily he founded various cities subjected one to another, both of long standing, and recently. By his disciples, some of whom were found in every city, he infused into them an aspiration for liberty; thus restoring to freedom Crotona, Sybaris, Catana, Rhegium, Himera, Agrigentum, Tauromenium, and others, on whom he imposed laws through Charondas the Catanean, and Zaleucus the Locrian, which resulted in a long era of good government, emulated by all their neighbours. Simichus the tyrant of the Centorupini, on hearing Pythagoras's discourse, abdicated his rule and divided his property between his sister and the citizens.

22. According to Aristoxenus, some Lucanians, Messapians, Peucetians and Romans came to him. He rooted out all dissensions, not only among his disciples and their successors, for many ages, but among all the cities of Italy and Sicily, both internally and externally. For he would continuously say, "We ought, to the best of our ability avoid, and even with fire and sword extirpate from the body, sickness; from the soul, ignorance; from the belly, luxury; from a city, sedition; from a family, discord; and from all things excess."

23. If we may credit what ancient and trustworthy writers have related of him, he exerted an influence even over irrational animals. The Daunian bear, who had committed extensive depredations in the neighbourhood, he seized; and after having patted her for a while, and given her barley and fruits, he made her swear never again to touch a living creature, and then released her. She immediately hid herself in the woods and the hills, and from that time on never attacked any irrational animal.

24. At Tarentum, in a pasture, seeing an ox [reaping] beans, he went to the herdsman, and advised him to tell the ox to abstain from beans. The countryman mocked him, proclaiming his ignorance of the ox-language. So Pythagoras himself went and whispered in the ox's ear. Not only did the bovine at once desist from his diet of beans, but would never touch any thenceforward, though he survived many years near

Hera's temple at Tarentum, until very old; being called the sacred ox, and eating any food given him.

25. While at the Olympic games, he was discoursing with his friends about auguries, omens, and divine signs, and how men of true piety do receive messages from the Gods. Flying over his head was an eagle, who stopped, and came down to Pythagoras. After stroking her awhile, he released her. Meeting with some fishermen who were drawing in their nets heavily laden with fishes from the deep, he predicted the exact number of fish they had caught. The fishermen said that if his estimate was accurate they would do whatever he commanded. They counted them accurately, and found the number correct. He then bade them return the fish alive into the sea; and, what is more wonderful, not one of them died, although they had been out of the water a considerable time. He paid them and left.

26. Many of his associates he reminded of the lives lived by their souls before it was bound to the body, and by irrefutable arguments demonstrated that he had bean Euphorbus, the son of Panthus. He specially praised the following verses about himself, and sang them to the lyre most elegantly:

"The shining circlets of his golden hair;
Which even the Graces might be proud to wear,
Instarred with gems and gold, bestrew the shore,
With dust dishonored, and deformed with gore.
As the young olive, in some sylvan scene,
Crowned by fresh fountains with celestial green,
Lifts the gay head, in snowy flowerets fair,
And plays and dances to the gentle air,
When lo, a whirlwind from high heaven invades,
The tender plant, and withers all its shades;
It lies uprooted from its genial head,
A lovely ruin now defaced and dead.
Thus young, thus beautiful, Euphorbus lay,
While the fierce Spartan tore his arms away."
(Pope, Homer's *Iliad*, Book 17).

27. The stories about the shield of this Phrygian Euphorbus being at Mycenae dedicated to Argive Hera, along with other Trojan spoils, shall here

be omitted as being of too popular a nature. It is said that the river Ca-icasus, while he with many of his associates was passing over it, spoke to him very clearly, "Hail, Pythagoras!" Almost unanimous is the re-port that on one and the same day he was present at Metapontum in Italy, and at Tauromenium in Sicily, in each place conversing with his friends, though the places are separated by many miles, both at sea and land, demanding many days' journey.

28. It is well known that he showed his golden thigh to Abaris the Hyper-borean, to confirm him in the opinion that he was the Hyperborean Apollo, whose priest Abaris was. A ship was coming into the harbor, and his friends expressed the wish to own the goods it contained. "Then," said Pythagoras, "you would own a corpse!" On the ship's ar-rival, this was found to be the true state of affairs. Of Pythagoras many other more wonderful and divine things are persistently and unani-mously related, so that we have no hesitation in saying never was more attributed to any man, nor was any more eminent.

29. Verified predictions of earthquakes are handed down, also that he immediately chased a pestilence, suppressed violent winds and hail, calmed storms both on rivers and on seas, for the comfort and safe pas-sage of his friends. As their poems attest, the like was often performed by Empedocles, Epimenides and Abaris, who had learned the art of do-ing these things from him. Empedocles, indeed, was surnamed Alex-anemos, as the chaser of winds; Epimenides, Cathartes, the lustrator. Abaris was called Aethrobates, the walker in air; for he was carried in the air on an arrow of the Hyperborean Apollo, over rivers, seas and inaccessible places. It is believed that this was the method employed by Pythagoras when on the same day he discoursed with his friends at Metapontum and Tauromenium.

30. He soothed the passions of the soul and body by rhythms, songs and in-cantations. These he adapted and applied to his friends. He himself could hear the harmony of the Universe, and understood the universal music of the spheres, and of the stars which move in concert with them, and which we cannot hear because of the limitations of our weak nature. This is testified to by these characteristic verses of Empedocles:

"Amongst these was one in things sublimest skilled,
His mind with all the wealth of learning filled,

Whatever sages did invent, he sought;
And whilst his thoughts were on this work intent,
All things existent, easily he viewed,
Through ten or twenty ages making search."

31. The words "sublimest things," and "he surveyed all existent things," and "the wealth of the mind," and the like, are indicative of Pythagoras' constitution of body, mind, seeing, hearing and understanding, which was exquisite, and surpassingly accurate. Pythagoras affirmed that the nine Muses were constituted by the sounds made by the seven planets, the sphere of the fixed stars, and that which is opposed to our earth, called "anti-earth." He called *Mnemosyne,* or Memory, the composition, symphony and connexion of then all, which is eternal and unbegotten as being composed of all of them.

32. Diogenes, setting forth his daily routine of living, relates that he advised all men to avoid ambition and vain-glory, which chiefly excite envy, and to shun the presences of crowds. He himself held morning conferences at his residence, composing his soul with the music of the lute, and singing certain old paeans of Thales. He also sang verses of Homer and Hesiod, which seemed to soothe the mind. He danced certain dances which he conceived conferred on the body agility and health. Walks he took not promiscuously, but only in company of one or two companions, in temples or sacred groves, selecting the quietest and pleasantest places.

33. His friends he loved exceedingly, being the first to declare that the goods of friends are common, and that a friend was another self. While they were in good health he always conversed with them; if they were sick, he nursed them; if they were afflicted in mind, he solaced them, some by incantations and magic charms, others by music. He had prepared songs for the diseases of the body, by the singing of which he cured the sick. He had also some that caused oblivion of sorrow, mitigation of anger and destruction of lust.

34. As to food, his breakfast was chiefly of honey; at dinner he used bread made of millet, barley or herbs, raw and boiled. Only rarely did he eat the flesh of victims; nor did he take this from every part of the anatomy. When he intended to sojourn in the sanctuaries of the divinities, he would eat no more than was necessary to still hunger and thirst. To

quiet hunger, he made a mixture of poppy seed and sesame, the skin of a sea-onion, well washed, till entirely drained of the outward juice; of the flower of the daffodil, and the leaves of mallows, of paste of barley and pea; taking an equal weight of which, and chopping it small, with Hymettian honey he made it into mass. Against thirst he took the seed of cucumbers, and the best dried raisins, extracting the seeds, and the flower of coriander, and the seeds of mallows, purslane, scraped cheese, wheat meal and cream; these he made up with wild honey.

35. He claimed that this diet had, by Demeter, been taught to Hercules, when he was sent into the Libyan deserts. This preserved his body in an unchanging condition; not at one time well, and at another time sick, nor at one time fat, and at another lean. Pythagoras's countenance showed the same constancy was in his soul also. For he was neither more elated by pleasure, nor dejected by grief, and no one ever saw him either rejoicing or mourning.

36. When Pythagoras sacrificed to the Gods, he did not use offensive profusion, but offered no more than barley bread, cakes and myrrh; least of all, animals, unless perhaps cocks and pigs. When he discovered the proposition that the square on the hypotenuse of a right angled triangle was equal to the squares on the sides containing the right angle, he is said to have sacrificed an ox, although the more accurate say that this ox was made of flour.

37. His utterances were of two kinds, plain or symbolical. His teaching was twofold: of his disciples some were called Students (*mathematekoi*), and others Hearers (*akousmatikoi*). The Students learned the fuller and more exactly elaborate reasons of science, while the Hearers heard only the chief heads of learning, without more detailed explanations.

38. He ordained that his disciples should speak well and think reverently of the Gods, muses and heroes, and likewise of parents and benefactors; that they should obey the laws; that they should not relegate the worship of the Gods to a secondary position, performing it eagerly, even at home; that to the celestial divinities they should sacrifice uncommon offerings; and ordinary ones to the inferior deities. (The world he divided into) opposite powers; the "one" was a better *monad*, light, right, equal, stable and straight; while the "other" was an inferior *Dyad*, darkness, left, unequal, unstable and movable.

39. Moreover, he enjoined the following. A cultivated and fruit-bearing plant, harmless to man and beast, should be neither injured nor destroyed. A deposit of money or of teachings should be faithfully preserved by the trustee. There are three kinds of things that deserve to be pursued and acquired; honourable and virtuous things, those that conduce to the use of life, and those that bring pleasures of the blameless, solid and grave kind, of course not the vulgar intoxicating kinds. Of pleasures there were two kinds; one that indulges the bellies and lusts by a profusion of wealth, which he compared to the murderous songs of the Sirens; the other kind consists of things honest, just, and necessary to life, which are just as sweet as the first, without being followed by repentance; and these pleasures he compared to the harmony of the Muses.

40. He advised special regard to two times; that when we go to sleep, and that when we awake. At each of these we should consider our past actions, and those that are to come. We ought to require of ourselves an account of our past deeds, while of the future we should have a providential care. Therefore he advised everybody to repeat to himself the following verses before he fell asleep:

"Nor suffer sleep to close thine eyes
Till thrice thy acts that day thou hast run o'er;
How slipt? What deeds? What duty left undone?"

On rising:

"As soon as ere thou wakest, in order lay
The actions to be done that following day"

41. Such things taught he, though advising above all things to speak the truth, for this alone deifies men. For as he had learned from the Magi, who call God Oremasdes, God's body is light, and his soul is truth. He taught much else, which he claimed to have learned from Aristoclea at Delphi. Certain things he declared mystically, symbolically, most of which were collected by Aristotle, as when he called the sea a *tear of Saturn;* the two bear (constellations) the *hand of Rhea;* the Pleiades, the *lyre of the Muses;* the Planets, the *dogs of Persephone;* and he called the sound caused by striking on brass the voice of a genius enclosed in the brass.

42. He had also another kind of symbol, such as, pass not over a balance; that is, shun avarice. Poke not the fire with a sword, that is, we ought not to excite a man full of fire and anger with sharp language. Pluck not a crown, meant not to violate the laws, which are the crowns of cities. Eat not the heart, signified not to afflict ourselves with sorrows. Do not sit upon a [pack]-measure, meant, do not live ignobly. On starting a journey, do not turn back, meant, that this life should not be regretted, when near the bourne of death. Do not walk in the public way, meant, to avoid the opinions of the multitude, adopting those of the learned and the few. Receive not swallows into your house, meant, not to admit under the same roof garrulous and intemperate men. Help a man to take up a burden, but not to lay it down, meant, to encourage no one to be indolent, but to apply oneself to labour and virtue. Do not carry the images of the Gods in rings, signified that one should not at once to the vulgar reveal one's opinions about the Gods, or discourse about them. Offer libations to the Gods, just to the ears of the cup, meant, that we ought to worship and celebrate the Gods with music, for that penetrates through the ears. Do not eat those things that are unlawful, sexual or increase, beginning nor end, nor the first basis of all things.

43. He taught abstention from the loins, testicle, pudenda, marrow, feet and heads of victims. The loins he called *basis,* because on them as foundations living beings are settled. Testicles and pudenda he called *generation,* for no one is engendered without the help of these. Marrow he called increase as it is the cause of growth in living beings. The beginning was the *feet,* and the head the *end*; which have the most power in the government of the body. He likewise advised abstention from beans, as from human flesh.

44. Beans were interdicted, it is said, because the particular plants grow and individualize only after (the earth) which is the principle and origin of things, is mixed together, so that many things underground are confused, and coalesce; after which everything rots together. Then living creatures were produced together with plants, so that both men and beans arose out of putrefaction whereof he alleged many manifest arguments. For if anyone should chew a bean, and having ground it to a pulp with his teeth, and should expose that pulp to the warm sun, for a short while, and then return to it, he will perceive the scent of human blood. Moreover, if at the time when beans bloom, one should take a little of the

flower, which then is black, and should put it into an earthen vessel, and cover it closely, and bury in the ground for ninety days, and at the end thereof take it up, and uncover it, instead of the bean he will find either the head of an infant, or the pudenda of a woman.

45. He also wished men to abstain from other things, such as a swine's paunch, a mullet, and a sea-fish called a "nettle," and from nearly all other marine animals. He referred his origin to those of past ages, affirming that he was first Euphorbus, then Aethalides, then Hermotimus, then Pyrrhus, and last, Pythagoras. He showed to his disciples that the soul is immortal, and to those who were rightly purified he brought back the memory of the acts of their former lives.

46. He cultivated philosophy, the scope of which is to free the mind implanted within us from the impediments and fetters within which it is confined; without whose freedom none can learn anything sound or true, or perceive the unsoundness in the operation of sense. Pythagoras thought that mind alone sees and hears, while all the rest are blind and deaf. The purified mind should be applied to the discovery of beneficial things, which can be effected by, certain artificial ways, which by degrees induce it to the contemplation of eternal and incorporeal things, which never vary. This orderliness of perception should begin from consideration of the most minute things, lest by any change the mind should be jarred and withdraw itself, through the failure of continuousness in its subject-matter.

47. That is the reason he made so much use of the mathematical disciplines and speculations, which are intermediate between the physical and the incorporeal realm, for the reason that like bodies they have a threefold dimension, and yet share the impassibility of incorporeals; [These disciplines he used] as degrees of preparation to the contemplation of the really existent things; by an artificial reason diverting the eyes of the mind from corporeal things, whose manner and state never remain in the same condition, to a desire for true (spiritual) food. By means of these mathematical sciences therefore, Pythagoras rendered men truly happy, by this artistic introduction of truly [consistent] things.

48. Among others, Moderatus of Gades, who [learnedly] treated of the qualities of numbers in seven books, states that the Pythagoreans specialized in the study of numbers to explain their teachings symbolically, as do geometricians, inasmuch as the primary forms and principles are

hard to understand and express, otherwise, in plain discourse. A similar case is the representation of sounds by letters, which are known by marks, which are called the first elements of learning; later, they inform us these are not the true elements, which they only signify.

49. As the geometricians cannot express incorporeal forms in words, and have recourse to the descriptions of figures, as that is a triangle, and yet do not mean that the actually seen lines are the triangle, but only what they represent, the knowledge in the mind, so the Pythagoreans used the same objective method in respect to first reasons and forms. As these incorporeal forms and first principles could not be expressed in words, they had recourse to demonstration by numbers. Number one denoted to them the reason of Unity, Identity, Equality, the purpose of friendship, sympathy, and conservation of the Universe, which results from persistence in Sameness. For unity in the details harmonizes all the parts of a whole, as by the participation of the First Cause.

50. Number two, or *Dyad*, signifies the two-fold reason of diversity and inequality, of everything that is divisible, or mutable, existing at one time in one way, and at another time in another way. After all these methods were not confined to the Pythagoreans, being used by other philosophers to denote unitive powers, which contain all things in the universe, among which are certain reasons of equality, dissimilitude and diversity. These reasons are what they meant by the terms *Monad* and *Dyad*, or by the words *uniform, biform,* or *diversiform.*

51. The same reasons apply to their use of other numbers, which were ranked according to certain powers. Things that had a beginning, middle and end, they denoted by the number Three, saying that anything that has a middle is triform, which was applied to every perfect thing. They said that if anything was perfect it would make use of this principle and be adorned, according to it; and as they had no other name for it, they invented the form *Triad; and whenever they tried to bring us to the knowledge of what is perfect they led us to that by the form of this Triad. So also with the other numbers, which were ranked according to the same reasons.*

52. All other things were comprehended under a single form and power which they called *Decad,* explaining it by a pun as *dechada* ("receptacle"), meaning comprehension. That is why they called Ten a perfect number, the most perfect of all as comprehending all difference of numbers, reasons, species and proportions. For if the nature of the uni-

verse be defined according to the reasons and proportions of members, and if that which is produced, increased and perfected, proceed according to the reason of numbers; and since the Decad comprehends every reason of numbers, every proportion, and every species, why should Nature herself not be denoted by the most perfect number, Ten? Such was the use of numbers among the Pythagoreans.

53. This primary philosophy of the Pythagoreans finally died out first, because it was enigmatical, and then because their commentaries were written in Doric, which dialect itself is somewhat obscure, so that Doric teachings were not fully understood, and they became misapprehended, and finally spurious, and later, they who published them no longer were Pythagoreans. The Pythagoreans affirm that Plato, Aristotle, Speusippus, Aristoxenus and Xenocrates; appropriated the best of them, making but minor changes (to distract attention from this their theft), they later collected and delivered as characteristic Pythagorean doctrines whatever therein was most trivial, and vulgar, and whatever had been invented by envious and calumnious persons, to cast contempt on Pythagoreanism.

54. Pythagoras and his associates were long held in such admiration in Italy, that many cities invited them to undertake their administration. At last, however, they incurred envy, and a conspiracy was formed against them as follows. Cylon, a Crotonian, who in race, nobility and wealth was the most preeminent, was of a severe, violent and tyrannical disposition, and did not scruple to use the multitude of his followers to compass his ends. As he esteemed himself worthy of whatever was best, he considered it his right to be admitted to Pythagorean fellowship. He therefore went to Pythagoras extolled himself, and desired his conversation. Pythagoras, however, who was accustomed to read in human bodies' nature and manners the disposition of the man, bade him depart, and go about his business. Cylon, being of a rough and violent disposition, took it as a great affront, and became furious.

55. He therefore assembled his friends, began to accuse Pythagoras, and conspired against him and his disciples. Pythagoras then went to Delos, to visit the Syrian Pherecydes, formerly his teacher, who was dangerously sick, to nurse him. Pythagoras's friends then gathered together in the house of Milo the wrestler; and were all stoned and burned when Cylon's followers set the house on fire. Only two escaped, Archippus and Lysis, according to the account of Neanthes. Lysis took refuge in Greece, with Epaminondas, whose teacher he had formerly been.

56. But Dicaearchus and other more accurate historians relate that Pythagoras himself was present when this conspiracy bore fruit, for Pherecydes had died before he left Samos. Of his friends, forty who were gathered together in a house were attacked and slain; while others were gradually slain as they came to the city. As his friends were taken, Pythagoras himself first escaped to the harbour of Caulonia, and thence visited the Locrians. Hearing of his coming, the Locrians sent some old men to their frontiers to intercept him. They said, "Pythagoras, you are wise and of great worth; but as our laws retain nothing reprehensible, we will preserve them intact. Go to some other place, and we will furnish you with any needed necessaries of travel." Pythagoras turned back, and sailed to Tarentum, where, receiving the same treatment as at Crotona, he went to Metapontum. Everywhere arose great mobs against him, of which even now the inhabitants make mention, calling them the Pythagorean riots, as his followers were called Pythagoreans.

57. Pythagoras fled to the temple of the Muses, in Metapontum. There he abode forty days, and starving, died. Others however state that his death was due to grief at the loss of all his friends who, when the house in which they were gathered was burned, in order to make a way for their master, they threw themselves into the flames, to make a bridge of safety for him, whereby indeed he escaped. When died the Pythagoreans, with them also died their knowledge, which till then than they had kept secret, except for a few obscure things which were commonly repeated by those who did not understand them. Pythagoras himself left no book; but some little sparks of his philosophy, obscure and difficult, were preserved by the few who were preserved by being scattered, as were Lysis and Archippus.

58. The Pythagoreans now avoided human society, being lonely, saddened and dispersed. Fearing nevertheless that among men the name of philosophy would be entirely extinguished, and that therefore the Gods would be angry with them, they made abstracts and commentaries. Each man made his own collection of written authorities and his own memories, leaving them wherever he happened to die, charging their wives, sons and daughters to preserve them within their families. This mandate of transmission within each family was obeyed for a long time.

59. Nichomacus says that this was the reason why the Pythagoreans studiously avoided friendship with strangers, preserving a constant friendship

among each other. Aristoxenus, in his book on the *Life of Pythagoras*, says he heard many things from Dionysius, the tyrant of Sicily, who, after his abdication, taught letters at Corinth. Among these were that they abstained from lamentations and grieving and tears; also from adulation, entreaty, supplication and the like.

60. It is said that Dionysius at one time wanted to test their mutual fidelity under imprisonment. He contrived this plan. Phintias was arrested, and taken before the tyrant, and charged with plotting against the tyrant, convicted, and condemned to death. Phintias, accepting the situation, asked to be given the rest of the day to arrange his own affairs, and those of Damon, his friend and associate, who now would have to assume the management. He therefore asked for a temporary release, leaving Damon as security for his appearance. Dionysius granted the request, and they sent for Damon, who agreed to remain until Phintias should return.

61. The novelty of this deed astonished Dionysius; but those who had first suggested the experiment, scoffed at Damon, saying he was in danger of losing his life. But to the general surprise, near sunset Phintias came to die. Dionysius then expressed his admiration, embraced them both, and asked to be received as a third in their friendship. Though he earnestly besought this, they refused this, though assigning no reason therefore. Aristoxenus states he heard this from Dionysius himself. [Hippobotus] and Neanthes relate about Myllia and Timycha...(here the manuscript ends)

Appendix 3

The Testimony of Johann Friedrich Schweitzer, known as Helvetius (1625–1709)[252]

On the 27 December, 1666, in the forenoon, there came to my house a certain man, who was a complete stranger to me, but of an honest, grave countenance, and an authoritative mien, clothed in a simple garb like that of a Mennonite. He was of middle height, his face was long and slightly pock-marked, his hair was black and-

---

252 Translated by A. E. Waite in *The Hermetic Museum*, 1893. The first English translation was published as *The Golden Calf, Which the World Adores, and Desires*. London, 1670.

straight, his chin close shaven, his age about 43 or 44, and his native province, as far as I could make out, North Holland.

After we had exchanged salutations, he asked me whether he might have some conversation with me. He wished to say something to me about the Pyrotechnic Art, as he had read one of my Tracts (directed against the Sympathetic Powder of Dr. Digby), in which I hinted a suspicion whether the Grand Arcanum of the Sages was not after all a gigantic hoax. He, therefore, took that opportunity of asking me whether I could not believe that such a grand mystery might exist in the nature of things, by means of which a physician could restore any patient whose vitals were not irreparably destroyed. I answered: "Such a Medicine would be a most desirable acquisition for any physician; nor can any man tell how many secrets there may be hidden in Nature; yet, though I have read much about the truth of this Art, it has never been my good fortune to meet with a real Master of the Alchemical Science." I also enquired whether he was a medical man, since he spoke so learnedly about the Universal Medicine. In reply, he modestly disclaimed my insinuation, and described himself as a brass founder, who had always taken a great interest in the extraction of medicinal potions from metals by means of fire. After some further conversation; the Artist Elias (for it was he) thus addressed me: "Since you have read so much in the works of the Alchemists about this Stone, its substance, its colour, and its wonderful effects, may I be allowed the question, whether you have not yourself prepared it?" On my answering his question in the negative, he took out of his bag a cunningly-worked ivory box, in which there were three large pieces of a substance resembling glass, or pale sulphur, and informed me that here was enough of the Tincture for the production of twenty tons of gold. When I had held the precious treasure in my hand for a quarter of an hour (during which time I listened to a recital of its wonderful curative properties), I was compelled to restore it to its owner, which I could not help doing with a certain degree of reluctance. After thanking him for his kindness in showing it to me, I then asked how it was that his Stone did not display that ruby colour which I had been taught to regard as characteristic of the Philosophers' Stone. He replied that the colour made no difference, and that the substance was sufficiently mature for all practical purposes. My request that he would give me a piece of his Stone (though it were no larger than a coriander seed), he somewhat brusquely refused, adding, in a milder tone, that he could not give it me for all the wealth I possessed, and that not on account of its great preciousness, but for some other reason which it was not lawful for him to divulge; nay, if fire could be destroyed in that way, he would immediately throw it all into the fire. Then, after a moment's consideration, he enquired whether I could not shew him into a room at the back of the house, where we should be less liable to the observation of passers-by. On my conducting him into the state parlour (which he entered without wiping his dirty boots), he demanded of me a gold coin, and while I was looking for it, he produced from his breast pocket a green silk handkerchief, in which were folded up five medals, the gold of which was infinitely superior to that of my gold piece. On the medals appeared the following inscriptions:—I was filled with admiration, and asked my visitor whence he had obtained that wonderful knowledge of the whole world? He replied that it was a gift freely bestowed on him by a friend who had stayed a few days at his house, who had also taught him to change common flints and crystals into stones more precious than rubies, chrysoliths, and sapphires; he also revealed to me the preparation of crocus of iron (an infallible cure for dysentery), of metallic liquid (an efficacious remedy for dropsy), and of many other infallible Medicines, to which, however, I paid no great heed, as I was impatiently anxious to have the chief secret of all revealed to me. The Artist told me that his Master had bidden him bring him a glass full of warm water, to which he had added a little white powder, and in which one ounce of silver had melted like ice in warm water. Of this draught he emptied one-half, and gave the rest to me. Its taste resembled that of fresh milk, and its effect was most exhilarating.

I asked my visitor whether the potion was a preparation of the Philosophers' Stone? But he answered: "You should not be so inquisitive."

Then he told me that, at the bidding of the Artist, he had taken down a piece of leaden water-pipe, and melted the lead in a pot, whereupon the Artist had taken some sulphureous powder out of a little box on the point of a knife, and cast it into the melted lead, and that after exposing the compound for a short time to a fierce fire, he had poured forth a great mass of molten gold upon the brick floor of the kitchen.

"The Master bade me take one-sixteenth of the gold for myself as a keepsake, and to distribute the rest amongst the poor; which I did by making over a large sum in trust to the Church of Sparrendam. At length, before bidding me farewell, my friend taught me this Divine Art."

When my strange visitor had concluded his narrative, I besought him to give me a proof of his assertion, by performing the transmutatory operation on some metals in my presence. He answered evasively, that he could not do so then, but that he would return in three weeks, and that, if he was then at liberty to do so, he would shew me something that would make me open my eyes. He appeared punctually to the promised day, and invited me to take a walk with him, in the course of which we discoursed profoundly on the secrets of Nature in fire, though I noticed that my companion was very chary in imparting information about the Grand Arcanum; he spoke very learnedly and gravely concerning the holiness of the Art (just as if he were a clergyman), and said that God had commanded the initiated to make the secret known only to the deserving. At last I asked him point blank to shew me the transmutation of metals. I besought him to come and dine with me, and to spend the night at my house; I entreated; I expostulated; but in vain. He remained firm. I reminded him of his promise. He retorted that his promise had been conditional upon his being permitted to reveal the secret to me. At last, however, I prevailed upon him to give me a piece of his precious Stone—a piece no larger than a grain of rape seed. He delivered it to me as if it were the most princely donation in the world. Upon my uttering a doubt whether it would be sufficient to tinge more than four grains of lead, he eagerly demanded it back. I complied, in the hope that he would exchange it for a larger piece; instead of which he divided it in two with his thumb, threw away one-half and gave me back the other, saying: "Even now it is sufficient for you." Then I was still more heavily disappointed, as I could not believe that anything could be done with so small a particle of the Medicine. He, however, bade me take two drachms, or half an-ounce of lead, or even a little more, and to melt it in the crucible; for the Medicine would certainly not tinge more of the base metal than it was sufficient for. I answered that I could not believe that so small a quantity of Tincture could transform so large a mass of lead. But I had to be satisfied with what he had given me, and my chief difficulty was about the application of the Tincture. I confessed that when I held his ivory box in my hand, I had managed to extract a few small crumbs of his Stone, but that they had changed my lead, not into gold, but only into glass. He laughed, and said that I was more expert at theft than at the application of the Tincture. "You should have protected your spoil with 'yellow wax,' then it would have been able to penetrate the lead and to transmute it into gold. As it was, your Medicine evaporated, by a sympathetic process, in the metallic smoke. For all metals, gold, silver, tin, and mercury, are corrupted by the fumes of lead, and degenerated into glass." I shewed him the crucible, and there he discovered the yellow piece of Medicine still adhering to it. He promised to return at nine o'clock the next morning, and then he would shew me that my Medicine could well be used for transmuting lead into gold. With this promise I had to declare myself satisfied. Still I asked him to favour me with some information about the preparation of the Arcanum. He would not tell me anything about the cost and the time; "as to its substance," he continued, "it is prepared from two metals or minerals; the minerals are better because they contain a larger quantity of mature Sulphur. The solvent is a certain celestial Salt, by means of which the Sages dissolve the earthy metallic body, and this process elicits the precious Elixir of the Sages. The work is performed from beginning to end in a crucible over an open fire; it is consummated in four days, and its cost is only about three florins. Neither the Min-

eral from the Egg nor the Solvent Salt are very expensive." I replied
that his statement was contradicted by the sayings of the Sages, who
assign seven or nine months as the duration of the Work. His only
answer was that the sayings of the Sages were to be understood in
a philosophical sense and no ignorant person could apprehend their
true meaning. I besought him that, as a stranger had made known
to him this precious mystery, so he would extend to me the same
kindness, and give me at least some information which would remove all the most formidable obstacles out of my path; for if one
knew one thing, other facts connected with it were more easily
discovered. But the Artist replied: "It is not so in our Magistery; if
you do not know the whole operation from beginning to end, you
know nothing at all. I have told you all; yet you do not know how
the crystal seal of Hermes is broken, and how the Sun colours it
with the marvellous splendour of its metallic rays, or in what mirror the metals see with the eyes of Narcissus the possibility of their
transmutation, or from what rays adepts collect the fire of perfect
metallic fixation." With these words, and a promise to return at nine
o'clock the next morning, he left me. But at the stated hour on the
following day he did not make his appearance; in his stead, however, there came, a few hours later, a stranger, who told me that
his friend the Artist was unavoidably detained, but that he would
call at three o'clock in the afternoon. The afternoon came; I waited
for him till half-past seven o'clock. He did not appear. Thereupon
my wife came and tempted me to try the transmutation myself. I
determined, however, to wait till the morrow, and in the meantime,
ordered my son to light the fire, as I was now almost sure that he
was an impostor. On the morrow, however, I thought that I might
at least make an experiment with the piece of "Tincture" which I
had received; if it turned out a failure, in spite of my following his
directions closely, I might then be quite certain that my visitor had
been a mere pretender to a knowledge of this Art. So I asked my
wife to put the Tincture in wax, and I myself, in the meantime, prepared six drachms of lead; I then cast the Tincture, enveloped as it
was in wax, on the lead; as soon as it was melted, there was a hiss-
ing sound and a slight effervescence, and after a quarter of an hour

I found that the whole mass of lead had been turned into the finest gold. Before this transformation took place, the compound became intensely green, but as soon as I had poured it into the melting pot it assumed a hue like blood. When it cooled, it glittered and shone like gold. We immediately took it to the goldsmith, who at once declared it to be the finest gold he had ever seen, and offered to pay fifty florins an ounce for it.

The rumour, of course, spread at once like wildfire through the whole city; and in the afternoon, I had visits from many illustrious students of this Art; I also received a call from the Master of the Mint and some other gentlemen, who requested me to place at their disposal a small piece of the gold, in order that they might subject it to the usual tests. I consented, and we betook ourselves to the house of a certain silversmith, named Brechtil, who submitted a small piece of my gold to the test called "the fourth": three or four parts of silver are melted in the crucible with one part of gold, and then beaten out into thin plates, upon which some strong aquafortis is poured. The usual result of this experiment is that the silver is dissolved, while the gold sinks to the bottom in the shape of a black powder, and after the aquafortis has been poured off, and melted once more in the crucible, resumes its former shape.... When we now performed this experiment, we thought at first that one-half of the gold had evaporated; but afterwards we found that this was not the case, but that, on the contrary, two scruples of the silver had undergone a change into gold.

Then we tried another test, viz., that which is performed by means of a septuple of Antimony; at first it seemed as if eight grains of the gold had been lost, but afterwards, not only had two scruples of the silver been converted into gold, but the silver itself was greatly improved both in quality and malleability. Thrice I performed this infallible test, discovering that every drachm of gold produced an increase of a scruple of gold, but the silver is excellent and extremely flexible. Thus I have unfolded to you the whole story from beginning to end. The gold I still retain in my possession, but I cannot tell you what has become of the Artist Elias. Before he left me, on that last day of our friendly intercourse, he told me that he was on the point of undertaking a journey to the Holy Land. May the Holy Angels of God watch over him wherever he is, and long preserve him as a source of blessing to Christendom! This is my earnest prayer on his and our behalf.

BIBLIOGRAPHY

Al-Bīrūnī: *The chronology of ancient nations. An English version of the Arabic text of the Athâr-ul-Bâkiya of Albîrûnî or "Vestiges of the past,"* (ed. Sachau, E.), USA: Andesite Press, 2015.

Albertus, Frater: *Alchemist's Handbook (Manual for Practical Laboratory Alchemy)*, York Beach, ME: Samuel Weiser, 1987.

Andrews, Munya: *The Seven Sisters of the Pleiades: Stories from Around the World*, North Melbourne: Spinifex Press, 2004.

Aristotle: *Metaphysics 1–5*, Translated by W.D. Ross, Oxford: Oxford University Press, 1942.

Ball, Philip: *The Devil's Doctor: Paracelsus and the World of Renaissance Magic and Science*, London: Heinemann, 2006.

Bergier, Jacques, and Pauwels, Louis: *The Morning of the Magicians*, New York: Stein and Day, 1964.

Betz, Hans Dieter (ed.): *The Greek Magical Papyri in Translation, Including the Demotic Spells*, Chicago and London: Chicago University Press, 1986.

Blavatsky, Helena: *The Secret Doctrine, the Synthesis of Science, Religion and Philosophy*, 1888.

Bowden, Hugh: *Classical Athens and the Delphic Oracle: Divination and Democracy*, UK: Cambridge University Press, 2005.

————. *Mystery Cults of the Ancient World*, US: Princeton University Press, 2010.

Boyle, Robert: *Of a Degradation of Gold made by an anti-elixir: a strange chymical narrative*. London, 1678.

Burkert, Walter: *Lore and Science in Ancient Pythagoreanism*, trans. Edwin L. Minar, Jr. Cambridge, MA: Harvard University Press, 1972.

————: *Greek Religion*, Cambridge, MA: Harvard University Press, 1985.

————: *Ancient Mystery Cults*, Cambridge, MA: Harvard University Press, 1987.

Burnet, John: *Early Greek Philosophy*, 3rd Edition, 1920.

Casanova de Seingalt, Jacques: *The Memoires of Casanova*. Translated by Arthur Machen. London: 1894.

Cline, Eric H.: *1177 B.C.: The Year Civilization Collapsed*. Princeton, NJ: Princeton University Press, 2014.

Conybeare, F. C.: *Philostratus: The Life of Apollonius of Tyana, the Epistles of Apollonius and the Treatise of Eusebius*, London: Heinemann, 1912.

Cook, Jill: *Ice Age Art; arrival of the modern mind*, London: British Museum Press, 2013.

Cooper-Oakley, Isabel: *The Comte de St. Germain*, Milan: Ars Regia, 1912.

Copenhaver, Brian (trans. and ed.): *The Greek Corpus Hermeticum and Latin Asclepius*. Cambridge, UK: Cambridge University Press, 1992.

Cornford, Francis Macdonald: *Plato and Parmenides. Parmenides' Way of Truth and Plato's Parmenides Translated, with an Introduction and a Running Commentary*. London: K. Paul, Trench, Trubner & Co. Ltd., 1939.

David-Neel, Alexandra: *Magic and Mystery in Tibet*, New York: Claude Kendall, 1932.

Deren, Maya: *Divine Horsemen, The Living Gods of Haiti*, New York: Vanguard Press, 1953.

Dickinson, Oliver: *The Aegean from Bronze Age to Iron Age: Continuity and Change Between the Twelfth and Eighth Centuries BC*, Routledge, 2007.

Diels, H., and W. Kranz: *Die Fragmente der Vorsokratiker*, Berlin, 1952.

Diodorus Siculus: *Bibliotheca Historica*, Volumes 1–6, translated by C. H. Oldfather, Loeb's Classical Library, Cambridge, MA: Harvard University Press, 1933–35.

Diogenes Laërtius: *The Lives and Opinions of Eminent Philosophers*. Translated by Charles Duke Yonge. London: H. G. Bohn. 1853.

Dobbs, Betty J.: *The Foundations of Newton's Alchemy: Or, "The Hunting of the Greene Lyon,"* New York and London: Cambridge University Press, 1975.

Dodds, E. R.: *The Greeks and the Irrational*, Berkeley, CA: 1951.

Dubuis, Jean: *The Jean Dubuis Collection*. Never published in book form. Formerly only available to members of The Philosophers of Nature; now freely available at archive.org.

Edmonds, Radford: *Myths of the Underworld Journey in Plato, Aristophanes, and the Orphic Gold Tablets: A Path Neither Simple Nor Single*, Cambridge University Press, 2004.

———: *The Orphic Gold Tablets and Greek Religion: Further Along the Path*, Cambridge University Press, 2011.

———: *Redefining Ancient Orphism: A Study in Greek Religion*, Cambridge University Press, 2013.

Eliade, Mircea: *The Forge and the Crucible*. London, Rider & Co., 1962.

———: *Shamanism: Archaic Techniques of Ecstasy*, Princeton, NJ: 1964.

———: *A History of Religious Ideas, Volume 2: From Gautama Buddha to the Triumph of Christianity*, Chicago and London: University of Chicago Press, 1982.

Empedocles: *The Complete Fragments*, translated by William Ellery Leonard, Oxford University Press, 1907.

Faivre, Antoine: *Access to Western Esotericism*, Albany, NY: SUNY Press, 1994.

———: *The Eternal Hermes, From Greek God to Alchemical Magus*, Grand Rapids, MI: Phanes Press, 1995.

Fontenrose, Joseph: *The Delphic Oracle: Its Responses and Operations - With a Catalogue of Responses*, University of California Press, 1978.

Fowden, G.: *The Egyptian Hermes*, Cambridge, UK: 1986.

Frazer, James George: *The Golden Bough: A Study in Magic and Religion*, 1900.

Freeman, Kathleen: *The Pre-Socratic Philosophers. A Companion to Diels 'Fragmente Der Vorsokratiker,'* 1946.

Gallop, David: *Parmenides of Elea: Fragments*. Toronto: University of Toronto Press, 1984.

Gardner, James: *The Faiths of the World*, Edinburgh: A. Fullarton & Co., 1858.

Geldard, Richard G.: *Parmenides and the Way of Truth*. Rhinebeck: Monkfish Book Publishing Company, 2007.

Godwin, Joscelyn: *The Golden Thread: The Ageless Wisdom of the Western Mystery Traditions*, Wheaton, IL: Quest Books, 2007.

Govinda, Lama Anagorika: *The Way of the White Clouds*, London: Hutchinson, 1966.

Graves, Robert: *The Greek Myths*, revised edition. London: Penguin, 1960.

Guénon, René: *Fundamental Symbols: The Universal Language of Sacred Science*, Cambridge, UK: Quinta Essentia, 1995.

Guirand, Felix: *New Larousse Encyclopaedia of Mythology*, UK: Hamlyn, 1976.

Guthrie, Kenneth Sylvan:*A History of Greek Philosophy*, Cambridge, UK: 1962-81.

————: *The Pythagorean Sourcebook and Library*, Grand Rapids, MI: Phanes Press, 1987.

Hanegraaff, Wouter J. (ed.): *Dictionary of Gnosis and Western Esotericism*, Leiden: Brill, 2006.

Hanegraaff, Wouter J., and Ruud M. Bouthoorn: *Lodovico Lazzarelli (1447–1500): The Hermetic Writings and Related Documents*. Tempe, AZ: Arizona Center for Medieval and Renaissance Studies (Medieval and Renaissance Texts and Studies 281), 2005.

Hartmann, Franz: *The Life of Philippus Theophrastus Bombast of Ho-henheim: Known by the Name of Paracelsus*, London: George Red-way, 1887.

van Helmont, Jan Baptista: *Oriatrike or, Physick Refined*. London, 1662.

Hermann, Arnold: *To Think Like God: Pythagoras and Parmenides*, Par-menides Publishing, 2004.

Herodotus: *The Histories*, translated by Robin Waterfield, London: Oxford University Press, 1998.

Hippolytus of Rome: *The Refutation of All Heresies*, translated by Rev. J. H. MacMahon, Edinburgh: T. and T. Clark, 1868.

Holmyard, E. J.: *Alchemy*. London: Penguin, 1957.

Iamblichus: *The Life of Pythagoras*. Various translations.

Inwood, Brad: *The Poem of Empedocles* (Revised Edition), University of Toronto Press, 2001.

Janko, Richard: *The Derveni Papyrus ("Diagoras of Melos, Apopyrgizontes Logoi"): A New Translation*, Classical Philology, Vol. 96, University of Chicago Press, January 2001.

———: *Empedocles, "On Nature" I 233–364: A New Reconstruction of "P. Strasb. Gr." Inv. 1665–6*, Zeitschrift für Papyrologie und Epigraphik, Bd. 150, Bonn, Germany, Verlag Rudolf Habelt, 2004.

Jay, Mike: *Stranger Than Fiction: Essays by Mike Jay*, UK: Daily Grail Publishing, 2018.

———: *Blue Tide*, NY: Autonomedia, 1999.

Jung, C. G.: *Collected Works of C.G. Jung, Volume 13: Alchemical Studies*. Princeton: Princeton University Press, 1983.

Junius, Manfred M.: *The Practical Handbook of Plant Alchemy*, New York: Inner Traditions International, 1985. Reprinted as: *Spagyrics: The Alchemical Preparation of Medicinal Essences, Tinctures, and Elixirs*, Rochester, Vermont: Healing Arts Press, 2007.

Kerenyi, Karl: *The Gods of the Greeks*, London: Thames & Hud-son, 1951.

———: *Dionysos Archetypal Image of the Indestructible Life*, USA: Prince-ton University Press, 1976.

Kingsley, Peter: *Poimandres: The Etymology of the Name and the Origins of the Hermetica*, Journal of the Warburg and Courtauld Institutes, Vol. 56 (1993), pp. 1–24.

————: *Ancient Philosophy, Mystery, and Magic: Empedocles and Pythagorean Tradition*, Oxford: Clarendon Press, 1995.

————: *In the Dark Places of Wisdom*, California: The Golden Sufi Center, 1999.

————: *Reality*, California: The Golden Sufi Center, 2004.

————: *A Story Waiting to Pierce You: Mongolia, Tibet and the Destiny of the Western World*, California: The Golden Sufi Centre, 2010.

Kirk, G. S., Raven, J. E., and Schofield, M.: *The Presocratic Philosophers. A Critical History with a Selection of Texts*, Second Edition, Cambridge University Press, 1983.

Lévi, Éliphas: *Transcendental Magic*. London: Rider & Company, 1896.

Martin, A., and O. Primaves: *L'Empédocle de Strasbourg*, Berlin / Strasbourg, 1998.

Martineau, John: *A Little Book of Coincidence*, Glastonbury, UK: Wooden Books, 2001.

Mackenzie, Donald A. : *Myths of Crete and Pre-Hellenic Europe*, London, 1917.

McKirahan, Richard D.: *Philosophy before Socrates*, Second Edition, Cambridge, USA: Hackett Publishing, 2011.

Melville, Francis: *The Book of Alchemy*, Beverly, MA: Fair Winds Press, 2002.

Nasr, S. H.: *Three Muslim Sages*, Cambridge, MA: 1964.

D'Olivet, Fabre, and Joscelyn Godwin (translator): *The Secret Lore of Music: The Hidden Power of Orpheus*, Rochester, Vermont: Inner Traditions Bear and Company, 1997.

Ogilvy, Guy: *The Alchemist's Kitchen*, Glastonbury, UK: Wooden Books, 2006.

Ovid: *Metamorphoses*, translated by A. S. Kline, USA: Borders Classics, 2004.

Paglia, Camille: *Sexual Personae*, Yale University Press, 1990.

Paton, W. R. (translator): *The Greek Anthology, Loeb Classical Library edition, in Greek and English*; London: W. Heinemann; New York, G.P. Putnam's Sons, c. 1916–1918.

Plato: *Phaedo. The Dialogues of Plato, in 5 volumes.* Translated by Benjamin Jowett, Oxford, 1892.

———: *Plato Complete Works*, ed. John M. Cooper, Indianapolis / Cambridge, Hackett Publishing Company, 1997.

Plutarch: *Moralia*, Loeb Classical Library, with an English translation by Frank Cole Babbitt, Harvard University Press, Cambridge, MA and London, England. First published 1936. Also in print under the title *Plutarch's Morals*.

———: *Plutarch's Morals, 5 vols.* Translator: William W. Goodwin, 1878.

———: *Lives of the noble Grecians and Romans (Complete and Unabridged)*, Oxford: Benediction Classics, 2015.

Polybius: *The Histories of Polybius, Vol. I*, Loeb Classical Library, 1922.

Porphyry: *Life of Pythagoras*, translated by Kenneth Sylvan Guthrie, 1920.

———: *Select Works of Porphyry: Containing His Four Books on Abstinence from Animal Food; His Treatise on the Homeric Cave of the Nymphs; And His Auxiliaries to the Perception of Intelligible Natures*, translated by Thomas Taylor, London, 1823.

Reames, Robin, ed.: *Logos without Rhetoric: The Arts of Language before Plato*, Columbia, South Carolina: University of South Carolina Press, 2017.

Russell, Bertrand: *A History of Western Philosophy*, first published 1945.

Shah, Idries: *The Secret Lore of Magic*, London: Frederick Muller, 1957.

Schibli, H. S.: *Pherekydes of Samos*, Oxford, UK: 1990.

Scott, W.: *Hermetica*, Oxford, UK: 1936.

Schultes, Richard Evans, and Hofmann, Albert: *Plants of the Gods, Origins of Hallucinogenic Use*, New York: McGraw-Hill Book Company, 1979.

Stamatellos, Giannis: *Introduction to Presocratics: A Thematic Approach to Early Greek Philosophy with Key Readings*, UK: John Wiley and Sons, 2012.

Strabo: *Geography*. Translated by H. C. Hamilton and W. Falconer, London: Henry G. Bohn, 1854.

Strassman, Rick: *DMT: The Spirit Molecule: A Doctor's Revolutionary Research into the Biology of Near-Death and Mystical Experiences*, USA: Park Street Press, 2001.

Sumach, Alexander: *A Treasury of Hashish*, Toronto: Stoneworks Publishing, 1976.

Szydło, Zbigniew: *Water Which Does Not Wet Hands: The Alchemy of Michael Sendivogius*. London-Warsaw, 1994.

Taran, Leonardo: *Parmenides*, USA: Princeton University Press, 1965.

Trépanier, S.: *Empedocles: An Interpretation*, New York and London: Routledge, 2004.

Ulmer Museum: *The Return of the Lion Man: History – Myth – Magic*, Germany: Jan Thorbecke Verlag, 2013.

Waite, A. E.: *The Hermetic Museum*, London, 1893.

————: *The Hermetic and Alchemical Writings of Aureolus Philippus Theophrastus Bombast, of Hohenheim, Called Paracelsus the Great*. London: James Elliott, 1894 (2 vols.).

————: *The Turba Philosophorum; or, Assembly of the Sages*, London: Redway, 1896.

Westerink, L. G.: *The Greek Commentators on Plato's* Phaedo, *vol. I: Olympiodorus*. Amsterdam: North-Holland Publishing Company, 1976.

Wright, M. R.: *Empedocles the Extant Fragments*, London, 1995.

Xenophanes: *Xenophanes. Fragments and Commentary: The First Philosophers of Greece*, Edited and translated by Arthur Fairbanks, London: K. Paul, Trench, Trubner, 1898.

Zuntz, Günther: *Persephone. Three Essays on Religion and Thought in Magna Graecia*, New York: Oxford University Press, 1971.

INDEX

A

Abaris, 111–114, 116–118, 123–125, 128–131, 134, 135, 144, 147, 163, 268

Abraham, 39

Acragas, 165, 166, 177, 188

Agrippa, Cornelius, 23

Akhmim, 167, 171, 204–206

Albertus Magnus, 214

Alexander the Great, 44, 49, 87, 207

Alexandria, 51, 64, 85, 111, 208, 209

al-Suhrawardi, 205

AMORC, 256

Anatolia, 42, 43, 156, 161, 162, 192

Anaxagoras, 168

Anaximander, 79, 80, 210, 261, 263

Aphrodite, 49, 181–183, 193

Apollo, 40, 42, 48, 57, 67, 69, 84–87, 95, 97, 98, 100, 104, 105, 107–113, 115–117, 119, 121, 125, 128–132, 134, 135, 143–145, 161–164, 177, 178, 192, 208, 261, 264, 268

Apollonius of Tyana, 85, 101, 224, 261, 286

Aquinas, Thomas, 214

Arabian Nights, xii, 209

Archaeus, 232

Argonauts, 40, 41, 46, 102, 202

Argot, 3, 218

Aristeas of Proconnesus, 128–130, 145, 160

Aristotle, 45, 98, 126, 136, 137, 141, 149, 154, 156, 166, 173, 178, 179, 188, 207, 225, 271, 275, 285

Arnold of Villanova, 214

Aslan, 33

Athena, 45, 51, 57, 80

Aurignacian, 15, 38, 53

Avars, 123, 128, 129, 134

Avicenna, 211, 212

Ayahuasca, 62

B

Bacchanalia, 56, 58, 59

Bacchus, 20, 50, 56, 58, 86, 129, 160

Banks, Sir Joseph, 237

Bez, 20–22, 32, 33

Bladud, 118, 119

Blagden, Charles, 237, 238, 240

Blavatsky, Helena, 37, 192, 223, 226, 285

Bolos of Mendes, 208

Boyle, Robert, 200, 239, 248, 252

Brahma, 33, 228

Burroughs, William, 14

C

Caduceus, 61

Casanova, Jacques, 221

Caves, ix, 13, 14, 18–23, 34, 38, 69, 75, 78, 81, 99, 100, 103–106, 108–110, 142, 143, 146, 155, 161, 162, 262, 264, 291

Celts, 115–117, 119–121, 134

Chaucer, 215

Chauvet cave, 22

Chavín de Huántar, 25, 30–32, 35, 60, 62

Chillout, 108

Chrysopoeia, ix, 204, 213

Cocteau, Jean, 42

Crete, 43, 100, 101, 103, 104, 119, 167, 176, 177, 182, 264, 290

Croton, 110, 130, 131, 135, 137, 139–141, 158

D

Dactyls, 96, 103–105, 163, 264

Dalai Lama, 124

David-Kneel, Alexandra, 146

Delphic Oracle, 84, 85, 87, 95, 97, 101, 285, 288

Demeter, 48, 51, 60, 133, 175, 191, 261, 270

Democritus, 45, 261

Derveni Papyrus, 63, 65–67, 74, 176, 255, 289

Descartes, René, 61

Dhul Nun al-Misri, 205

Dionysus, 46–52, 56–59, 61–65, 67, 69, 85–87, 95, 104, 105, 107, 108, 110, 131, 161, 191, 192, 208, 255

Dippel, Conrad, 232

DMT, 31, 62, 108, 292

Doctrine of Signatures, 227

Dragon, 41, 48, 85–87, 256

Druids, 39, 116, 117, 119–121, 173

Dubuis, Jean, 54, 55, 257, 287

E

Elements, 40, 51, 63, 67, 80, 87, 98, 114, 137, 144, 172–175, 177, 179, 182, 201, 204, 206, 210, 218, 222, 226, 239, 256, 274

Eleatic School, 167

Eleusinian Mysteries, 32, 47, 59, 60, 62–65, 67, 83, 94, 103, 158, 162, 192, 228

Eleusis, 59, 60, 62

Elias Artista, 250

Elysian Fields, 62

Empedocles, 127, 139, 141, 144, 165–169, 171–193,
    204, 205, 207, 224, 268, 287, 289, 290, 292

Eno, Brian, 108

Enoch, 39

Epimenides, 97, 100–105, 109, 114, 125, 144, 155,
    160, 163, 164, 168, 177, 187, 268

Ergot, 60

Euripedes, 56, 193

Eurydice, 41, 45, 68, 73

F

Ficino, Marsilio, 39, 41, 158, 159

Frankenstein, 232

Frederick the Great, 221

Freemasonry, 29, 61, 222

Freud, Sigmund, 21, 253, 254

Fulcanelli, 3, 217–220

G

Galen, 225

Glastonbury, 21, 35, 170, 290

Gnosis, 137, 154, 210, 288

Goethe, 232

Golem, 232

Gorgias the Sophist, 192

Great Mother, 133, 202

Green Man, 47

H

Hades, 45, 46, 60, 62, 66, 73, 74, 133, 138, 161, 169,
    173–179, 190

Hahn, Joachim, 14

Harun al-Rashid, 209

Hecate, 191, 193

Heisenberg, Werner, 80

Hera, 51, 76, 119, 173–176, 193, 208, 261, 267

Hercules, 40, 109, 130, 264, 270

Hermes, 6, 36, 37, 39, 40, 48, 51, 61, 76, 208, 282, 287, 288

Hermes Trismegistus, 6, 37, 39

Hermeticism, 207–209, 218

Hermotimus of Clazomenae, 126–128, 160, 163, 273

Herodotus, 101, 107, 121–123, 129–131, 143, 289

Himmler, Heinrich, 13

Hippocrates, 225, 244

Hipponium, 74

Hofmann, Albert, 60

Holy Grail, 55, 213, 218

Homer, 42–44, 48, 49, 66, 110, 131, 157, 166, 167, 180, 267, 269

Hyperborea, 87, 114, 115, 119, 128–131, 134, 147

Iamblichus, 82, 83, 97, 98, 100, 110, 134, 135, 139, 160, 167, 289

I

Ibiza, 21

Ibn Arabi, 205

Ibn Suwaid, 204–206

Icaros, 24

J

Jābir ibn Ḥayyān, 205, 208, 209

Jay, Mike, 31, 289

Jègues-Wolkiewiez, Chantal, 34

Jesus, 14, 33, 39, 97, 104, 146

Jung, C. G., 33, 200, 228, 231, 253–255, 289

Junius, Manfred, xiv, 29, 254, 257

K

Kabbalah, 6, 54, 173, 257

Karmapa, 124, 125

Kent's Cavern, 16

Kervran, Louis, 201, 256

Kirwan, Richard, 237–238, 240, 245–246, 252

Knights Templar, 218

Kolisko, Lili, 256

Kronos, 104, 182

Kykeon, 60, 62

L

Lama Anagorika Govinda, 147

Lascaux, 34, 38

Leopard Society, 31

Linear B script, 43, 48, 131

Lion Man, ix, 13, 15–22, 32, 35–38, 46, 52, 53, 127, 171, 187, 202, 255, 292

Lord of the Rings, 5

LSD, 60

M

Macbeth, 180, 191

Maclise, Hetty, 125

Maclise, Ossian, 124

Maenads, 46, 48, 57, 67, 68

MDMA, 60

Merlin, 23, 118

Metapontum, 129, 130, 141, 145, 268, 276

Metempsychosis, 75, 78, 79, 81

Minoan culture, 176, 177

Minotaur, 119, 182

Mithras, 33, 255

Mongolia, 43, 135, 290

Moors, 213

Morienus, 209, 214

Moses, 39, 54

Mt. Etna, 176, 190

N

Narasimha, 33

Narnia, 33, 48

Neith, 45

Newton, Isaac, 37, 200, 240, 287

Nietzsche, Friedrich, 67

Noah, 39

O

Omophagia, 63, 64

Orpheus, ix, 39–42, 44–47, 53, 55, 56, 60–68, 73, 84, 107,
    108, 125, 137, 184, 290

Orphic Mysteries, 65, 79, 255

Orphism, 41, 42, 62, 74, 107, 109, 120, 255, 287

Osiris, 20, 50, 61, 104

P

Pancaldi, Augusto, 257

Paracelsus, 36, 216, 224–232, 250, 256, 285, 289, 292

Paris Magical Papyrus, 167, 190

Parmenides, 139, 150–160, 162–164, 167, 168, 172, 177,
    178, 181, 185–187, 191, 286, 288, 289, 292

Pausanias, 129, 130, 169, 179, 188, 189

Persephone, 45, 51, 60, 62, 133, 155, 161, 173–175, 271,
    292

Persia, 205, 211

Pherekydes, 78–81, 102, 140, 291

Philosophers of Nature, 257, 287

Philosophers' Stone, 33, 175, 201, 204, 211, 214, 216, 219,
    220, 223, 235, 246, 248, 278, 279

Phocaea, 156, 161

Phoenicians, 77, 262

Pico della Mirandola, Giovanni, 39

Plato, 39, 41–45, 51, 63–66, 76, 80, 101, 128, 137, 138,
141–143, 147, 153, 154, 158, 159, 167, 168, 173, 188,
207, 230, 259, 275, 286, 287, 291, 292

Pleiades, 34, 35, 79, 116, 271, 285

Plutonium, 161

Potter, Harry, xiii, xiv, 4, 201

Price, James, 215, 233, 237, 245, 248, 253

Pythagoras, 39, 41, 76–84, 87, 97–100, 103, 105, 107, 109,
110, 112–114, 118–123, 125–127, 129–131, 133–141,
143–145, 149, 157, 158, 163, 164, 167, 168, 177, 184,
187, 189, 204, 205, 210, 224, 260–270, 273, 275–277,
289, 291

Pythagoreanism, 138, 139, 141, 275, 286

Pythagoreans, 103, 108, 136, 138–141, 144, 147, 167, 168,
174, 178, 273–276

Pytheas the Phocaean, 114, 156

Pythia, 85, 87–97, 130, 162

R

Ra, 33

Rabelais, 224

Rappenglück, Michael, 33

Rastafarians, 33

Rhazes, 188, 211, 212

Riedel, Albert, 256

Rosicrucians, 250

Royal Society, 234, 237–243, 245–247

Ryle, Gilbert, 81

S

Saint-Germain, Count, 220–223

San Pedro, 25–28, 30, 31, 62

Santorini, 176

Sappho, 68

Schweitzer, Johann Friedrich (aka Helvetius), 215, 217, 248–250, 252, 277

Scythians, 101, 107, 112, 120, 121, 124

Sechin Alto, 27, 30

Sendivogius, Michael, 250, 292

Seton, Alexander, 249

Shakespeare, 44, 88, 118, 180

Shamanism, 18, 19, 23, 26, 31, 53, 56, 64, 73, 102, 107, 120, 123–126, 128, 132, 133, 137, 173, 174, 189, 190, 231, 287

Shelley, Mary, 232

Shiva, 50, 108

Shulgin, Alexander, 60

Sibyls, 39

Sicily, 115, 145, 166, 168, 176, 207, 266, 268, 277

Sikkim, 124, 146

Silk Road, 43

Simhamukha, 33

Socrates, 45, 64, 68, 137, 142, 158, 207, 290

Solomon, 26, 39, 193, 226

Solon, 45, 101, 259, 260

Sophocles, 45, 56, 67

Spagyrics, 54, 229, 231, 258, 289

Sparagmos, 63, 64

St Anthony's Fire, 60

St. Paul, 101, 104

Stonehenge, 14, 116, 119

Strasbourg Papyrus, 171, 172, 180, 190, 205

Stromboli, 176

Sufis, 166, 205, 207

Syrian Rue, 62

T

Tarot, 6

Tartarus, 86, 190–192

Thales, 79, 98, 109, 264, 269

Thebes, 45, 167, 208

Themistoclea, 84, 97, 100

Theogenesis, 51

Theriomorphism, 32

Thor, 36, 170, 171

Thyrsus, 48, 61

Tower of Babel, 3

Transmutation, 5, 201, 209, 212, 215, 216, 219, 233, 234, 238, 239, 246, 248–250, 256, 280, 282

Transylvania, 220

Trithemius, Johannes, 224

Troy, 42, 110

Tuatha Dé Danann, 117

Tulku, 123–125, 135

U

Underworld, 41, 45, 51, 53, 60, 62, 74, 102, 104, 133, 143, 155, 174–176, 181, 189–192, 287

V

Vampires, 223

van Helmont, Jan Baptista, 200, 215–217, 248, 252, 289

Venus, 19, 21–23, 181, 182

Vikings, 121

Voltaire, 221

von Bernus, Alexander, 258

Voodoo, 48, 52

W

Wetzel, Robert, 13

Witches, 2, 6, 7, 23, 112, 180, 181, 191

X

Xenophanes, 144, 156, 157, 159, 160, 168, 292

Y

Yaghuth, 33
Yeats, W. B., 5
Young, Francis Brett, xiv

Z

Zagreus, 49, 51
Zalmoxis, 109, 120, 122, 123, 143
Zeno, 158, 168, 186
Zeus, 36, 48, 50, 51, 60, 63, 64, 67, 85–87, 100, 103, 104,
    109, 155, 166, 170, 171, 173–176, 182, 255, 265
Zoroaster, 39, 83
Zosimus of Panopolis, 200, 206, 207

To Write to the Author

If you wish to contact the author or would like more information about this book, please write to the author in care of Llewellyn Worldwide Ltd. and we will forward your request. Both the author and publisher appreciate hearing from you and learning of your enjoyment of this book and how it has helped you. Llewellyn Worldwide Ltd. cannot guarantee that every letter written to the author can be answered, but all will be forwarded. Please write to:

Guy Ogilvy
℅ Llewellyn Worldwide
2143 Wooddale Drive
Woodbury, MN 55125-2989

Please enclose a self-addressed stamped envelope for reply,
or $1.00 to cover costs. If outside the U.S.A., enclose
an international postal reply coupon.

Many of Llewellyn's authors have websites with additional information and resources. For more information, please visit our website at http://www.llewellyn.com.

GET MORE AT LLEWELLYN.COM

Visit us online to browse hundreds of our books and decks, plus sign up to receive our e-newsletters and exclusive online offers.

- • Free tarot readings • Spell-a-Day • Moon phases
- • Recipes, spells, and tips • Blogs • Encyclopedia
- • Author interviews, articles, and upcoming events

GET SOCIAL WITH LLEWELLYN

Find us on  🐦 @LlewellynBooks
www.Facebook.com/LlewellynBooks

GET BOOKS AT LLEWELLYN

LLEWELLYN ORDERING INFORMATION

 Order online: Visit our website at www.llewellyn.com to select your books and place an order on our secure server.

 Order by phone:
- • Call toll free within the US at 1-877-NEW-WRLD (1-877-639-9753)
- • We accept VISA, MasterCard, American Express, and Discover.
- • Canadian customers must use credit cards.

 Order by mail:
Send the full price of your order (MN residents add 6.875% sales tax) in US funds plus postage and handling to: Llewellyn Worldwide, 2143 Wooddale Drive, Woodbury, MN 55125-2989

POSTAGE AND HANDLING

STANDARD (US):
(Please allow 12 business days)
$30.00 and under, add $6.00.
$30.01 and over, FREE SHIPPING.

INTERNATIONAL ORDERS,
INCLUDING CANADA:
$16.00 for one book, plus $3.00 for each additional book.

Visit us online for more shipping options.
Prices subject to change.

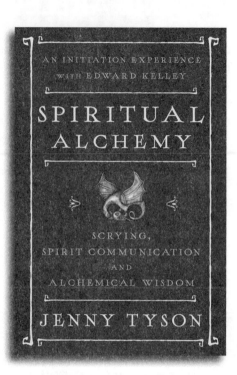

AN INITIATION EXPERIENCE
WITH EDWARD KELLEY

SPIRITUAL ALCHEMY

SCRYING,
SPIRIT COMMUNICATION
AND
ALCHEMICAL WISDOM

JENNY TYSON

Spiritual Alchemy

Scrying, Spirit Communication, and Alchemical Wisdom

JENNY TYSON

Transcend ordinary consciousness and undergo a personal, life-altering transformation through Jenny Tyson's amazing journey of spirit communication and instruction. This remarkable book presents Jenny's yearlong training and the intense three-day initiation that turned her minimal psychic abilities into full-blown clairvoyance and clairaudience. Along the way she contacted several guides, including famed Elizabethan magicians John Dee and Edward Kelley.

Providing detailed accounts of Jenny's experiences and the ghost box and other tools she used, *Spiritual Alchemy* guides your own spirit communication. Discover Jenny's unique analysis of the Emerald Tablet of Hermes Trismegistus, her process of awakening and raising Kundalini energy, and her work with the angels and gateways to divine unity. With powerful new training methods, a unique interview with Edward Kelley, and more, this book revolutionizes the interactions between humans and spirits.

978-0-7387-4976-1, 312 pp., 6 x 9 $19.99

pathways to enlightenment

The Path of
Alchemy

ENERGETIC HEALING AND THE
WORLD OF NATURAL MAGIC

Mark Stavish

The Path of Alchemy
Energetic Healing & the World of Natural Magic
Mark Stavish

Alchemy offers tremendous insight into alternative therapies, new medicines, and the depths of the human mind. Illuminating a truly esoteric practice, Mark Stavish reveals how to create and apply "medicines for the soul" in this remarkable guide to plant and mineral alchemy.

The Path of Alchemy introduces the history and basic laws of this ancient practice, and explains how it ties into Qabala, tarot, astrology, and the four elements. Safe, modern techniques—based on spagyrics (plant alchemy)—for producing distillations, stones, tinctures, and elixirs are given, along with their uses in physical healing, spiritual growth, psychic experiments, initiation, consecration, spellwork, and more. Each chapter includes meditations, projects, and suggested reading as aids to "inner transformation," an equally important aspect of alchemy. Tools, rituals, lunar and solar stones, and the elusive Philosopher's Stone are all covered in this comprehensive guide to alchemy.

978-0-7387-0903-1, 264 pp., 6 x 9 $17.99

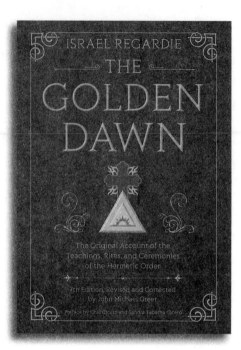

ISRAEL REGARDIE

THE
GOLDEN
DAWN

The Original Account of the
Teachings, Rites, and Ceremonies
of the Hermetic Order

7th Edition, Revised and Corrected
by John Michael Greer

Preface by Chic Cicero and Sandra Tabatha Cicero

The Golden Dawn
The Original Account of the Teachings, Rites, and Ceremonies of the Hermetic Order
ISRAEL REGARDIE AND JOHN MICHAEL GREER

First published in 1937, Israel Regardie's *The Golden Dawn* has become the most influential modern handbook of magical theory and practice. In this new, definitive edition, noted scholar John Michael Greer has taken this essential resource back to its original, authentic form. With added illustrations, a twenty-page color insert, additional original material, and refreshed design and typography, this powerful work returns to its true stature as a modern masterpiece.

An essential textbook for students of the occult, *The Golden Dawn* includes occult symbolism and Qabalistic philosophy, training methods for developing magical and clairvoyant powers, rituals that summon and banish spiritual potencies, secrets of making and consecrating magical tools, and much more.

978-0-7387-4399-8, 960 pp., 7 x 10 **$65.00**

THE WISDOM OF

HYPATIA

Ancient Spiritual Practices for a More Meaningful Life

BRUCE J. MACLENNAN, PhD

The Wisdom of Hypatia
Ancient Spiritual Practices for a More Meaningful Life
BRUCE J. MacLENNAN, PhD

Hypatia was one of the most famous philosophers of the ancient world. The mix of classical philosophies she taught to Pagans, Jews, and Christians in the fourth century forms the very foundation of Western spirituality as we know it today. *The Wisdom of Hypatia* is a hands-on guide to using the principles of philosophy to bring purpose, tranquility, and spiritual depth to your life.

To the ancients, philosophy was a spiritual practice meant to help the seeker achieve a good life and maintain mental tranquility. Bruce J. MacLennan, PhD, provides a concise history of philosophy up to Hypatia's time and a progressive, nine-month program of spiritual practice based on her teachings. Explore the three most important philosophical schools of the Hellenistic Age. Lead a more serene, balanced life. Experience self-actualization through union with the divine. Discover the techniques described in the historical sources, and put into practice the profound insights of the world's greatest minds.

978-0-7387-3599-3, 384 pp., 7½ x 9⅛ $21.99

A HANDBOOK OF

SAXON
SORCERY
& MAGIC

WYRDWORKING,
RUNE CRAFT,
DIVINATION &
WORTCUNNING

ALARIC ALBERTSSON

A Handbook of Saxon Sorcery & Magic
Wyrdworking, Rune Craft, Divination & Wortcunning
Alaric Albertsson

Discover the secrets of Saxon sorcery, and learn how to craft rune charms, brew potions, cast effective spells, and use magical techniques to find love and prosperity. Exploring the practices and customs of the Anglo-Saxons hidden in English folk traditions, this book shares techniques for making wands and staffs, consecrating and using a ritual *seax* (knife), healing with herbs (wortcunning), soothsaying, and creating your own set of runes. The meaning and magical properties of the thirty-three Old English Futhorc runes are classified by theme, helping you in your quest to know yourself and influence your world for the better.

Previously published as *Wyrdworking*.

978-0-7387-5338-6, 360 pp., 6 x 9 $19.99